Graphic Design to Beat the Clock

Time-saving software secrets, online resources, and desktop tips

Stephen Beale

Focal Press
Taylor & Francis Group

Contents

Chapter One

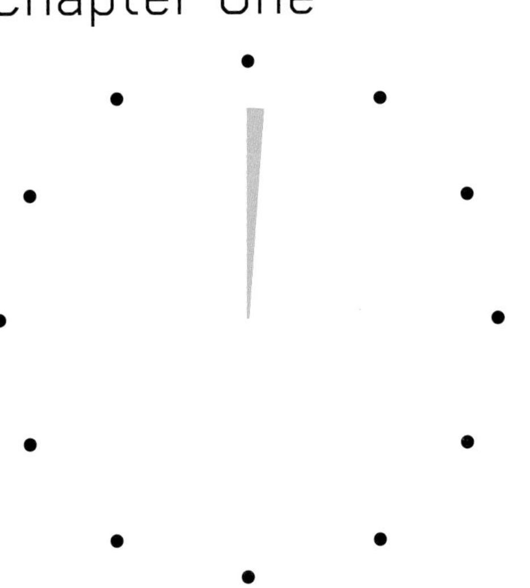

QUICK SHORTCUTS

Chapter Two

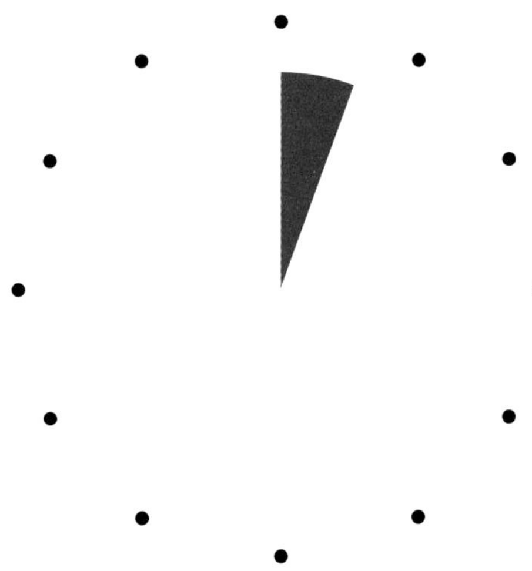

FAST FIXES

Chapter Three

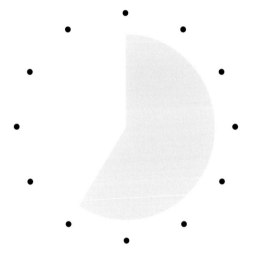

Chapter Four

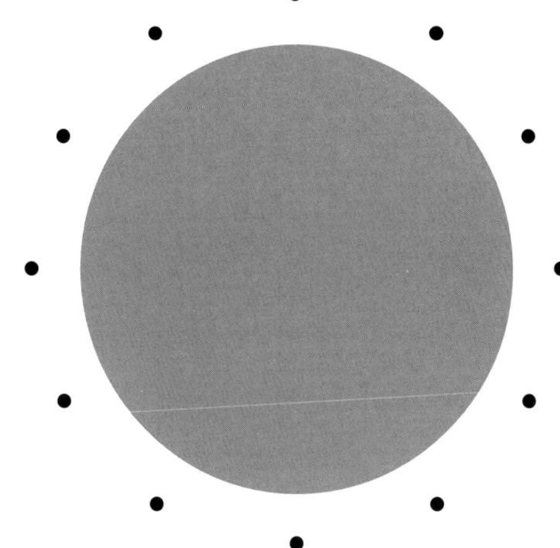

Introduction

Programs such as Adobe Photoshop, InDesign, Illustrator, and Dreamweaver have numerous shortcuts, quick fixes, hidden tricks, and other features that can dramatically improve productivity. The purpose of this book is to help you uncover and use them.

We're focusing primarily on Adobe's Creative Suite because those are the tools typically used by most designers. We've included the latest release, Creative Suite 6, but most of the information will apply equally well to earlier versions, especially CS 5 and CS 5.5. Furthermore, you'll also find tips for maximizing productivity in Mac OS X and Windows.

The book is organized into four sections, each offering progressively greater time savings. Of course, the time you save depends in large part on the nature of your design work.

Here's a quick rundown of some of the steps you can take to work faster (and more effectively):

01. **Shortcuts:** You're probably familiar with many of the keyboard shortcuts used for accessing items in the menus, but the Creative Suite includes a host of other shortcuts that will help you work more efficiently.

02. **Presets:** Many functions can be saved as presets and reused later with one or two mouse clicks. Even tools such as brushes, patterns, and swatches support presets that can be saved and shared with others, or downloaded from the web.

03. **Styles:** Styles are useful for more than just formatting type. In Photoshop, Illustrator, and InDesign, styles provide an efficient means of changing the look of layers or graphic objects.

04. **Reusable Content:** Templates and object libraries can save lots of time by letting you store design elements and reuse them whenever they're needed. You can also use built-in libraries to access ready-made content.

05. **Actions and Batch Processing:** These features act like little robots that can execute a series of operations while you sit back and watch.

06. **Scripting:** Scripting takes automation to a higher level by letting you write simple programs to execute commands in Photoshop, Illustrator, and InDesign. You can also use built-in scripts or find them on the web.

07. **Extensions and Plugins:** A host of companies offers products that add even more functionality to the Creative Suite. Some can even be downloaded for free.

Tip

This book assumes that you already have a basic familiarity with most of these programs, though you'll find a brief overview on pages 10–15. This will help you determine which programs are the best choices for specific kinds of projects.

Finally, a note about style conventions in this book: when we refer to keyboard shortcuts, we'll list the Mac shortcut followed by the Windows shortcut in parentheses if it's different. For example, Cmd-S (Ctrl+S) means you should press the Command key and the letter S on a Mac, and the Control key plus S on a Windows PC.

How to Use This Book

This book is designed to help you save time. No need to waste precious minutes flicking back and forth between the table of contents and the page you're after. At any given time, on any given page, you should know where you are, what you're looking at, and where you need to go to find the next tip.

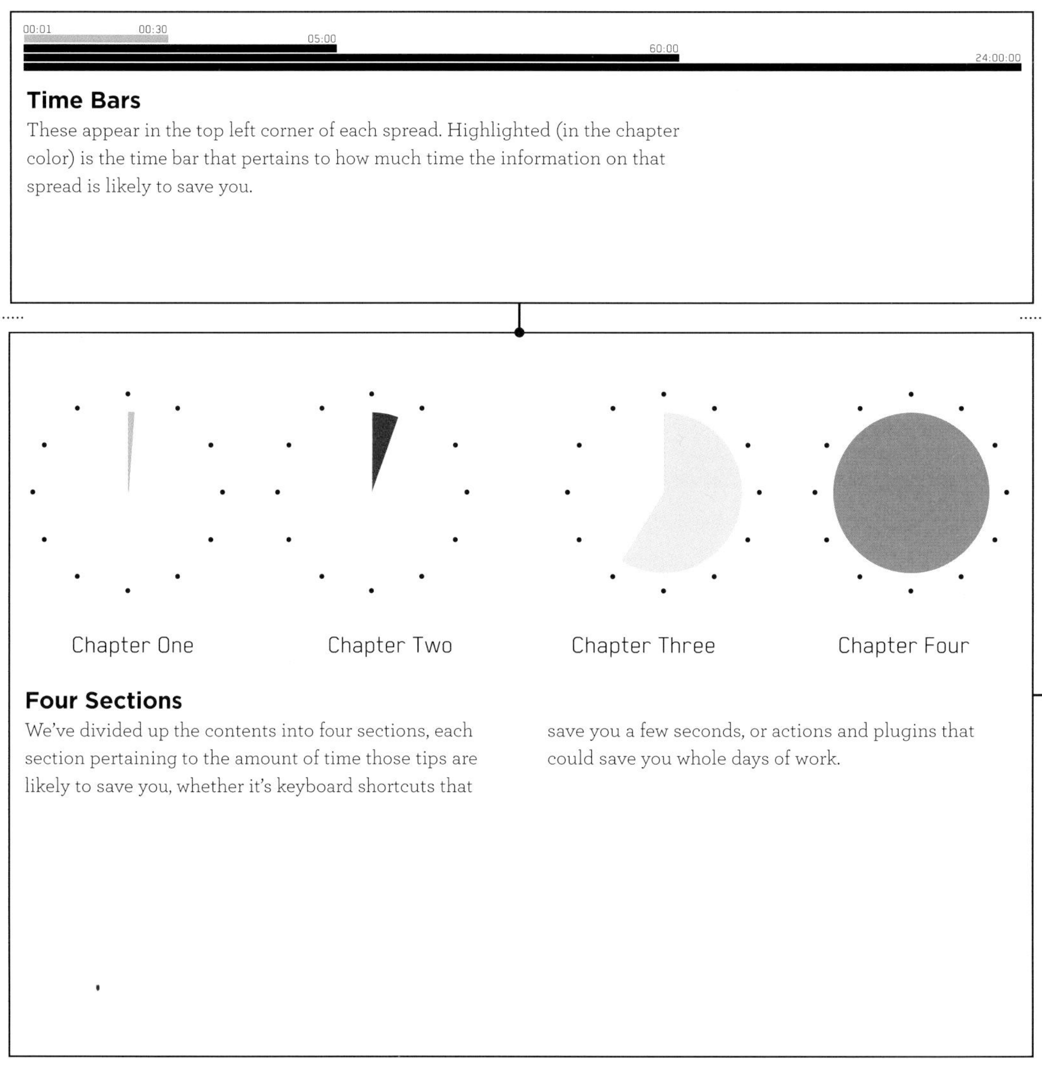

Time Bars

These appear in the top left corner of each spread. Highlighted (in the chapter color) is the time bar that pertains to how much time the information on that spread is likely to save you.

Four Sections

We've divided up the contents into four sections, each section pertaining to the amount of time those tips are likely to save you, whether it's keyboard shortcuts that save you a few seconds, or actions and plugins that could save you whole days of work.

Creative Suite 6
Photoshop
Illustrator
InDesign
Dreamweaver
Flash Professional
Edge
Fireworks
Muse
Acrobat Professional
Bridge
Kuler
Online
Mac
Windows

Color Coding

Colored dots run along the top right corner of each spread. Each color relates to a software package, Mac or PC desktop, or online resource. If you're looking for a quick tip in Adobe Illustrator, simply flick to a page with the orange dot highlighted at the top.

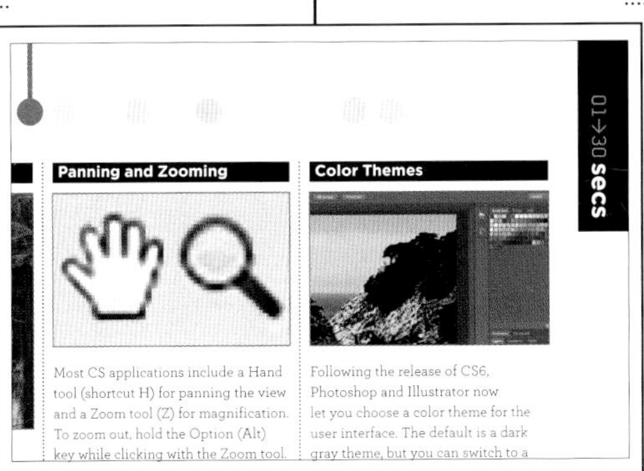

01→30 secs
Panning and Zooming
Color Themes
Most CS applications include a Hand tool (shortcut H) for panning the view and a Zoom tool (Z) for magnification. To zoom out, hold the Option (Alt) key while clicking with the Zoom tool.
Following the release of CS6, Photoshop and Illustrator now let you choose a color theme for the user interface. The default is a dark gray theme, but you can switch to a

Tabs

Black tabs run along the right-hand side of each spread. The wider the tab, the more time you're likely to save.

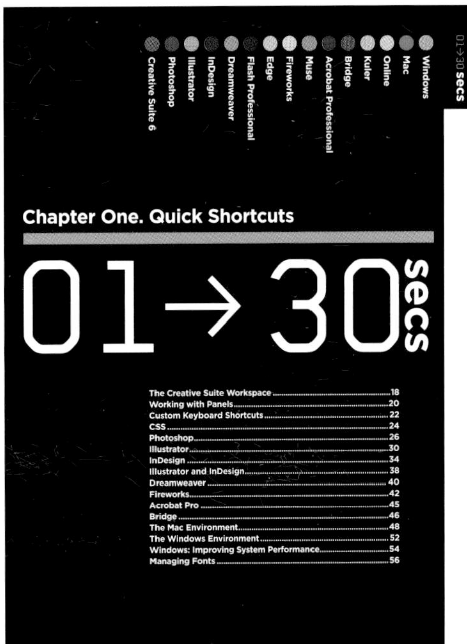

Chapter Content Lists

Each new chapter has a dedicated contents list with page numbers listed. You can flick straight to that page and look up the tip you need.

The Designer's Toolbox

The first step in any project is selecting the right tool for the job. Here's a rundown of the applications in Adobe's Creative Suite.

Photoshop

Photoshop is the premier application for working with digital photos and other raster-based images.

Specific uses of Photoshop include photo correction, compositing, design comps, type treatments, logos, web graphics, digital fine art, broadcast graphics, and 3D graphics. It includes tools for creating type and vector graphics, but it's still oriented primarily toward pixel-based images. It is available in two versions: Photoshop Standard and Photoshop Extended. The latter includes features for creating 3D graphics along with specialized functions for scientists, engineers, and medical professionals. Except where noted, this book focuses on Photoshop Standard.

Of all the programs covered in this book, Photoshop has the steepest hardware requirements, especially if you work with large images. For maximum productivity, you should run it on a relatively new computer (preferably with Intel's I5 or I7 chip) stocked with plenty of RAM and a fast hard drive. You'll also need a speedy graphics processor to take advantage of scrubby zoom, view rotation, and Photoshop Extended's 3D features.

Illustrator

This is the Creative Suite's primary tool for creating vector graphics. Unlike digital photos, in which the primary building block is the pixel, vector graphics are built from lines and curves, which Illustrator refers to as "paths." The main advantage of vector graphics is that they can be scaled, rotated, and modified in other ways with no loss of quality. The files also tend to be smaller than image files, though this depends in part on the nature of the graphic.

Illustrator is ideally suited for maps, diagrams, line drawings, logos, type treatments, and other graphics that require scalability and a high degree of precision. It's also a popular tool for creating print ads and packaging, and it's a good starting point for graphics that you want to animate in Flash or Adobe's new web-animation tool, Edge.

Traditionally, vector graphics tools haven't been all that intuitive, requiring users to work with anchor points and direction handles to modify paths, but in recent versions, Illustrator has added features such as the Blob Brush, Eraser, and Live Paint Bucket that behave more like Photoshop's painting tools.

InDesign

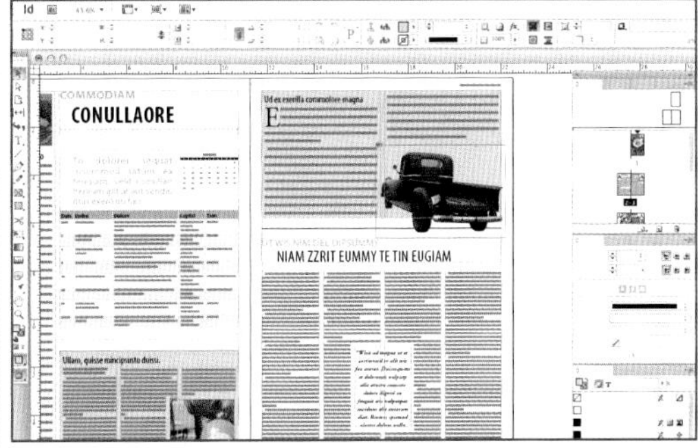

InDesign is the Creative Suite's page-layout tool. Traditionally used for print projects such as books, magazines, newspapers, and brochures, it can also create web pages and e-books.

InDesign is primarily a meeting place for content created in other programs, and works particularly well with Photoshop and Illustrator. For example, if an imported graphic needs additional work, you can use InDesign's Edit Original feature to reopen the file in one of those programs. After you make the edits and save the file, the changes are instantly reflected in the page layout.

The latest frontier for InDesign is "digital publishing," Adobe's term for content geared toward mobile devices such as Apple's iPad. Using InDesign, you can create layouts for different screen sizes and orientations within the same document. You can also add video clips, slide shows, and other multimedia elements, then upload the file to Adobe's Digital Publishing Suite.

InDesign's main competitor is QuarkXPress, which once dominated the page layout market but has fallen behind in recent years. A free open-source alternative is Scribus.

Dreamweaver

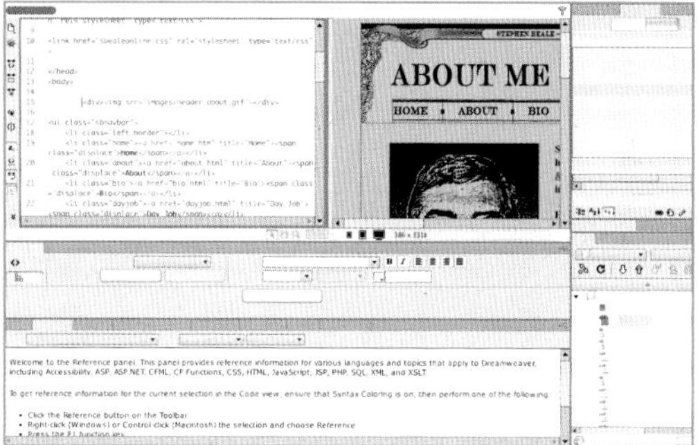

Dreamweaver is the Creative Suite's primary tool for website development. It provides a WYSIWYG ("what you see is what you get") design environment along with features for developing code in HTML, CSS, JavaScript, and PHP.

One of Dreamweaver's strengths is its ability to hide some of the complexities of coding while providing full access to the code for experienced developers. For example, a designer with little or no programming knowledge can use Spry Effects to build JavaScript behaviors such as tooltips and accordion menus. And designers can use the CSS Styles panel to create, modify, and manage Cascading Style Sheets, with any changes automatically reflected in the underlying code.

Many of the new features in Dreamweaver CS5.5 and CS6 are geared toward HTML5 and CSS3, the latest versions of the key web standards. This is especially important for designers targeting mobile devices.

Flash Professional

Flash Professional provides a set of tools for creating Flash content. Flash originated as a technology for producing vector-based web animations that could be quickly downloaded to a user's browser via the Flash Player plugin. It has since evolved into a comprehensive application-development environment based on Adobe's ActionScript language. Designers can still use it as an animation tool, while programmers can create sophisticated online applications such as games.

Flash continues to be a popular technology for viewing rich-media content in desktop browsers, but it's not well supported on mobile devices. However, the new Toolkit for JS extension for Flash Professional CS6 can export animations as JavaScript code that runs in HTML5.

Most Flash content on websites is encoded in the Shockwave Flash format (SWF). However, Flash projects can also be exported as AIR (Adobe Integrated Runtime) applications. These applications behave like desktop programs and can be packaged as apps for mobile devices.

Edge

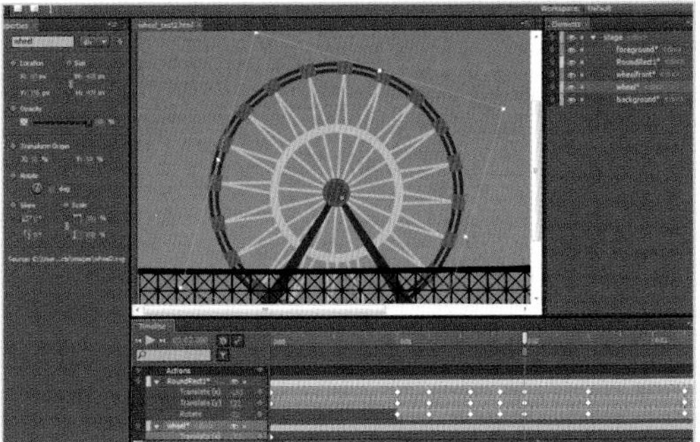

Edge allows you to create interactive web animations similar to those produced in Flash Professional. However, instead of generating SWF files, Edge produces animations using HTML5, CSS3, and JavaScript. Since these are open web standards, Edge content can be viewed in browsers without the need for the Flash Player plugin.

It's best suited for content aimed at mobile devices such as Apple's iPad and iPhone. Browsers for these devices support the new features in HTML5 and CSS3 that enable animation.

Edge uses an animation timeline similar to the one in Adobe After Effects. You can import images in standard web formats such as GIF, JPEG, and PNG, then use keyframes in the timeline to animate motion, rotation, scaling, and other attributes. The program uses JavaScript in place of Adobe's ActionScript language to enable interactive behaviors, such as pressing a button to launch an animation.

Alternatives to Edge include Sencha Animator, which runs on Windows PCs, and Tumult Hype, which runs on the Mac.

Fireworks

Fireworks is an all-purpose program for producing graphics targeted at websites and mobile devices. It combines vector and bitmap tools, so it functions in some ways like a hybrid of Illustrator and Photoshop. However, it has additional features specific to interactive projects. For example, you can create graphics with embedded links and JavaScript rollovers, and immediately preview them in a web browser. And with the new CSS Code Extraction feature in CS6, you can apply attributes such as gradient fills, stroke colors, and rounded corners to an object, and then copy automatically-generated CSS code into a style sheet.

In recent versions, Adobe has positioned Fireworks as a rapid-prototyping tool for web development. You can mock up a website with multiple pages, add interactive elements, and export it as a PDF file for client presentations. The same workflow can also be used to develop games, mobile apps, and other interactive projects.

Muse

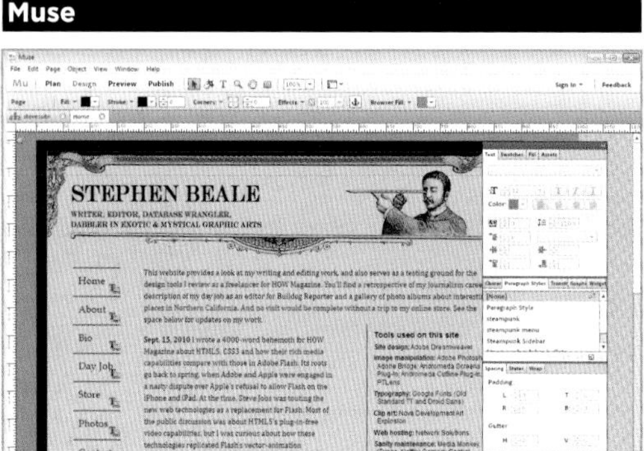

Another new program, Muse is aimed at print designers who'd like to create websites without learning the intricacies of HTML, CSS, or JavaScript. It provides a set of tools similar to those in InDesign that let you build web pages in much the same way you would create print layouts. For example, you can set up character or paragraph styles for formatting text, and use Master Pages for recurring design elements. As you build your site, Muse generates HTML, CSS, and JavaScript code that you can export or upload. Unlike Dreamweaver, you can't modify the underlying code, nor can you see the code unless you export it or preview the site in a browser.

Acrobat Professional

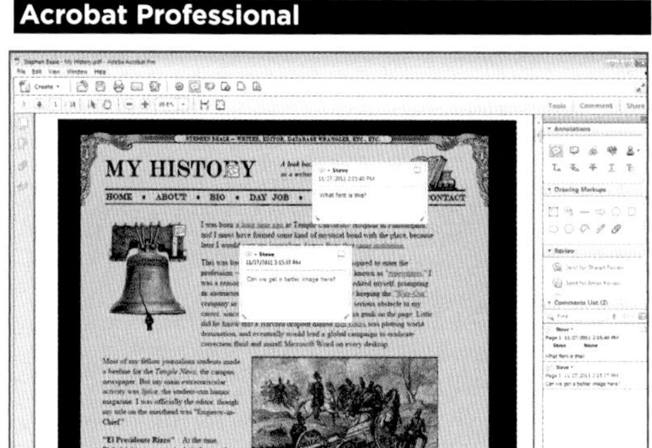

This is Adobe's tool for creating, modifying, and managing PDF files. It's included in the Creative Suite, but doesn't conform to the standard CS interface and has many uses outside of design.

Designers typically use Acrobat for client presentations and to manage the review process. With the Acrobat Portfolio feature, you can import documents in various formats and distribute them as PDF files. Acrobat's commenting tools allow others to add electronic "sticky notes" and annotations to documents and then email them to other participants.

Bridge

This is an asset-management program included with Photoshop, Illustrator, InDesign, Flash Professional, Premiere, and After Effects. It's most useful for browsing, viewing, and organizing media, such as photos, illustrations, movies, PDFs, and InDesign documents. You can apply labels, ratings, and keywords to your assets and then sort or filter them based on those values.

Bridge also functions as a substitute for the file managers in Windows and the Mac OS—you can browse, move, copy, or rename files or folders regardless of what program created them.

Through its Tools menu, Bridge provides access to batch-processing functions in Photoshop, Fireworks, and Illustrator. For example, you can select a batch of images in Bridge and run Photoshop's Image Processor to convert them to a different format.

InDesign and Photoshop also include a stripped-down version called Mini Bridge that lets you browse and open assets from a panel within those programs.

Kuler

Kuler is a set of tools that enable designers to create harmonized color themes and share them with others. It's available in multiple forms:

- as an online service (www.adobe.com/products/kuler)
- as an app for Android tablets.
- as a panel in Photoshop, Illustrator, InDesign, Fireworks, and Flash Professional. The panel automatically downloads themes from the online Kuler community.

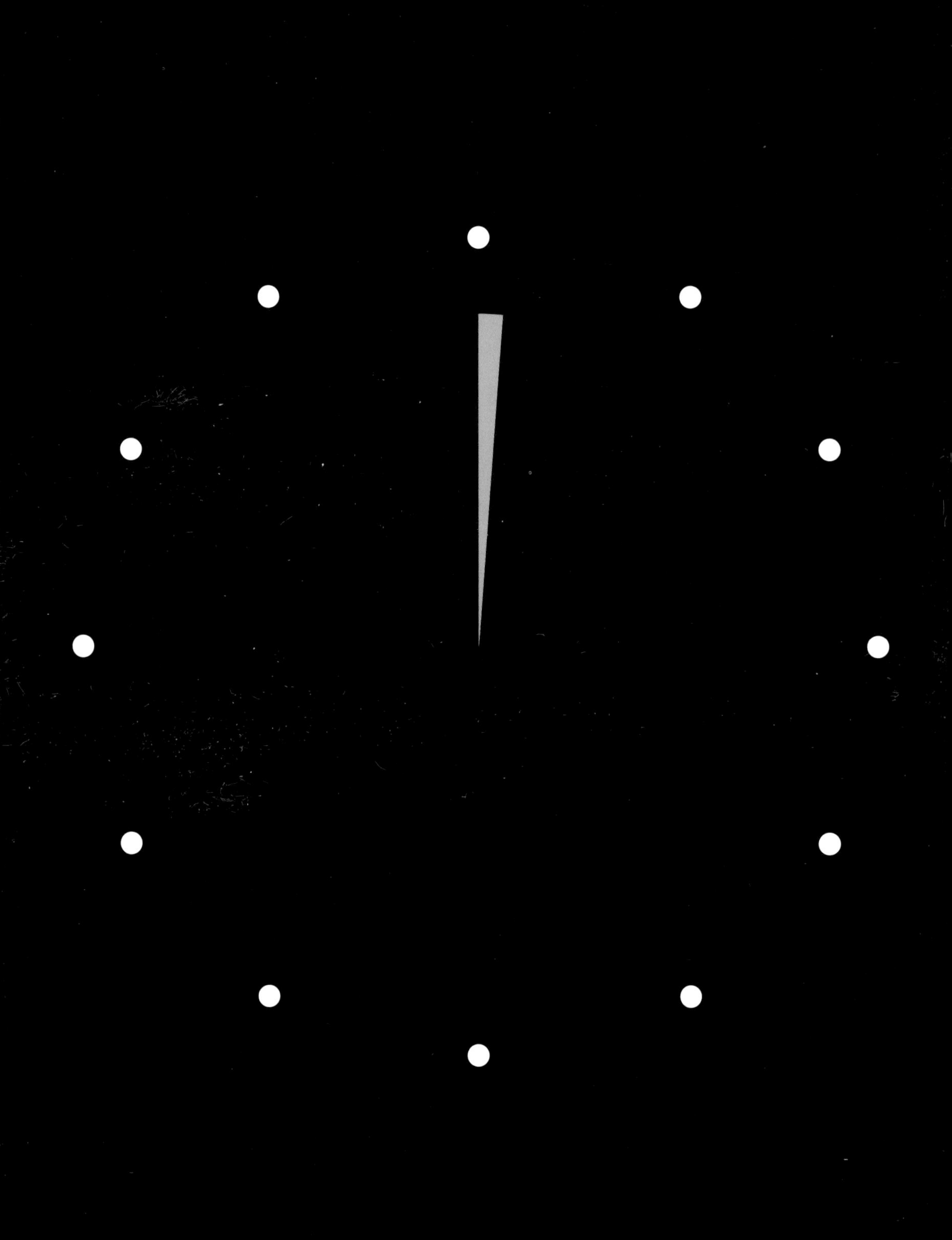

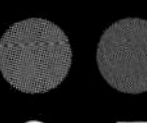
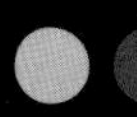
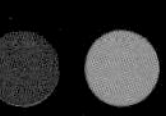
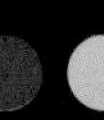
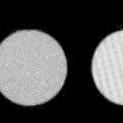

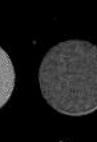

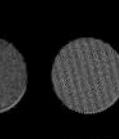

Creative Suite 6
Photoshop
Illustrator
InDesign
Dreamweaver
Flash Professional
Edge
Fireworks
Muse
Acrobat Professional
Bridge
Kuler
Online
Mac
Windows

Chapter One. Quick Shortcuts

01→30 secs

Quick Shortcuts

The Creative Suite Workspace

Most Creative Suite applications share common interface features, including tabbed documents, collapsible panels, and tools that behave in similar ways. Follow these tips to take control of your workspace and operate more efficiently.

Managing Window Views

Tabbed Windows

By default, multiple documents appear in tabbed windows similar to the tabs in web browsers. The windows sit in a container known as a "dock."

Click on a tab to activate a window, or use ⌘-Tab (Ctrl-Tab) to cycle through open documents.

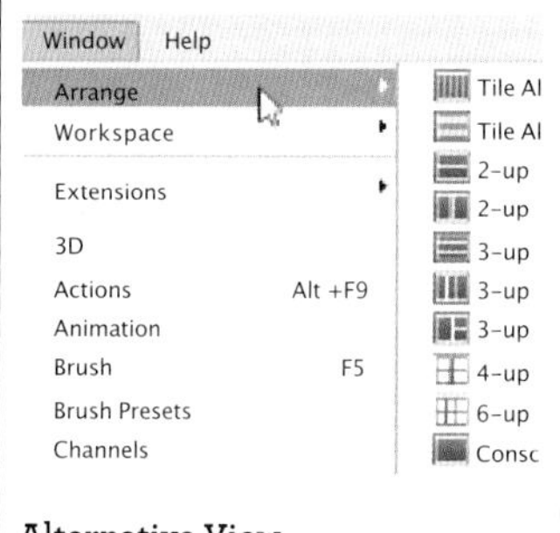

Alternative View

The Window > Arrange menu lets you switch to an alternative view. You can tile documents vertically or horizontally, or choose from a variety of other layouts. Click on Consolidate All to Tabs to return to the default tabbed view.

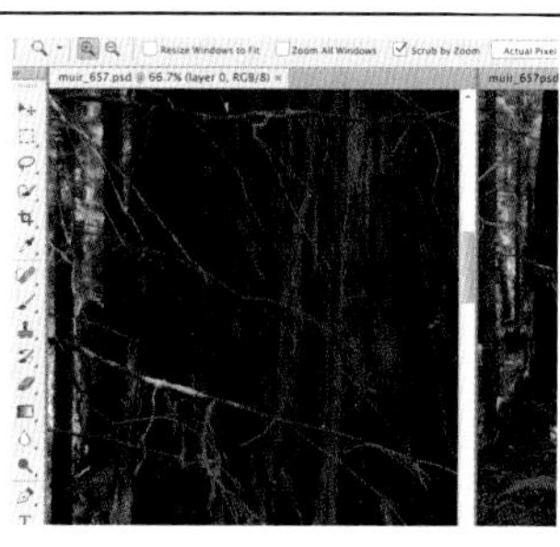

Multiple Views

Use the New Window option at the bottom of the Arrange menu to show multiple views of the same document. This is useful if you want to zoom in while retaining a larger view in a second window.

Screen Modes

In the standard screen mode, your view of a document can be obstructed by panels or other document windows. Some CS apps provide a remedy by means of alternative screen modes. For example, Photoshop's Full Screen Mode with Menu Bar expands the current document window so it fills the screen, but retains menus and panels. Photoshop's Full Screen mode and InDesign's Presentation Mode hide all menus, panels, and tools.

The Toolbar

By default, the toolbar appears in a single column, but you can switch to a two-column layout by clicking on the double arrow at the top. InDesign also gives you the option of a horizontal layout. In Fireworks and Flash, the toolbar is limited to a single column.

The tiny triangle to the lower right of a tool icon indicates that it's part of a group. Hold down the mouse button to see the grouped tools. The keyboard shortcut (if the tool has one) appears on the right. If you frequently use a tool that doesn't have a shortcut, you can assign one using the Keyboard Shortcuts feature.

See Also page 22

Panning and Zooming

Most CS applications include a Hand tool (shortcut H) for panning the view and a Zoom tool (Z) for magnification. To zoom out, hold the Option (Alt) key while clicking with the Zoom tool.

You can use these other keyboard shortcuts to zoom:

- **Zoom In ⌘-**Plus (Ctrl+Plus)
- **Zoom Out** ⌘-Minus (Ctrl+Minus)
- **Zoom to 100%**
  ⌘-Option-1 (Ctrl+Alt+1)
- **Fit All on Screen**
  Shift-⌘-0 (Shift+Ctrl+0)

Color Themes

Following the release of CS6, Photoshop and Illustrator now let you choose a color theme for the user interface. The default is a dark gray theme, but you can switch to a different theme. Go to [Application Name] > Preferences > Interface on the Mac or Edit > Preferences > Interface on Windows to make your choice.

The Control Panel

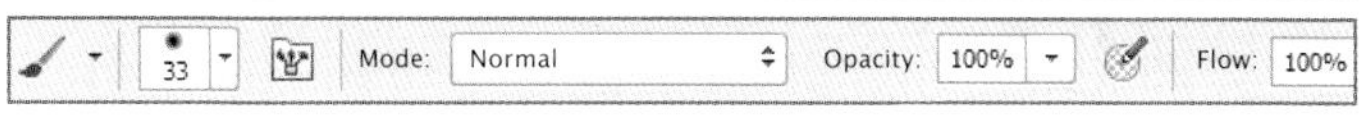

This panel shows options for the currently selected tool, object, or element. It goes by different names depending on the application. In Photoshop, it's called the Options bar, while in Dreamweaver, Fireworks, and Flash, it's known as the Property Inspector.

Context-Sensitive Menus

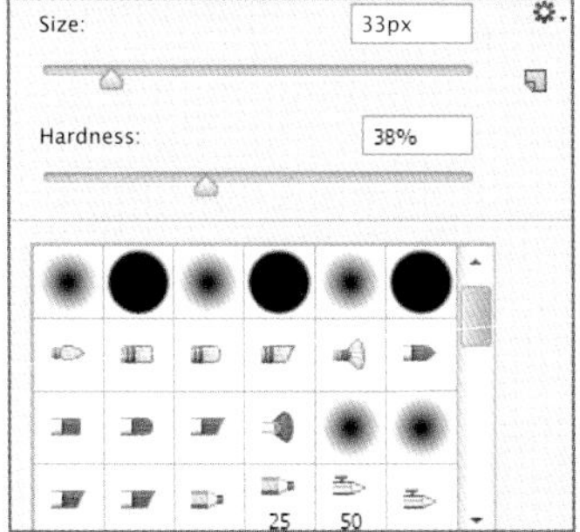

Also known as shortcut menus, these menus are among the most-overlooked timesavers. They appear when you right-click or Ctrl-click with the mouse, displaying options relevant to the tool or panel you're currently using. This is not only often a faster way to choose a menu item, you might also see options you weren't even aware of.

For example, in Photoshop, right-clicking or Ctrl-clicking with the Brush opens the Brush Preset Picker. Or you can right-click on the canvas with the Move tool to select any layer underneath the cursor.

Quick Shortcuts

Working with Panels

Panels are such a central part of the Creative Suite that they can easily get in the way. Smart panel managment will help you work more efficiently.

Anatomy of a Panel

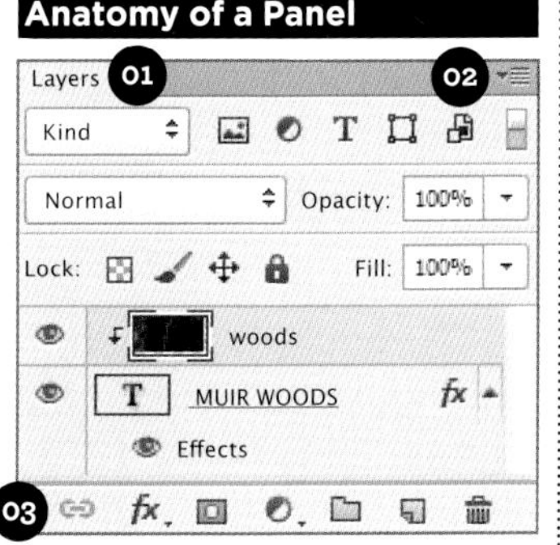

01. Tab: Drag to move a panel to a different group or its own floating window. Double click to collapse the panel.

02. Fly-out Menu: Provides panel-specific options, such as duplicating a layer or changing its properties.

03. Icons: Provide handy access to often-used features. The Trash can on the right works across all programs as a delete button. Here, it will delete selected layers. The icon next to it, resembling a page with a turned corner, creates a new item. Depending on the panel, it might create a new layer, page, style, or color. Hover over each icon with the mouse to see a description of its function.

Organizing Panels

04. Panel Arrangement: A typical arrangement is shown here. On the right are three groups of panels arranged vertically. On the left are six panels that have been collapsed to icons. All of these are contained within a single dock. Dragging on the bar at the top moves them all in unison.

05. Panel Tab: Click and drag on a tab to float the panel out of the dock or move it to a different group.

06. Blue Border: When you drag a panel to a group, it becomes transparent and this border appears, indicating that you can drop the panel into place.

07. Dock: Move groups in or out of the dock by dragging on the empty area next to their tabs.

A panel group can be docked to any side of another group, but it's best to stack them vertically. The blue line indicates the drop zone where the group will appear when you let go of the mouse button.

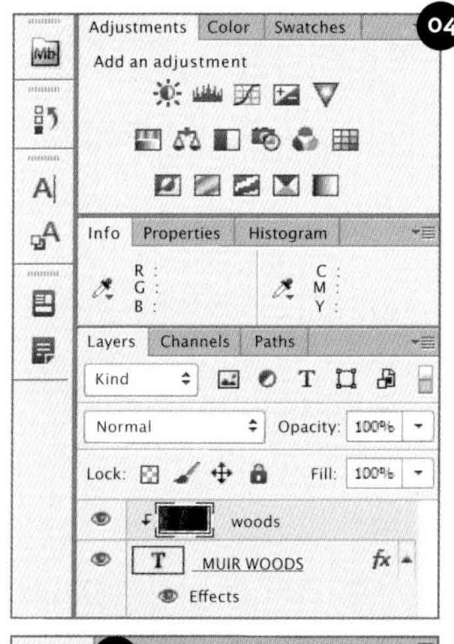

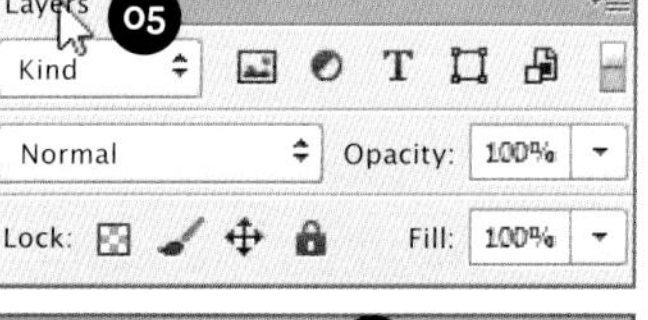

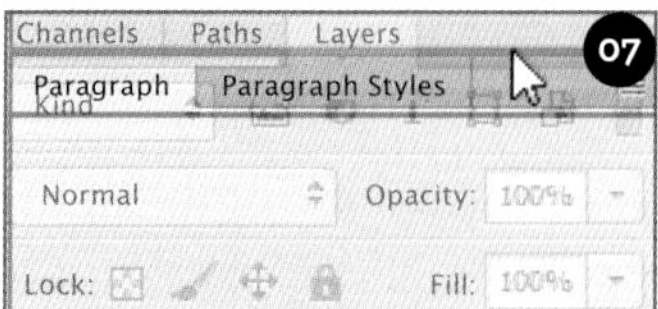

Expanding and Collapsing Panels

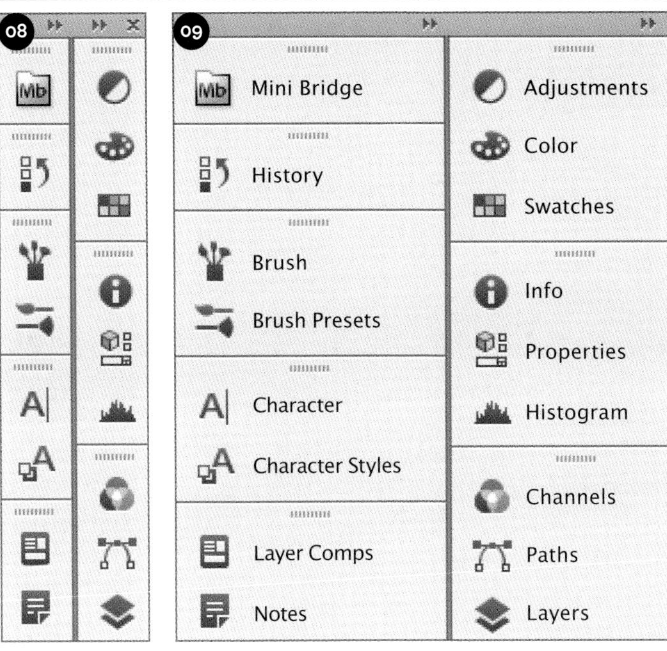

08. Panel Icons: To gain screen space, collapse panels to icons. Do this by clicking on the double-arrow in the title bar.

09. Panel Names: Viewing only the icons can make it difficult to tell which panels they represent. Drag on the right or left edges of the collapsed panels to widen the column and see their names.

To expand a single panel, click on its icon. Click on the double-arrow to expand all panels in that column.

Additional Panel Options

In CS6, close a dock or floating panel by clicking on the X in the upper left (on the right in Windows). In some programs, you can also close a panel or tab group via the panel menu. In the Mac version of CS5, the button is a small circle instead of an X.

- Open or close panels by clicking on their names in the Window menu.
- Double-click on a panel's tab to collapse its group to a single line.
- Click once on the tab to expand it.
- In Illustrator, InDesign, and Photoshop, hit the Tab key to hide or show all open panels, or hit Shift-Tab to hide or show all except the Tools and Control panels. Press F4 to hide or show open panels in Dreamweaver or Flash. Tab and F4 both work in Fireworks.

Customizing the Workspace

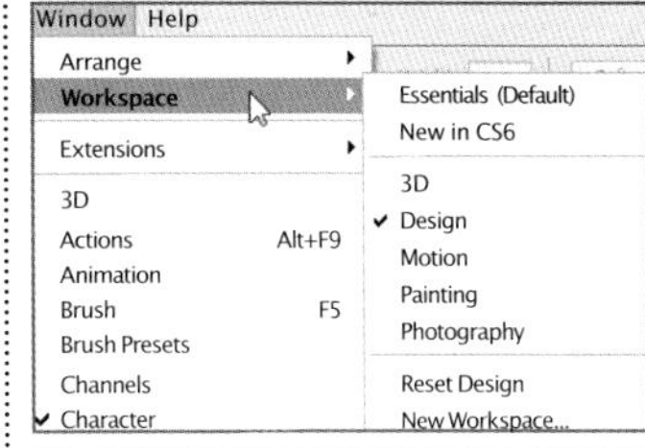

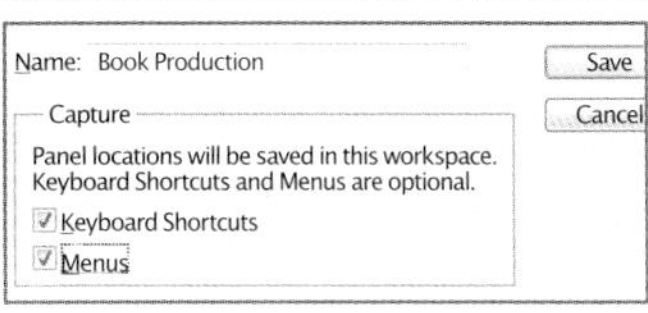

Once you've organized the panels to your liking, save the arrangement as a custom workspace, or create multiple workspaces for different tasks.

You can also use one of the built-in workspaces as a starting point for your own. For example, Photoshop ships with a default workspace—Essentials—plus workspaces for 3D graphics, design, video, painting, and photography. InDesign has workspaces for books, interactive projects, print production, and typography.

Saving a workspace is simple: choose Window > Workspace > New Workspace and give your workspace a name. You have the option to include custom keyboard shortcuts or menus.

Once you've saved a workspace, it will appear at the top of the Window > Workspace menu.

Quick Shortcuts

Custom Keyboard Shortcuts

If you don't like the default keyboard shortcuts, you can create your own. The steps are similar in each program. Here's how it's done in InDesign.

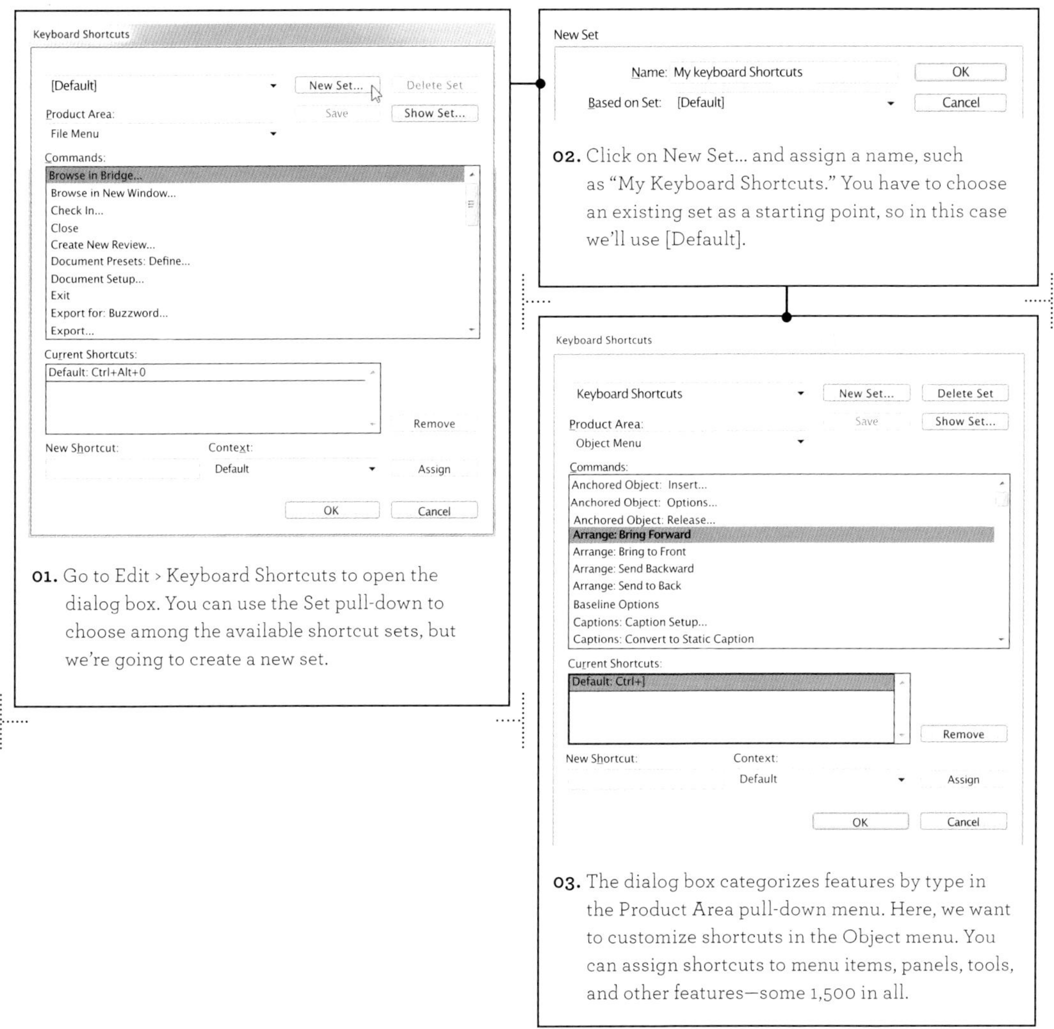

01. Go to Edit > Keyboard Shortcuts to open the dialog box. You can use the Set pull-down to choose among the available shortcut sets, but we're going to create a new set.

02. Click on New Set... and assign a name, such as "My Keyboard Shortcuts." You have to choose an existing set as a starting point, so in this case we'll use [Default].

03. The dialog box categorizes features by type in the Product Area pull-down menu. Here, we want to customize shortcuts in the Object menu. You can assign shortcuts to menu items, panels, tools, and other features—some 1,500 in all.

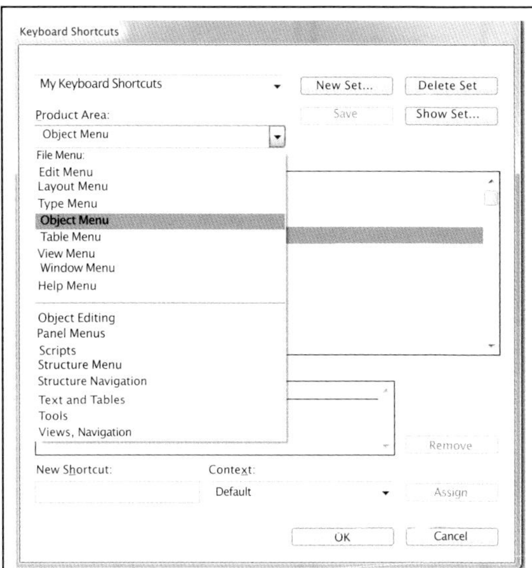

04. We want to add a new shortcut for the Arrange: Bring Forward option. When you click on that command, you can see that the default shortcut is ⌘+] (Ctrl+]).

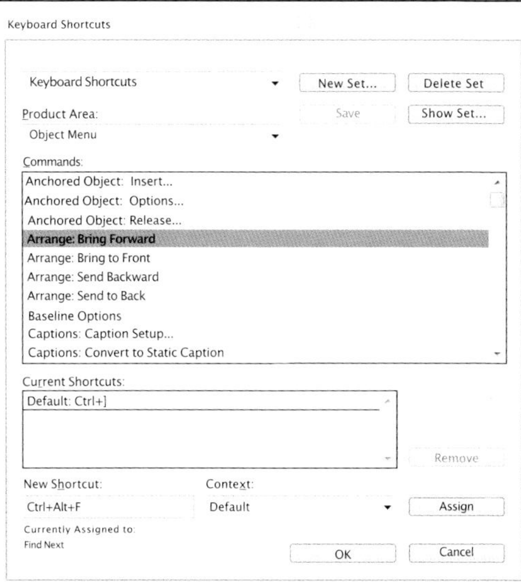

05. To add a shortcut, place the cursor in the New Shortcut field and hit the key combination you want to use. Usually, this is one or two modifier keys in combination with a letter, number, punctuation mark, or function key. On Windows, permitted modifier keys are Ctrl, Shift, and Alt. On the Mac, you can use ⌘, Shift, Ctrl, or Option as modifiers. In this case, we'll try ⌘+Option+F (Ctrl+Alt+F). InDesign will let you know if the key combo is already assigned. Be careful here—you may want to try a different shortcut if the one you've chosen is assigned to another frequently used feature.

06. Click the Assign button to assign the new keyboard shortcut. You can proceed to assign shortcuts to other commands, then click OK.

Quick Shortcuts

CSS

Instead of This	Use This
font-size: 12px; line-height: 1.4; font-weight: bold; font-style: italic; font-family: Verdana, sans-serif	font: 12px/1.4 bold italic Verdana, sans-serif
background-color: #999; background-image: url(image.png); background-repeat: no-repeat; background-position: top left;	background: #999 url(image.png) no-repeat top left
list-style-type: disc; list-style-position: outside	list-style: disc outside
margin-top: 6px; margin-right: 12px; margin-bottom: 4px; margin-left: 8px	margin: 6px 12px 4px 8px (top, right, bottom, left)
margin-top: 8px; margin-right: 12px; margin-bottom: 6px; margin-left: 12px	margin: 8px 12px 6px (top, right/left, bottom)
margin-top: 0; margin-right: 6px; margin-bottom: 0; margin-left: 6px%	margin: 0 6px (top/bottom, right/left)
margin-top: 6px; margin-right: 6px; margin-bottom: 6px; margin-left: 6px	margin: 6px (all margins have same width)
padding-top: 4em; padding-right: 2em; padding-bottom: 3em; padding-left: 1em	padding: 4em 2em 3em 1em (top, right, bottom, left)
padding-top: 3em; padding-right: 2em; padding-bottom: 1em; padding-left: 2em	padding: 3em 2em 1em (top, right/left, bottom)
padding-top: 3em; padding-right: 2em; padding-bottom: 3em; padding-left: 2em	padding: 3em 2em (top/bottom, right/left)
padding-top: 1em; padding-right: 1em; padding-bottom: 1em; padding-left: 1em	padding: 1em (all padding has same width)
border-top: 4px; border-right: 2px; border-bottom: 3px; border-left: 1px	border: 4px 2px 3px 1px (top, right, bottom, left)
border-top: 4px; border-right: 2px; border-bottom: 3em; border-left: 2px	border: 4px 2px 3px (top, right/left, bottom)
border-top: 2px; border-right: 0; border-bottom: 2px; border-left: 0	border: 2px 0 (top/bottom, right/left)
border-top: 1px; border-right: 1px; border-bottom: 1px; border-left: 1px	border: 1px (all borders have same width)
bor border-width: 2px; border-color: #fff; border-style: solid	border: 2px #fff solid
border-left-width: 1px; border-left-color: blue; border-left-style: solid	border-left: 1px blue solid

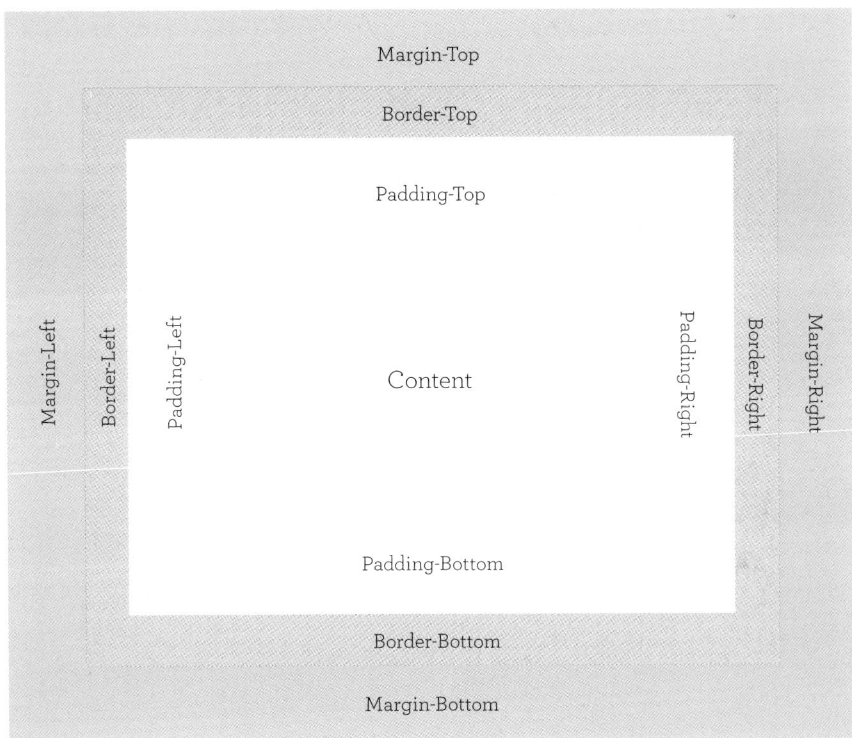

The Box Model

In CSS layouts, boxes replace tables as the primary building blocks. The Box Model determines how padding, margins, and borders affect the overall box dimensions.

Quick Shortcuts

Photoshop

The Tools Panel

Open the Info panel (Window > Info or F8) to see a description of the selected tool. If tools in a group share the same shortcut, you can cycle through by pressing Shift and the shortcut. Use the Keyboard Shortcuts feature (see page 22) to assign custom shortcuts for tools. Mac users can Ctrl-click to replicate right-click actions if they have a one-button mouse.

Tool	Shortcut	Tool Options
Move	V	Press the Option (Alt) key to copy an item as you move it. Press Shift to constrain movements to 45 degrees. Right-click on the canvas to select an underlying layer. When using most other tools, you can temporarily switch to the Move tool by pressing ⌘ (Ctrl). When the Move tool is selected, you can use the arrow keys instead of the mouse to move a layer or selection. Press Shift with the arrow keys to move in 10-point increments.
Rectangular/ Elliptical Marquee	M	Hold the Shift key to constrain proportions. Hold the Option (Alt) key to draw from the center or to deselect part of an existing marquee. Hold the Space bar to move the marquee while making a selection. With any selection tool, right-click to choose selection options.
Lasso	L	When using the Polygonal Lasso tool, double-click to close the polygon. When using the Magnetic Lasso tool, press the right or left angle brackets (> or <) to increase or decrease the contrast used to detect borders. Press the semicolon or apostrophe to increase or decrease the frequency of anchor points. Press the plus or minus keys to increase or decrease the width of the detection area.
Quick Selection	W	To decrease or increase the brush size: for Mac, hold down both Ctrl-Option keys, then click and drag the cursor left or right. For Windows, press Alt key then right-click and drag left or right.
Magic Wand	W	Use the tool options bar to set tolerance level. A higher number selects more pixels.
Crop	C	Press Return (Enter) to crop the image. Hit Esc to abandon the crop. Use forward slash (/) to show or hide the crop area.
Eyedropper	I	Click on a color in the canvas to set a new foreground color. Option-click (Alt-click) to set a new background color. Right-click to change the sampling area. When using the Brush, Pencil, Paint Bucket, or Shape tools, you can temporarily switch to the Eyedropper tool by holding the Option (Alt) key.
Spot Healing Brush/Healing Brush	J	To decrease or increase the brush size: for Mac, hold down both Ctrl-Option keys, then click and drag the cursor left or right. For Windows, press Alt key then right-click and drag left or right. Click on the Content-Aware button in the tool options bar to apply a content-aware fill.
Patch	J	Set Source and Destination area in the tool options bar. In CS6, click on Content-Aware button in the tool options bar to apply a content-aware fill.
Red Eye	J	Set Pupil Size and Darken Amount in the tool options bar.
Brush	B	Right-click on the canvas to open the Brush panel. Press the Option (Alt) key to switch temporarily to the Eyedropper tool. To increase or decrease brush size on the Mac, press Ctrl-Option and drag left or right. On Windows, press Alt and Right-click. Drag up or down to increase or decrease softness.
Pencil, Color Replacement, and Mixer Brush	B	Use the same modifiers as the Brush tool to increase or decrease brush size. Press the Option (Alt) key to switch temporarily from the Pencil to the Eyedropper tool.

Tool	Shortcut	Tool Option
Clone Stamp	S	Option (Alt) click to select the area to sample. Open the Clone Source panel for additional controls. To decrease or increase the brush size: for Mac, hold down both Ctrl-Option keys, then click and drag the cursor left or right. For Windows, press Alt key then right-click and drag left or right.
History Brush, Art History Brush	Y	These tools use the same modifiers as the Pencil tool for resizing.
Eraser	E	Uses the same modifiers as the Brush tool for resizing unless the Block Mode is selected in the tool options bar.
Background Eraser	E	Uses the same modifiers as the Brush for resizing.
Gradient	G	Hold shift key to constrain gradient angles to 45 degrees. Right-click to open the Gradient panel. Choose other options from the Option panel.
Paint Bucket	G	Right-click on the canvas to choose a blend mode. Press the Option (Alt) key to switch temporarily to the Eyedropper tool.
Dodge	O	Uses the same modifiers as the Brush tool for resizing. Use with Shift-Option-S (Shift+Alt+S) to lighten shadows; Shift-Option-M (Shift+Alt+M) to lighten midtones; and Shift-Option-H (Shift+Alt+H) to lighten highlights.
Burn	O	Uses the same modifiers as the Brush tool for resizing. Use with shortcuts listed above to darken shadows, midtones, or highlights.
Dodge	O	Uses the same modifiers as the Brush tool for resizing. Use with Shift-Option-D (Shift+Alt+D) to desaturate; Shift-Option-S (Shift+Alt+S) to saturate.
Pen Tool/ Freeform Pen	P	Press ⌘-Option (Ctrl+Alt) while dragging to duplicate path. Press ⌘ (Ctrl) to temporarily switch to the Direct Selection tool.
Type	T	Click on the canvas for point text. Click and drag for area text.
Path Selection	A	Press ⌘ (Ctrl) to temporarily switch to the Direct Selection tool. Press ⌘-Option (Ctrl+Alt) while dragging to duplicate path.
Direct Selection	A	Option-click (Alt-click) to select the entire path. Shift-click to select multiple anchor points. Press ⌘-Option (Ctrl+Alt) while dragging to duplicate path.
Shape	U	Hold the Shift key to constrain proportions. If shape is set to Fill Pixels, press Option (Alt) to temporarily switch to the Eyedropper.
Hand	H	Shift-drag to pan multiple documents simultaneously. When using other tools, temporarily switch to the Hand tool by pressing the spacebar. Double-click on the tool to fit image in window. Press H and hold down the mouse button to zoom in or out temporarily.
Rotate View	R	Enter the rotation angle in the tool options bar or Option-drag (Alt-drag) to rotate to the desired angle. Hit Esc to reset view. This tool works only when Enable OpenGL Drawing is checked in Edit > Preferences > Performance.
Zoom	Z	Hold Option (Alt) to zoom out. When using other tools, zoom in by pressing ⌘-Spacebar (Ctrl+Spacebar). Zoom out by pressing Option-spacebar (Alt+Spacebar).

Quick Shortcuts

Painting and Retouching

Action	Shortcut
Navigate brushes	Comma (,) selects the previous brush. Period (.) selects the next brush. Left angle bracket (<) selects the first brush. Right angle bracket (>) selects the last brush.
Lock or unlock transparent areas	Hit forward slash (/) to toggle back and forth. If transparent areas are locked, painting tools will have no effect on them.
Paint in a straight line	Select a brush. Shift-click at the start point of the line, then shift-click again at the end point.
Foreground/Background Colors	Hit X to switch foreground and background colors. Hit D to reset foreground color to black and background color to white.

Viewing the Workspace

Action	Shortcut
Change cursor to cross-hairs	Press Caps Lock (useful when extra precision is needed.)
Scroll vertically	Page Up or Page Down to scroll one screen at a time. Shift+Page Up or Shift+Page Down to scroll 10 pixels at a time.
Scroll horizontally	⌘-Page Up (Ctrl+Page Up) to scroll left. ⌘-Page Down (Ctrl+Page Down) to scroll right.
Move view to corners	Home to move to upper left. Option-Home (Alt+Home) to move to upper right. End to move to lower right. Option-End (Alt+End) to move to lower left.
Show/Hide Grid	⌘-' (Ctrl+'). Set grid size in Edit › Preferences › Guides, Grids & Slices.
Show/Hide Guides	⌘-; (Ctrl+;). Place guides by dragging from rulers.
Show/Hide Rulers	⌘-R (Ctrl+R)
Turn Snap On/Off	Shift-⌘-; (Shift+Ctrl+;)
Screen Modes	F to cycle through. Esc or F to exit Full Screen Mode.
Canvas colors	Spacebar+F to cycle forward between canvas colors, Shift+spacebar+F to cycle backward.

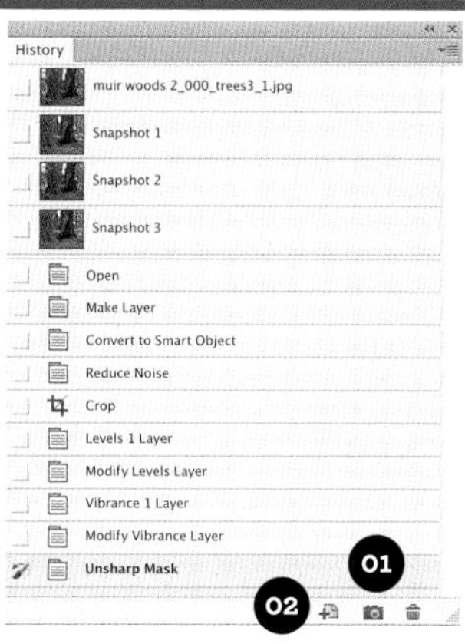

The History Panel

Use this panel as a quick way to undo previous steps and return to earlier states of the image:

01. Snapshots: Click here to create snapshots at important points in the project.
02. New Document: Click here to create a new document based on the current state.

History Brush: Click in the box next to a state to create a source for the History brush.
Navigation: You can also use keyboard shortcuts to navigate through the states: ⌘-Option-Z (Ctrl+Alt+Z) to step backward Shift-⌘-Z (Shift+Ctrl+Z) to step forward.

Selections

Action	Shortcut
Add to selection	Hold Shift key as you apply any selection tool.
Subtract from selection	Hold Option (Alt) key as you apply any selection tool.
Intersect a selection	Hold Shift-Option (Shift+Alt) as you apply a selection tool. Doesn't work with Quick Selection tool.
Select All	⌘-A (Ctrl+A)
Deselect All	Shift-⌘-I (Shift+Ctrl+I) or Shift+F7
Reselect	Shift-⌘-D (Shift+Ctrl+D)
Select Inverse	⌘-D (Ctrl+D)
Hide/Show selection marquee	⌘-H (Ctrl+H). Toggles back and forth.
Refine Mask	⌘-Option-R (Ctrl+Alt+R)
Feather selection	Shift+F6
Transform selected area	⌘-T (Ctrl+T)
Repeat last transformation	Shift-⌘-T (Shift+Ctrl+T)
Quick Mask Mode	Q (toggles on and off)
Group (selected) Layers	⌘-G (Ctrl+G)
Ungroup Layers	Shift-⌘-G (Shift+Ctrl+G)
Select All Layers	⌘-Option-A (Ctrl+Alt+A)

Quick Shortcuts

Illustrator

Tool	Shortcut	Tool Options
Selection	V	Double-click on an object to enter Isolation mode. Press Esc to exit Isolation mode. When using any tool, press ⌘ (Ctrl) to switch to the Selection, Direct Selection, or Group Selection tool, depending on which was last used.
Direct Selection	A	Press Option (Alt) to switch temporarily to the Group Selection tool.
Magic Wand	Y	Click on an object to select others with similar attributes. Shift-click to add to the selection. Option-click (Alt-click) to subtract from the selection. Caps Lock changes the cursor to crosshairs.
Lasso	Q	Draw around objects to select them. Shift-drag to add to the selection. Option-drag (Alt-drag) to subtract from the selection. Caps Lock changes the cursor to crosshairs.
Pen	P	Press Spacebar and drag to move the current anchor point. Press Option (Alt) to switch to Convert Anchor Point tool. Caps Lock changes the cursor to crosshairs.
Add Anchor Point	+	Press Option (Alt) to switch between this and Delete Anchor Point tool. Caps Lock changes the cursor to crosshairs.
Delete Anchor Point	-	Press Option (Alt) to switch between this and Add Anchor Point tool. Caps Lock changes the cursor to crosshairs.
Convert Anchor Point	Shift+C	When using the Pen tool, press Option (Alt) to switch to this tool temporarily.
Blob Brush	Shift+B	Double-click on the tool to customize its behavior.] increases size, [decreases size. Shift constrains movement to 45 degree angles. Caps Lock changes the cursor to crosshairs. Press Option (Alt) to switch to Smooth tool.
Type	T	Option (Alt) switches to Area Type tool. Shift switches to Vertical Type tool.
Line Segment	\	Shift constrains to 45 degree angle.
Rectangle	M	Shift constrains the shape to a square. Option (Alt) draws from center.
Ellipse	L	Shift constrains the shape to a circle. Option (Alt) draws from center.

Tool	Shortcut	Tool Options
Paintbrush	B	Double-click on the tool to set options. Option (Alt) switches temporarily to Smooth tool. Caps Lock changes the cursor to crosshairs.
Pencil	N	Double-click on the tool to set options. Option (Alt) switches temporarily to Smooth tool. Caps Lock changes the cursor to crosshairs.
Rotate	R	Option-click (Alt-click) on an object to set the origin point and open the Rotate dialog. Click on the origin point and Option-drag (Alt-drag) to make a copy as you rotate. Shift constrains rotation to 45 degree angles.
Reflect	O	Option-click (Alt-click) on an object to set the origin point and open the Reflect dialog. Shift constrains reflection to 45 degree angles.
Scale	S	Option-click (Alt-click) on an object to set the origin point and open the Scale dialog. Click on the origin point and Option-drag (Alt-drag) to make a copy as you scale. Shift constrains proportions.
Warp	Shift+R	Press Option (Alt) to resize the tool. Press Shift-Option (Shift-Alt) to resize proportionally.
Width	Shift+W	This is a tool introduced in CS5 that adds variable widths to strokes. Shift-click to select multiple width points. Esc to deselect a width point. Shift-drag to move multiple width points. Option-drag (Alt-drag) to make nonuniform widths. Option-drag (Alt-drag) a width point to copy it.
Free Transform	E	When resizing: Shift constrains proportions. When rotating: Shift constrains to 45 degree angles.
Shape Builder	Shift+M	Creates objects from selected overlapping shapes. Click inside a region to extract. Drag over regions to merge paths. Option-click (Alt-click) on a region to delete. Caps Lock changes the cursor to crosshairs.
Live Paint Bucket	K	Click on selected objects to create a Live Paint Group. Press Shift to switch between fill and stroke colors. Caps Lock changes the cursor to crosshairs.
Live Paint Selection	Shift+L	Selects areas within a Live Paint Group. Shift-click to add to selection. Use Direct Selection tool to reshape areas. Caps Lock changes the cursor to crosshairs.
Perspective Grid	Shift+P	Adds perspective grid to layout. Shift-⌘-I (Shift+Ctrl+I) toggles grid display on and off.
Perspective Selection	Shift+V	⌘-Alt-drag (Ctrl+Alt-drag) to copy selected objects as you move them
Symbol Sprayer	Shift+S	When any symbolism tool is selected, press Shift+} to increase intensity. Press Shift+{ to decrease intensity. Caps Lock changes the cursor to crosshairs.
Column Graph	J	Shift constrains graph to a square. Option (Alt) draws from center. These shortcuts apply to other graph tools.

Quick Shortcuts

Tool	Shortcut	Tool Options
Mesh	U	Click within a path to add mesh points. Option-click (Alt-click) to delete mesh points. Use Direct Selection tool to adjust mesh points. This tool does not work with compound paths or a single line.
Gradient	G	Press Shift to constrain gradient to 45 degree angles.
Eyedropper	I	Click on an object to sample all appearance attributes, including fills, strokes, and text styles, and apply them to selected object. Shift-click to sample only the color. Shift-Option-click (Shift+Alt-click) to append attributes. Double-click on the tool to customize which attributes are sampled or applied.
Blend	W	Double-click on the tool to set options.
Slice	Shift+K	Press shift to constrain the slice to a square. Press Option (Alt) to draw from center.
Eraser	Shift+E	Option-drag (Alt-drag) to erase a rectangular area.
Scissors	C	Press Option (Alt) to switch to the Add Anchor Point tool.
Artboard	Shift+O	Press Shift to constrain the artboard's proportions. Option-drag (Alt-drag) to duplicate an artboard.
Hand	H	Double-click on tool to fit imageable area in window. When using other tools, press Spacebar to switch to the Hand tool.
Zoom	Z	Press Option (Alt) to zoom out. When drawing zoom marquee, press Spacebar to move the zoom area. When using other tools, Press ⌘-Spacebar

Other Toolbox Features

Feature	Shortcut
Toggle Fill/Stroke	X
Swap Fill and Stroke colors	Shift+X
Restore to Default Fill and Stroke	D
Apply Color	, (comma)
Apply Gradient	. (period)
Apply No Color	/ (forward slash)
Cycle Draw Modes (Normal, Draw Behind, Draw Inside)	Shift-D

Grids, Guides, and Rulers

Action	Shortcut
Show/Hide Guides	⌘-; (Ctrl+;)
Show/Hide Perspective Grid	Shift-⌘-I (Shift+Ctrl+I)
Show/Hide Rulers	⌘-R (Ctrl+R)
Toggle Rulers to Artboard Rulers	⌘-Option-R (Ctrl+Alt+R)
Show/Hide Transparency Grid	Shift-⌘-D (Shift+Ctrl+D)
Smart Guides On/Off	⌘-U (Ctrl+U)
Lock Guides	⌘-Option-; (Alt+Ctrl+;)
Make Guides	⌘-5 (Ctrl+5)
Release Guides	⌘-Option-5 (Alt+Ctrl+5)
Show Grid	⌘-' (Ctrl+')
Snap to Grid	Shift-⌘-' (Shift+Ctrl+')
Snap to Point	⌘-Option-' (Alt+Ctrl+')

Opening Panels

Panel	Shortcut
Align	Shift-F7
Appearance	Shift-F6
Attributes	⌘-F11 (Ctrl+F11)
Brushes	F5
Color	F6
Color Guide	Shift-F3
Gradient	⌘-F9 (Ctrl+F9)
Graphic Styles	Shift-F5
Info	⌘-F8 (Ctrl+F8)
Layers	F7
Pathfinder	Shift-⌘-F9 (Shift+Ctrl+F9))
Stroke	⌘-F10 (Ctrl+F10)
Symbols	Shift-⌘-F11 (Shift+Ctrl+F11)
Transform	Shift-F8
Transparency	Shift-⌘-F10 (Shift+Ctrl+F10)
Character	⌘-T (Ctrl+T)
Paragraph	⌘-Option-T (Alt+Ctrl+T)
Tabs	Shift-⌘-T (Shift+Ctrl+T)

Viewing the Workspace

Action	Shortcut
View all artboards in window	⌘-Option-0 (Ctrl+Alt+0)
Preview	⌘-Y (Ctrl+Y)
Pixel Preview	⌘-Option-Y (Alt+Ctrl+Y)
Go to next document	⌘-F6 (Ctrl+F6)
Go to previous document	⌘-Shift-F6 (Ctrl+Shift+F6)
Go to next document group	⌘-Option-F6 (Ctrl+Alt+F6)
Go to previous document group	⌘-Option-Shift-F6 (Ctrl+Alt+Shift+F6)
Show/Hide Artboards	⌘-Shift-H (Ctrl+Shift+H)
Show/Hide Bounding Box	Shift-⌘-B (Shift+Ctrl+B)
Show/Hide Edges	⌘-H (Ctrl+H)
Show/Hide Gradient Annotator	⌘-Option-G (Alt+Ctrl+G)
Show/Hide Template	Shift-⌘-W (Shift+Ctrl+W)
Show/Hide Unselected Artwork	⌘-Option-Shift-3 (Ctrl+Alt+Shift+3)
(Normal, Full Cycle Screen ModesScreen with Menu Bar, Full Screen)	F
Exit Full Screen mode	Esc

Quick Shortcuts

InDesign

The Toolbox Panel

Open Tool Hints (Window > Utilities > Tool Hints) to see a description of the selected tool and instructions for using it. Tools are shown here only if they have shortcuts. You can assign custom shortcuts to the Smooth, Erase, and other tools using Edit > Keyboard Shortcuts... (see page 22).

Selection Tools

Tool	Shortcut
Selection	V or Esc
Direct Selection	A
Page	Shift+P
Gap	U
Content Collector	B
Content Placer	B
Pencil	N
Rectangle Frame	F

Drawing and Type Tools

Tool	Shortcut
Type	T
Type on a Path	Shift+T
Line	\ (back slash)
Pen	P
Add Anchor Point	+ (plus)
Delete Anchor Point	- (minus)
Convert Direction Point	Shift+C
Rectangle	M

Transformation Tools

Tool	Shortcut
Scissors	C
Free Transform	E
Rotate	R
Scale	S
Shear	O
Gradient Swatch	G
Gradient Feather	Shift+G
Ellipse	L

Temporary Tool Selection

Temporary Select	Shortcut
Any tool	Hold down the tool's shortcut key. Release it to return to the previous tool.
Hand	In Layout mode: Spacebar. In Text mode: Option (Alt). In any mode: Option-Spacebar (Alt+Spacebar)
Convert Direction Point When using Direct Selection tool	Option-Command (Ctrl+Alt).
Convert Direction Point	When using Direct Selection tool: Option-Command (Ctrl+Alt). When using Pen tool: Option (Alt)

Temporary Select	Shortcut
Zoom Out	Option-⌘-Spacebar or Option-Zoom In tool (Ctrl+Alt+Spacebar or Alt+Zoom In).
Selection or Direct Selection	⌘ (Ctrl). This will switch to the last-used selection tool.
Add Anchor Point	Option (Alt). This shortcut applies only when you're using the Scissors or Delete Anchor Point tool.
Delete Anchor Point	Option (Alt). This shortcut applies only when you're using the Add Anchor Point tool.
Zoom In	⌘-Spacebar (Ctrl+Spacebar)

Modification and Navigation

Tool	Shortcut
Eyedropper	I
Measure	K
Hand	H
Zoom	Z

Other Toolbox Features

Feature	Shortcut
Fill/Stroke (toggle)	X
Measure	K
Swap Fill and Stroke colors	Shift+X
Restore to Default Fill and Stroke	D
Formatting Affects Container/ Content (toggle)	J
Apply Color	, (comma)
Apply Gradient	. (period)
Apply No Color	/ (forward slash)
Normal View/ Preview Mode (toggle)	W

Opening Panels

Panel	Shortcut
Align	Shift-F7
Character	⌘-T (Ctrl+T)
Character Styles	Shift-F11 or Shift-⌘-F11 (Shift+F11 or Shift+Ctrl+F11)
Color	F6
Control	⌘-Option-6 (Ctrl+Alt+6)
Drop Shadow	⌘-Option-M (Ctrl+Alt+M)
Effects	Shift-⌘-F10 (Shift+Ctrl+F10)
Glyphs	Shift-Option-F11 (Shift+Alt+F11)
Index	Shift+F8)
Links	Shift-⌘-D (Shift+Ctrl+D)
Object Styles	⌘-F7 (Ctrl+F7)
Pages	F12 or ⌘-F12 (F12 or Ctrl+F12)
Paragraph Styles	F11 or ⌘-F11 (F11 or Ctrl+F11)
Preflight	Shift-⌘-Option-F (Shift+Ctrl+Alt+F)
Preview	Shift-⌘-Return (Shift+Ctrl+Enter)
Scripts	⌘-Option-F11 (Ctrl+Alt+F11) (Shift+Ctrl+Alt+F)
Separations Preview	Shift+F6
Stroke	F10 or ⌘-F10 (F10 or Ctrl+F10)
Swatches	F5
Table	Shift+F9
Tabs	Shift-⌘-T (Shift+Ctrl+T)
Text Wrap	⌘-Option-W (Ctrl+Alt+W)
Hide/Show Panels and Toolbox	Tab
Hide/Show Panels Only	Shift-Tab. Does not hide Control panel or Toolbox.
Tabs	Shift-⌘-T (Shift+Ctrl+T)

Most panels can also be opened via the Window menu.

Quick Shortcuts

Navigating the Layout

Go to	Shortcut
Any Page	⌘-J (Ctrl+J). Enter page number. Go to a Master Page by entering its prefix.
First Page	Shift-⌘-Page Up (Shift+Ctrl+Page Up)
Last Page	Shift-⌘-Page Down (Shift+Ctrl+Page Down)
Next Page	Shift+Page Down, Text: Shift+Page Down
Previous Page	Shift+Page Up
First Spread	Home or Shift-Option-Page Up (Shift+Alt+Page Up)
Last Spread	End or Shift-Option-Page Down (Shift+Alt+Page Down)
Next Spread	Option-Page Down (Alt+Page Down)
Previous Spread	Option-Page Up (Alt+ Page Up)
Go Forward	⌘-Page Down (Ctrl+Page Down). Goes to next page visited.
Go Back	⌘-Page Up (Ctrl+Page Up). Goes to last page visited.

All but the last four actions are available via View menu.

Grids, Guides, and Rules

Action	Shortcut
Show/Hide Guides	⌘-; (Ctrl+;)
Show/Hide Rulers	⌘-R (Ctrl+R)
Lock Guides	⌘-Option-; (Ctrl+Alt+;)
Snap to Guides	Shift-⌘-; (Shift+Ctrl+;)
Enable/Disable Smart Guides	⌘-U (Ctrl+U)
Show/Hide Baseline Grid	⌘-Option-' (Ctrl+Alt+')
Show/Hide Document Grid	⌘-' (Ctrl+')
Snap to Document Grid	Shift-⌘-' (Shift+Ctrl+')
Temporarily turn snap on or off	Press ⌘ (Ctrl) as you're dragging an object
Snap guide to ruler increments	Press Shift as you're dragging the guide
Select all Guides	⌘-Option-G (Ctrl+Alt+G)
Cycle through measurement units	Shift-⌘-Option-U (Ctrl+Shift+Alt+U)

Containers

Action	Shortcut
Select graphics container	Click with the Selection tool.
Select text container	Click with the Selection tool or Direct Selection tool.
Select content in graphics container	Click with the Direct Selection tool, or use the Selection tool to click on the donut-shaped grabber in the middle of the container.
Select content in text container	Click inside container with Text tool. You can also double-click with the Selection tool or triple-click with the Direct Selection tool.
Switch selection from content to container	Esc or double-click
Switch selection from container to content	Shift-Esc or double-click

View Settings

Action	Shortcut
Zoom In	⌘-+ (plus) (Ctrl++ [plus])
Zoom Out	⌘- – (minus) (Ctrl+–[minus])
Zoom to 50%, 200%, or 400%	⌘-5, 2 or 4 (Ctrl+5, 2 or 4)
View Actual Size	⌘-1 (Ctrl+1)
Fit Pasteboard in Window	Shift-⌘-Option-0 (Shift+Ctrl+Alt+0)
Fit Page in Window	⌘-0 (Ctrl+0)
Fit Selection in Window	⌘-Option-+(plus) (Ctrl+Alt++[plus])
Fit Spread in Window	⌘-Option-0 (Ctrl+Alt+0) or double-click Hand tool.
Current/previous view	⌘-Option-2 (Ctrl+Alt+2). Toggles between the two views.
Overprint Preview	Shift-⌘-Option-Y (Shift+Ctrl+Alt+Y)
Show/Hide Frame Edges	⌘-H (Ctrl+H)
Display Performance: High Quality	⌘-Option-H (Ctrl+Alt+H)
Display Performance: Typical	⌘-Option-Z (Ctrl+Alt+Z)
Display Performance: Fast	Shift-⌘-Option-Z (Shift+Ctrl+Alt+Z)
Clear Display Settings for Objects	Shift-⌘-F2 (Shift+Ctrl+F2). When you apply this shortcut, objects will revert to global settings for display performance.

Most actions are also available via the View menu.

Working with Text

Action	Shortcut
Autoflow when placing text	Shift-click. This shortcut automatically adds pages and frames as text is flowed.
Fixed-page autoflow when placing text	Shift-Option (Shift+Alt). Automatically adds frames, but does not add pages.
Semi-autoflow when placing text	Option-click (Alt-click). Automatically adds a frame to the current page and reloads text icon.
Show/Hide Text Threads	⌘-Option-Y (Ctrl+Alt+Y)
Go to first frame in thread	Shift-⌘-Option-Page Up (Shift+Ctrl+Alt+Page Up)
Go to last frame in thread	Shift-⌘-Option-Page Down (Shift+Ctrl+Alt+Page Down)
Go to next frame in thread	⌘-Option-Page Down (Ctrl+Alt+Page Down)
Go to previous frame in thread	⌘-Option-Page Up (Ctrl+Alt+Page Up)
Edit in Story Editor	⌘-Y (Ctrl+Y)
Find/Change	⌘-F (Ctrl+F)
Check Spelling	⌘-I (Ctrl+I)

Quick Apply

Use the Quick Apply panel (Edit > Quick Apply) for instant access to styles, scripts, menu commands, and other features that you can apply to the current selection. The keyboard shortcut is ⌘-Return (Ctrl+Enter).

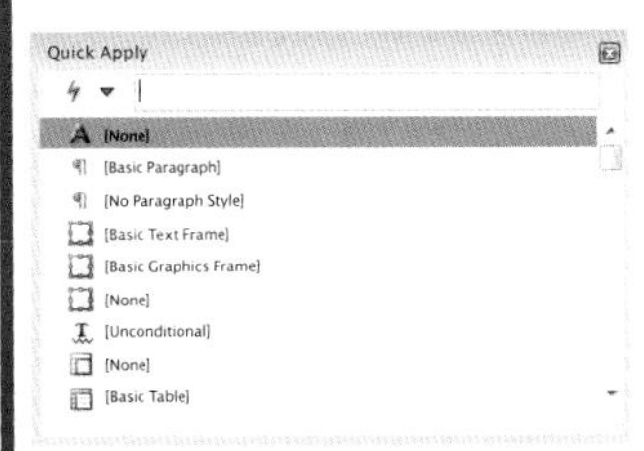

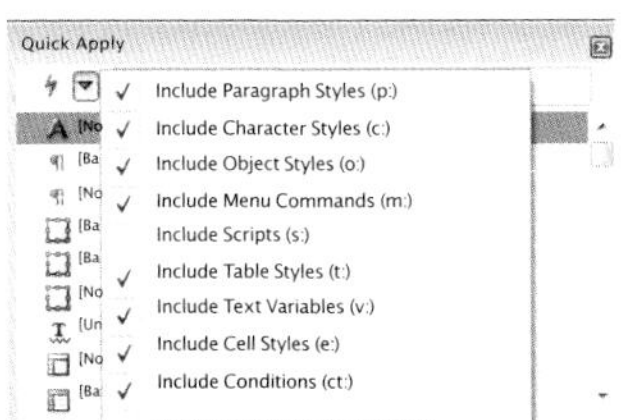

- Type in a few letters of the style or command to narrow the list.
- Type in a prefix, such as p: for Paragraph Styles, to narrow the list to specific types.
- Click on the triangle to specify which styles to include in the list.

Quick Shortcuts

Illustrator and InDesign

Formatting Type

Action	Shortcut
Align Left	⌘-Shift-Option-L (Ctrl+Alt+Shift+L)
Align Right	⌘-Shift-Option- R (Ctrl+Alt+Shift+R)
Align Center	⌘-Shift-Option-C (Ctrl+Alt+Shift+C)
Justify	⌘-Shift-Option-J (Ctrl+Alt+Shift+J)
Justify All Lines	⌘-Shift-Option-F (Ctrl+Alt+Shift+F)
Increase point size	⌘-> (Ctrl+>). Press Shift to increase by 5 points.
Decrease point size	⌘-< (Ctrl+<). Press Shift to decrease by 5 points.
Increase leading	Option-Up Arrow (Alt+Up Arrow). Press Shift to increase 5 times.
Decrease leading	Option-Down Arrow (Alt+Down Arrow). Press Shift to decrease 5 times.
Auto leading	Shift-⌘-Option-A (Shift+Ctrl+Alt+A)
Auto-hyphenate	Shift-⌘-Option-H (Shift+Ctrl+Alt+H). Toggles on and off.

Action	Shortcut
Increase kerning and tracking	Option-Right Arrow (Alt+Right Arrow). Press ⌘ (Ctrl) to increase 5 times.
Decrease kerning and tracking	Option-Left Arrow (Alt+Left Arrow). Press ⌘ (Ctrl) to decrease 5 times.
Increase kerning between words	⌘-Option-\ (Ctrl+Alt+\). Press Shift to increase 5 times.
Decrease kerning between words	⌘-Option-Del (Ctrl+Alt+Back). Press Shift to decrease 5 times.
Reset kerning and tracking	⌘-Option-Q (Ctrl+Alt+Q)
Increase baseline shift	Shift-Option-Up Arrow (Shift+Alt+Up Arrow). Press Shift to increase 5 times.
Decrease baseline shift	Shift-Option-Down Arrow (Shift+Alt+Down Arrow). Press Shift to decrease 5 times.
Reset horizontal scale	Shift-⌘-X (Shift+Ctrl+X)
Reset vertical scale	Shift-⌘-Option-X (Shift+Ctrl+Alt+X)
Show Hidden Characters	⌘-Option-I (Ctrl+Alt+I)
Set Tabs	Shift-⌘-T (Shift+Ctrl+T)

Transforming Objects

Action	Shortcut
Move object	Use arrow keys to move left, right, up or down. Press Shift to move 10 times base amount. Press Shift-⌘ (Shift+Ctrl) to move 1/10th base amount. Set base amount in Preferences.
Move... (dialog box)	Shift-⌘-M (Shift+Ctrl+M).
Duplicate	Shift-⌘-Option-D (Shift+Ctrl+Alt+D)
Duplicate and offset	With Selection or Direct Selection tool: Option-drag (Alt-drag). Press Shift to constrain to 45° angles. With Arrow keys: Option (Alt). Press Shift to increase offset distance 10 times.
Duplicate and transform	Choose a transformation tool and Option-drag (Alt-drag)
Decrease scale	⌘-< (Ctrl+<). Press Option (Alt) to decrease by 5 percent.
Increase scale	⌘-> (Ctrl+>). Press Option (Alt) to increase by 5 percent.
Transform Again	⌘-D (Ctrl+D) (Illustrator only)
Transform Sequence Again	⌘-Option-4 (Ctrl+Alt+4) (InDesign only)

Selecting Objects

Action	Shortcut
Add to/subtract from selection	Shift-Click with Selection or Direct Selection tool.
Select first object above	Shift-⌘-Option-] (Shift+Ctrl+Alt+]).
Select last object below	Shift-⌘-Option-[(Shift+Ctrl+Alt+[).
Select next object above	⌘-Option-] (Ctrl+Alt+]). Or with Selection tool: ⌘-Option-click (Ctrl+Alt-click)
Select next object below	⌘-Option-[(Ctrl+Alt+[). Or with Selection tool: ⌘-click (Ctrl-click)

Arranging Objects

Action	Shortcut
Bring to Front	Shift-⌘-] (Shift+Ctrl+])
Bring Forward	⌘-] (Ctrl+])
Send Backward	⌘-[(Ctrl+[)
Send to Back	Shift-⌘-[(Shift+Ctrl+[)

Quick Shortcuts

Dreamweaver

Opening Panels

Action	Shortcut
Show/Hide Panels	F4
AP Elements	F2
Behaviors	Shift+F4
Bindings	⌘-F10 (Ctrl+F10)
Business Catalyst	Shift-⌘-B (Shift+Ctrl+B)
Code Inspector	F10
Components	⌘-F7 (Ctrl+F7)
CSS Styles	Shift+F11
Databases	Shift-⌘-F10 (Shift+Ctrl+F10)
Files	F8
Frames	Shift+F2
History	Shift+F10
Insert	⌘-F2 (Ctrl+F2)
Properties	⌘-F3 (Ctrl+F3)
Search	F7
Server Behaviors	⌘-F9 (Ctrl+F9)
Snippets	Shift+F9
Tag Inspector	F9

Navigation

Action	Shortcut
Go to next document	⌘-Tab (Ctrl+Tab)
Go to previous document	Shift-⌘-Tab (Shift+Ctrl+Tab)
Switch Code/Design Views	⌘-` (Ctrl+`)
Open New Document in Same Window	Shift-⌘-N (Shift+Ctrl+N)
Browse in Bridge...	⌘-Option-O (Ctrl+Alt+O)

Select/Find

Action	Shortcut
Select All	⌘-A (Ctrl+A)
Select Parent Tag	⌘-[(Ctrl+[)
Select Child	⌘-] (Ctrl+])
Find and Replace	⌘-F (Ctrl+F)
Find Selection	Shift+F3
Find Next	F3

Formatting

Action	Shortcut
Indent	⌘-Option-] (Ctrl+Alt+])
Outdent	⌘-Option-[(Ctrl+Alt+[)
Align Left, Right, Center, Justify	⌘-Shift-Option-L, R, C, J (Ctrl+Alt+Shift-L, R, C, J)
Bold	⌘-B (Ctrl+B)
Italic	⌘-I (Ctrl+I)
Make Link...	⌘-L (Ctrl+L)
Remove Link	Shift-⌘-L (Shift+Ctrl+L)

Paragraph Formatting

Action	Shortcut
None	⌘-0 (Ctrl+0)
Paragraph	Shift-⌘-P (Shift+Ctrl+P)
Heading 1	⌘-1 (Ctrl+1)
Heading 2	⌘-2 (Ctrl+2)

Insert

Action	Shortcut
Line Break	Shift-Return
Non-Breaking Space	Shift-⌘-Spacebar (Shift+Ctrl+Spacebar)
SWF	⌘-Option-F (Ctrl+Alt+F)
Editable Region	⌘-Option-V (Ctrl+Alt+V)
Image	⌘-Option-I (Ctrl+Alt+I)
Named Anchor	⌘-Option-A (Ctrl+Alt+A)
Table	⌘-Option-T (Ctrl+Alt+T)
Tag...	⌘-E (Ctrl+E)

Site Testing

Action	Shortcut
Live View	Option-F11 (Alt+F11)
Freeze JavaScript	F6. Works only in Live View
Follow Link	⌘-Click Link (Ctrl+Click Link)
Refresh Design View	F5
Enter/Exit Inspect Mode	Shift-Option-F11 (Alt+Shift-F11)
Preview in Primary Browser	F12
Preview in Secondary Browser	Shift+F12

Quick Code Editing

Action	Shortcut
Modify Page Properties	⌘-J (Ctrl+J)
Open Quick Tag Editor	⌘-T (Ctrl+T)
Go to Source Code	⌘-Option-` (Ctrl+Alt+`)
Open Code Navigator	⌘-Option-N (Ctrl+Alt+N)

Editing in Code View

Action	Shortcut
Go to Line	⌘-G (Ctrl+G)
Show Code Hints	⌘-Spacebar (Ctrl+Spacebar)
Refresh Code Hints	⌘-. (Ctrl+.)
Balance Braces	⌘-' (Ctrl+')
Indent Code	Shift-⌘-> (Shift+Ctrl+>)
Outdent Code	Shift-⌘-< (Shift+Ctrl+<)
Select Child	⌘-] (Ctrl+])
Select Parent Tag	⌘-[(Ctrl+[)
Surround with #	Shift-⌘-3 (Shift+Ctrl+3)

Grids, Guides, and Rulers

Action	Shortcut
Show/Hide Grid	⌘-Option-G (Ctrl+Alt+G)
Show/Hide Rulers	⌘-Option-R (Ctrl+Alt+R)
Show/Hide Guides	⌘-; (Ctrl+;)
Lock Guides	⌘-Option-; (Ctrl+Alt+;)
Show/Hide All	Shift-⌘-I (Shift+Ctrl+I)
Snap To Grid	⌘-Shift-Option-G
Snap To Guides	Shift-⌘-; (Shift+Ctrl+;)
Guides Snap To Elements	Shift-⌘-/ (Shift+Ctrl+/)

Quick Shortcuts

Fireworks

The Tools Panel

If multiple tools share the same shortcut, you can cycle through them by repeatedly pressing the shortcut key. For example, press V twice to choose the Select Behind tool. If a tool doesn't have a default shortcut, you can assign one using Keyboard Shortcuts (see page 22).

Tool	Shortcut	Tool Options
Pointer	V, 0	When using most other tools, press ⌘ (Ctrl) to switch to the Pointer or Subselection tool, depending on which was last used. The Subselection tool doesn't have a default shortcut, but you can assign one in Keyboard Shortcuts.
Select Behind	V, 0	Press the shortcut key to toggle between Pointer and Select Behind.
Scale/Skew/ Distort/9-slice scaling	Q	Click and drag within the selected object to move it. When using Scale or 9-slice scaling tools, press Shift to constrain proportions.
Crop	C	Press Shift to constrain proportions. Double-click inside the selected area to apply the crop. Hit Esc or double-click outside the selected area to remove the crop marquee.
Export Area	J	Click and drag to select the area you want to export. Press Shift to constrain proportions. Double-click inside the selected area to open the Image Preview dialog and export the selection. Hit Esc or double-click outside the selected area to remove the export marquee.
Marquee/Oval Marquee	M	Press Shift to constrain proportions to square or circle. Press Option (Alt) to draw from center. Press Spacebar to move marquee while making a selection. When refining selections, press Shift to add to selection and Option (Alt) to subtract.
Lasso/Polygon Lasso	L	When refining selections, press Shift to add to selection and Option (Alt) to subtract. When using Polygon Lasso, press Shift to constrain lines to 45 degrees. Double-click to close the polygon.
Magic Wand	W	Press Shift to add to selection and Option (Alt) to subtract.
Brush	B	Press Option (Alt) to sample color. Press Shift and drag to constrain angles to 45 degrees.
Pencil	Y	Press Shift and drag to constrain angles to 45 degrees. Shift-click to draw connected line segments.
Eraser	E	Press Shift to constrain angles to 90 degrees.
Blur/Sharpen/ Smudge	R	Press Option (Alt) to switch temporarily between Blur and Sharpen.
Dodge/Burn	R	Press Option (Alt) to switch temporarily between Dodge and Burn.
Rubber Stamp	S	Click once to select the source area, then click or drag in the areas you want to paint. Option-click (Alt-click) to select a new source area.
Replace Color	S	Select options for this tool in the Properties panel. Press Option (Alt) to sample a color. Press Shift to constrain angles to 90 degrees.
Red Eye Removal	S	Select options for this tool in the Properties panel. Press Shift to constrain proportions.
Line	N	Press Shift to constrain angle to 45 degrees. Press Option (Alt) to sample a color with the Eyedropper.

Tool	Shortcut	Tool Options
Pen	P	Press Shift to constrain angle to 45 degrees.
Vector Path/ Redraw Path	B	Press Shift to constrain angle to 45 degrees. Press Option (Alt) to sample a color with the Eyedropper.
Rectangle/ Ellipse	R	Press Shift to constrain proportions to square or circle. Press Option (Alt) to draw from center. Press Spacebar to move shape as it's being created.
Polygon	G	Select shape and number of sides in the Properties panel. Press Shift to constrain orientation to 45 degrees. Press Option (Alt) to draw from center. Press Spacebar to move shape as it's being created. You can also use this tool in conjunction with the Auto Shape Properties panel.
Text	T	Click and drag to select the text area.
Freeform	F	Press Right Arrow key as you drag to increase the reshape area. Press Left Arrow key to reduce. Press Shift to constrain movement to 45 degrees.
Reshape Area	F	Press Right Arrow key as you drag to increase the reshape area. Press Left Arrow key to reduce.
Path Scrubber	U	Set options in the Properties panel. Press the shortcut key to toggle between additive and subtractive. These tools require a pressure-sensitive tablet.
Rectangular Hotspot	J	Press Shift to constrain proportions to square or circle. Press Option (Alt) to draw from center. Press Spacebar to move hotspot while making a selection.
Slice Tool	K	Press Shift to constrain proportions. Press Option (Alt) to draw from center. Press Spacebar to move slice while making a selection.
Eyedropper	I	Press Caps Lock to change cursor to crosshairs.
Paint Bucket	K	Press Option (Alt) to sample a color.
Hand	H	When using most other tools, press Spacebar to temporarily switch to Hand. Double-click on the tool to fit artwork in window.
Zoom	Z	Press Option (Alt) to zoom out. Click and drag within the document to zoom in on that area.

Opening Panels

All default shortcuts for opening panels changed in CS6. Both old and new are noted below.

Panel	Shortcut
Tools	CS6: ⌘-Option-F2 (Ctrl+Alt+F2). CS5: ⌘-Option-T (Ctrl+Alt+T)
Properties	CS6: ⌘-Option-F3 (Ctrl+Alt+F3)
Optimize	CS6: F6
Layers	CS6: F2. CS5: ⌘-Option-L (Ctrl+Alt+L)
Common Library	CS6: F7. CS5: ⌘-Shift-L (Ctrl+Shift+L)
Pages	CS6: F5. CS5: ⌘-Option-O (Ctrl+Alt+O)
States	CS6: Shift+F2. CS5: ⌘-Option-K (Ctrl+Alt+K)

Panel	Shortcut
History	CS6: Shift+F10.
Styles	CS6: ⌘-F11 (Ctrl+F11). CS5: ⌘-Option-J (Ctrl+Alt+J)
URL	CS6: Shift-Option-F11 (Shift+Alt+F11). CS5: ⌘-Option-U (Ctrl+Alt+U)
Color Mixer	CS6: Shift+F9. CS5: ⌘-Option-M (Ctrl+Alt+M)
Swatches	CS6: ⌘-F9 (Ctrl+F9). CS5: ⌘-Option-S (Ctrl+Alt+S)
Behaviors	CS6: Shift+F3. CS5: ⌘-Option-H (Ctrl+Alt+H)

00:01 00:30 05:00 60:00 24:00:00

Quick Shortcuts

Fireworks

Viewing the Workspace

Action	Shortcut
Hide Selection	CS6: ⌘-L (Ctrl+L). CS5: ⌘-M (Ctrl+M).
Show All	CS6: ⌘-Shift-L (Ctrl+Shift+L). CS5: ⌘-Shift-M (Ctrl+Shift+M)
Show/Hide Slices and Hotspots	CS6: 2
Show/Hide Edges	⌘-H (Ctrl+H)
Show/Hide Tooltips	⌘-] (Ctrl+])
Show/Hide Rulers	⌘-Option-R (Ctrl+Alt+R)
Show/Hide Grid	⌘-' (Ctrl+')
Snap to Grid	⌘-Shift-' (Ctrl+Shift+')
Edit Grid	⌘-Option-G (Ctrl+Alt+G)
Show/Hide Guides	⌘-; (Ctrl+;)
Lock Guides	⌘-Option-; (Ctrl+Alt+;)
Snap to Guides	⌘-Shift-; (Ctrl+Shift+;)
Show/Hide Smart Guides	⌘-\ (Ctrl+\)
Snap to Smart Guide	⌘-Shift-\ (Ctrl+Shift+\). Toggles on and off.

Working with Objects

Action	Shortcut
Free Transform	⌘-T (Ctrl+T)
Numeric Transform	⌘-Shift-T (Ctrl+Shift+T)
Rotate 90°	⌘-9 (Ctrl+9) to rotate clockwise, ⌘-7 (Ctrl+7) to rotate counterclockwise
Align Left	⌘-Option-1 (Ctrl+Alt+1)
Align Center Vertical	⌘-Option-2 (Ctrl+Alt+2)
Align Right	⌘-Option-3 (Ctrl+Alt+3)
Align Top	⌘-Option-4 (Ctrl+Alt+4)
Align Center Horizontal	⌘-Option-5 (Ctrl+Alt+5)
Align Bottom	⌘-Option-6 (Ctrl+Alt+6)
Distribute Widths	⌘-Option-7 (Ctrl+Alt+7)
Distribute Heights	⌘-Option-9 (Ctrl+Alt+9)
Bring to Front	CS6: ⌘-Shift-Up Arrow (Ctrl+Shift+Up Arrow). CS5: ⌘-F (Ctrl+F)
Bring Forward	CS6: ⌘-Up Arrow (Ctrl+Up Arrow). CS5: ⌘-Shift-F (Ctrl+Shift+F)
Send Backward	CS6: ⌘-Down Arrow (Ctrl+Down Arrow). CS5: ⌘-Shift-B (Ctrl+Shift+B)
Send to Back	CS6: ⌘-Shift-Down Arrow (Ctrl+Shift+Down Arrow). CS5: ⌘-B (Ctrl+B)
Align Text Left, Right, Center, Justify	⌘-Option-Shift-L, R, C, J (Ctrl+Alt+Shift+L, R, C, J)
Stroke/Fill Colors	Press X to swap stroke and fill colors. Press D to restore strokes to black and fills to white. You can change the color defaults in Preferences › General.

Quick Shortcuts

Acrobat Pro

Action	Shortcut
Go to Page	Shift-⌘-N (Shift+Ctrl+N)
Go to First Page	Home
Go to Last Page	End
Go to Next Page	Right Arrow
Go to Previous Page	Left Arrow
Show/Hide Menu Bar	F9
Add Sticky Note	⌘-6 (Ctrl+6)

Single-Key Accelerators

To enable these shortcuts, go to Edit > Preferences > General and check "Use single-key accelerators to access tools."

Navigation Tool	Shortcut
Hand	H
Select	V
Zoom	Z
Take A Snapshot	G

Tools Tool	Shortcut
Pages > Crop	C
Content > Edit Document Text	T
Content > Insert Link	L
Content > Select Object	R
Analyze > Object Data	O
Analyze > Measuring	B

Quick Tools Toolbar

- Press Spacebar to temporarily select Hand tool
- Press ⌘-Spacebar (Ctrl+Spacebar) to temporarily select Zoom tool.
- When Zoom tool is selected, you can draw a marquee to zoom in. Press ⌘ (Ctrl) to zoom out.

Comment Tool	Shortcut
Annotations > Add Sticky Note	S
Annotations > Highlight Text	U
Annotations > Stamp tool	K
Annotations > Text Edits	E
Drawing Markups > Add Text Box	X
Drawing Markups > Add Text Callout	P

Quick Shortcuts

Bridge

File/Folder Operations

Action	Shortcut
New Folder	Shift-⌘-N (Ctrl+Shift+N)
Open file in Camera Raw	⌘-R (Ctrl+R) or double-click image.
Open Raw Image File in Photoshop	Shift+double-click image. Bypasses Camera Raw.
Return to CS Application	⌘-Alt+O (Ctrl+Alt+O) This reopens Photoshop, Illustrator, or whatever other program was used to summon Bridge.
View Info on Selected Files	⌘-I (Ctrl+I)
Find Files	⌘-F (Ctrl+F)
Delete File	⌘-Del (Ctrl+Del)
Batch Rename	Shift-⌘-R (Ctrl+Shift+R)
Rotate image 90 degrees clockwise	⌘-] (Ctrl+])
Rotate image 90 degrees counterclockwise	⌘-[(Ctrl+[)

View/Navigation Option

Action	Shortcut
Cycle forward between thumbnail, details, and list views	⌘-\ (Ctrl+\)
Cycle backward between views	Shift-⌘-\ (Ctrl+Shift+\)
Increase/decrease thumbnail size	⌘-+ (plus) (Ctrl++ [plus])/⌘- - (minus) (Ctrl+- [minus]). Hold down Shift key for bigger increase or decrease in size.
Full Screen Preview	Space
Slideshow	⌘-L (Ctrl+L)
Slideshow Options	Shift-⌘-L (Ctrl+Shift+L)
Review Mode	⌘-B (Ctrl+B)
Compact Mode	⌘-Enter (Ctrl+Enter)
Show/hide panels	Tab
Move left or right one file	Left or Right Arrow
Move to first or last file	Home or End

Selecting Files

Action	Shortcut
Add to selection (contiguous)	Shift + Arrow Key
Add to selection (discontiguous)	⌘-click (Ctrl-click).
Open Raw Image File in Photoshop	Shift-⌘-A (Ctrl+Shift+A)
Invert Selection	Shift⌘-I (Shift+Ctrl+I)

Ratings and Labels

Action	Shortcut
Apply star ratings to selection	⌘-rating (Ctrl+rating). Rating is a number from 1 to 5
Decrease rating	⌘-, (Ctrl+,)
Increase Rating	⌘-. (Ctrl+.)
Remove Rating	⌘-0 (Ctrl+0)
Show files with high ratings	⌘-Option-Rating (Ctrl+Alt+Rating) to show files with that rating or higher. Example: ⌘-Option-4 shows files rated 4 or 5.
Show files with a specified rating	⌘-Option-Shift-rating (Ctrl+Alt+Shift+rating). Example: ⌘-Option-4 shows files rated 4
Apply Label: Select	⌘-6 (Ctrl+6)
Apply Label: Second	⌘-7 (Ctrl+7)
Apply Label: Approved	⌘-8 (Ctrl+8)
Apply Label: Review	⌘-9 (Ctrl+9))
Show files based on label	⌘-Option-6 through 9 (Ctrl+Alt+6 through 9)
Reject file	Del

Stacks

Action	Shortcut
Group Files as Stack	⌘-G (Ctrl+G)
Ungroup Files from Stack	Shift-⌘-G (Ctrl+Shift+G)
Open Stack	⌘-Right Arrow (Ctrl+Right Arrow)
Close Stack	⌘-Left Arrow (Ctrl+Left Arrow)
Open Stack	⌘-Alt+Right Arrow (Ctrl+Alt+Right Arrow)
Collapse All Stacks	⌘-Alt+Left Arrow (Ctrl+Alt+Left Arrow)
Select all files in stack Option-click	(Alt-click)

Filters

Action	Shortcut
Clear filters	⌘-Option-A (Ctrl+Alt+A)
Select inverse	Option-click (Alt-click) on a filter to select all other filters in that category.
Show files with selected rating or higher	Shift-click on the rating in filter panel. Example: Click on 3 stars to show files rated 3, 4 or 5 stars.

Quick Shortcuts

The Mac Environment

Mac OS X is the preferred environment for most creative professionals. Recent versions—Lion and Mountain Lion—introduce behaviors from the iPad along with new features such as the Launchpad, App Store, and Mission Control.

Introducing Finger Gestures

If you have a laptop trackpad or Apple's Magic Trackpad, you can use finger gestures as shortcuts, much as you can on the iPad and iPhone. For example, with two fingers, you can:

- Scroll up, down, left, or right
- Click to replicate a right-click
- Pinch to zoom out
- Spread to zoom in
- Rotate a photo or PDF document

Go to > System Preferences > Trackpad to see all default gestures or to customize them.

The Dock

The Dock is the most efficient way to open frequently used applications, folders, or documents. Applications always appear on the left, and folders and documents on the right.

- Add items to the Dock by dragging them from the Finder. You can also drag to remove or rearrange items.
- To see options for each application in the Dock, right-click or hold down the mouse button for a few seconds. Right-click to see options for each folder.
- Go to > System Preferences > Dock to modify Dock settings. To conserve space in the Dock, you can insert a folder containing aliases for applications or documents.

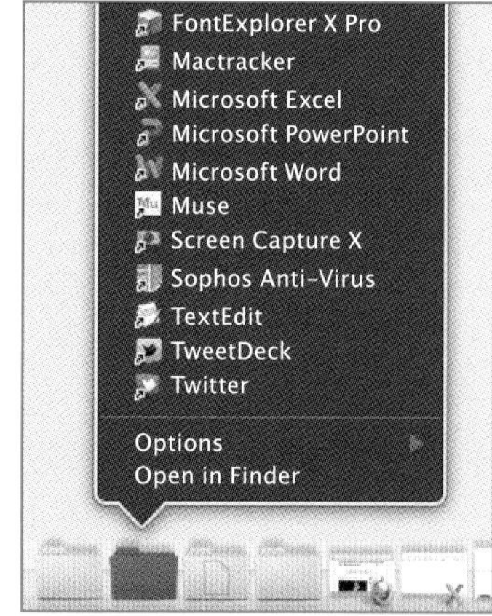

Launchpad

This is another new feature in OS X Lion that replicates iPad functionality. It provides a single location for launching any installed application. As each screen fills up, the program inserts new screens to accommodate additional apps.

- To navigate through the screens, click on the dots at the bottom, scroll with the mouse or hit the Right or Left Arrow keys.
- To move an app between screens, drag it to the edges. You can also drag to rearrange apps.
- If you use the Finder to create an alias of an application, the alias will appear in the Launchpad. Removing the alias from the Applications folder will remove it from the Launchpad—just be sure you're removing the alias and not the application itself.
- You can consolidate Launchpad apps into folders to conserve space. To create a folder, drag one app over another. To open a folder, click on it. To rename a folder, open it and click on the name.

Quick Shortcuts

Contextual Menus

These menus appear when you right-click or Ctrl-click on an item in the Mac OS or an application. It's an efficient way to choose options that are available for the tool or feature you've selected. All of Apple's recent-vintage mice support right-clicking, as do most mice from other vendors.

In OS X, the right-click is referred to as the "secondary click." You can choose whether the right- or left-click is the secondary click by going to > System Preferences > Mouse.

Spaces

Mission Control enables OS X's Spaces feature, which lets you organize your workspace into multiple desktops. For example, you can have InDesign running in one desktop and Safari running in another, and then switch between them by pressing Ctrl-Right or Left Arrow. You can also navigate the desktops via Mission Control.

To Create a New Desktop

- Go to the upper-right corner of Mission Control and click on the plus sign.
- Drag the app's window to the upper-right corner.

Mission Control

This new app, which replaces many features in Exposé, makes it easier to navigate through open windows on your desktop. You can open it from the Dock, or use one of several shortcuts: the Exposé key on an Apple keyboard, Ctrl-Up Arrow, a three-finger upward swipe on a trackpad, or a double-tap on the Magic Mouse. To exit Mission Control, hit Esc, the Exposé key or Ctrl-Up Arrow, or swipe down with three fingers.

Mission Control shows the currently running applications, but won't let you navigate the documents open in each program. Instead, use these shortcuts:

- To view open windows in the currently active application, press Ctrl-Down Arrow.
- To view open windows in other applications, press ⌘-Tab to open the application switcher, navigate to the application, and press the Up or Down Arrow.

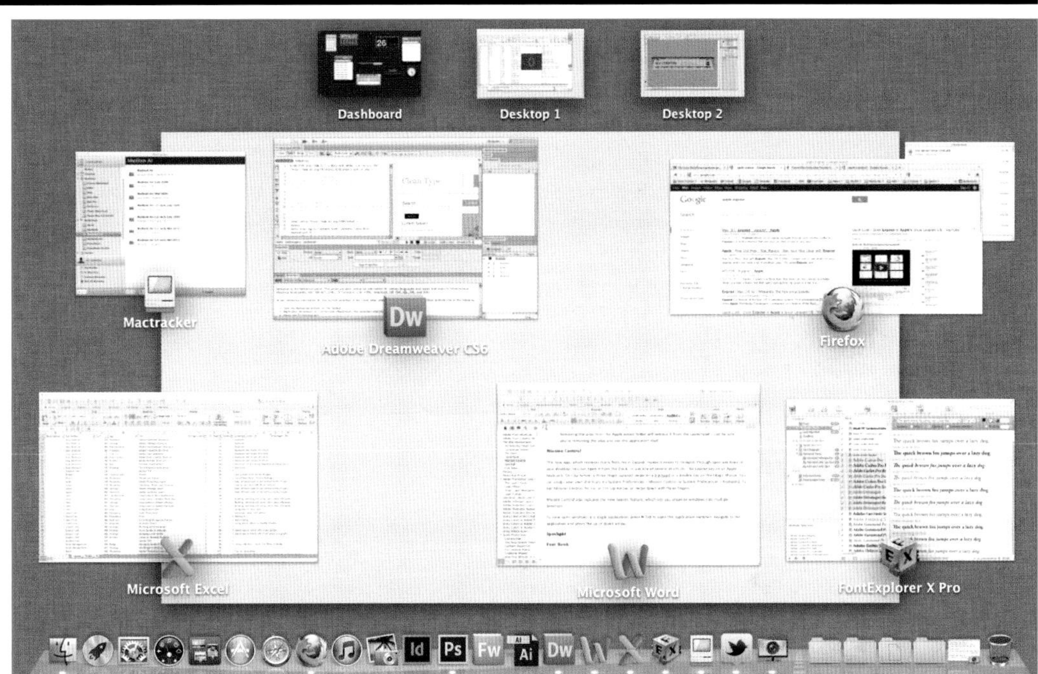
Dashboard
Desktop 1
Desktop 2
Mactracker
Adobe Dreamweaver CS6
Firefox
Microsoft Excel
Microsoft Word
FontExplorer X Pro

Quick Shortcuts

The Windows Environment

The latest versions of Windows, particularly Windows 7, make it a snap to access frequently used programs and documents.

Exploring the Taskbar

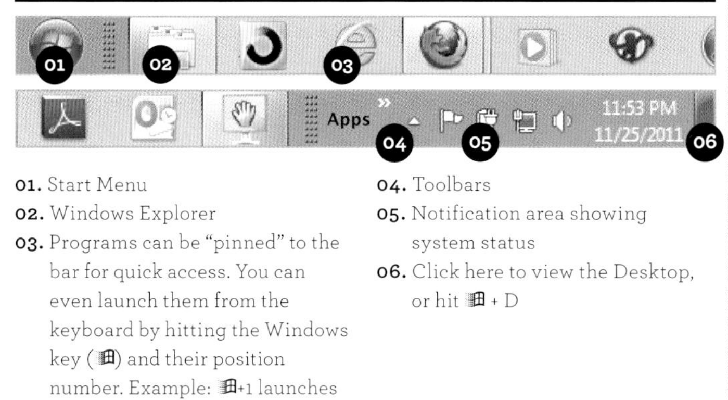

01. Start Menu

02. Windows Explorer

03. Programs can be "pinned" to the bar for quick access. You can even launch them from the keyboard by hitting the Windows key (⊞) and their position number. Example: ⊞+1 launches Windows Explorer.

04. Toolbars

05. Notification area showing system status

06. Click here to view the Desktop, or hit ⊞ + D

Quick Access to Documents

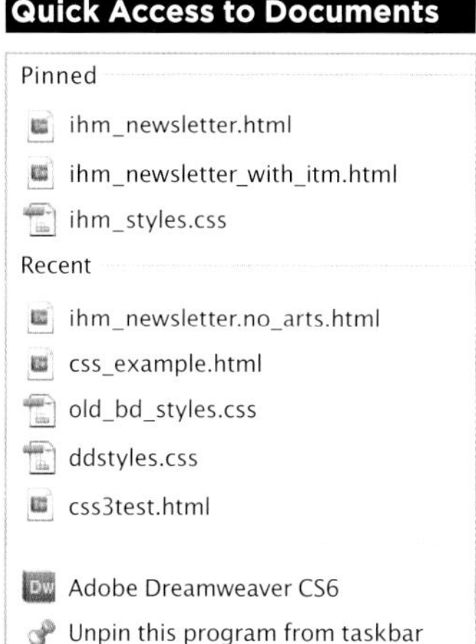

Once a program is pinned to the Taskbar, you can right-click on its icon to see a list of recently opened documents. You can pin a document to the list so it's always a couple of clicks away. You might do this with frequently used templates, or you can temporarily pin a current project.

To pin a document, right-click on its name in the Recent list and choose Pin to this List. You can also right-click to remove a document from the list.

Quick Access to Programs

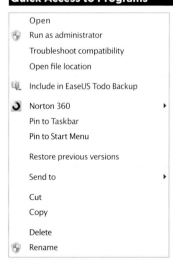

Open
Run as administrator
Troubleshoot compatibility
Open file location
Include in EaseUS Todo Backup
Norton 360
Pin to Taskbar
Pin to Start Menu
Restore previous versions
Send to
Cut
Copy
Delete
Rename

Windows 7 offers many ways to launch programs, but for maximum efficiency it's best to use the Taskbar and/or Start Menu. By default, the Taskbar sits on the bottom of the screen. You can move it to the top, right, or left edges, but you'll probably find it's quicker to access programs and documents if you keep it on the bottom. The Taskbar shows all currently running programs, but you can also "pin" the ones you use most often so they're always available. Drag the program's shortcut to the Taskbar, or right-click on the program's name and choose Pin to Taskbar.

Quick Access to Folders

Pinned
_Story Notes-Current - Shortcut
ihm
GDHalf the Time
Frequent
bmps
windows interface
cs interface
vector graphics
Grid systems
Windows Explorer

You cannot pin folders to the Taskbar, but you can pin them to the Windows Explorer list. Just drag the folder to the Taskbar and let go when you see the Pin to Windows Explorer message.

Another option is to add a folder as a Toolbar. Right-click in an empty area of the Taskbar and choose Toolbars > New Toolbar. Select a folder, and it will appear on the right side of the Taskbar. Keep in mind that this can use up a lot of space in the bar. To remove a folder, right-click on its name and choose Close Toolbar.

Customizing the Taskbar

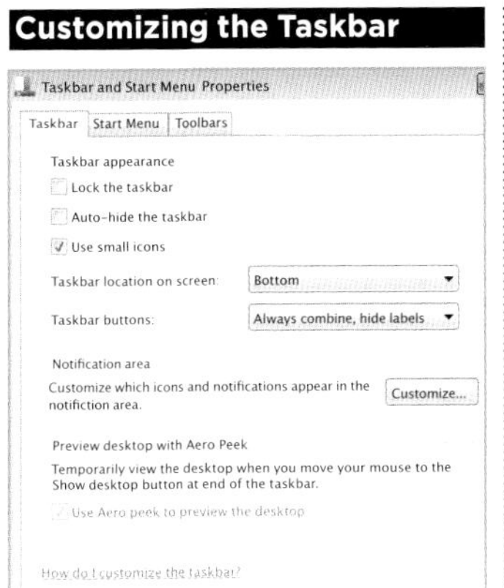

You can customize the Taskbar's appearance through the Properties dialog. Find an empty area of the Taskbar, right-click, and choose Properties. The options include Small Icons, which take up less space, and Auto-hide. When you Auto-hide the Taskbar, it appears only when you hover over its location.

The Start Menu

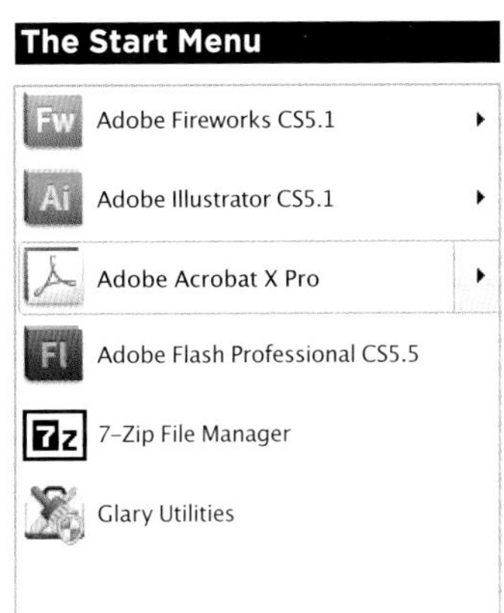

Just as you can pin programs to the Taskbar, you can use the same procedure—right-clicking or dragging—to pin them to the Start Menu. Pinned applications appear at the top of the menu. Click on the arrow next to the program to see recently opened documents. As with the Taskbar, you can pin documents to the list by right-clicking on their names.

In Windows 8, the Start menu has been replaced by the Start screen.

Windows 8

If you buy a new PC, chances are it will be running Windows 8, the latest version of Microsoft's operating system. It's the first Microsoft OS designed to co-exist on desktop computers and mobile devices such as smartphones and tablets. It thus enables navigation via finger gestures, though you can also use a mouse or other pointing device.

The most prominent feature is the new Metro user interface. Instead of booting up to the traditional Windows desktop, the OS presents the new Start screen, which replaces the Start menu in older Windows versions. Each application appears on the screen as a tile that can present live information, such as a summary of the last-received email message. Also new is the Charm Bar, which provides access to the search function and system settings.

The old Windows desktop hasn't gone away. You can access it by clicking on the desktop tile, and at that point Windows 8 behaves more like Windows 7, with the familiar taskbar on the bottom of the screen.

Quick Shortcuts

Windows: Improving System Performance

The latest versions of Windows don't perform well on older computers, and even newer hardware can benefit from changing some of the system settings.

Turn off Aero

Control Panel Home
Change desktop icons
Change mouse pointers
Change your account picture

Change the visuals and sounds on your computer
Click a theme to change the desktop background, window color, sounds, and screen saver all at once.

VAIO Theme 5
Basic and High Contrast Themes (6)
Windows 7 Basic
Windows classic
High Contrast #1
High Contrast #2
High Contrast Black
High Contrast White

See also
Display
Taskbar and Start menu
Ease of Access Center

Desktop Background
Solid Color
Window Color
Windows 7 Basic
Sounds
Windows Default
Screen Saver
None

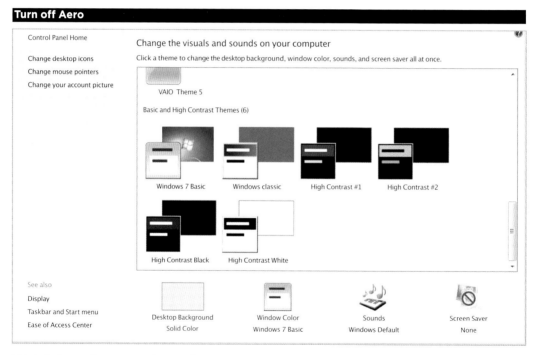

This is the feature that gives Windows fancy-looking special effects such as transparent borders and icons that display document contents. Turning it off can make the system more responsive, but has minimal impact on the appearance of programs.

The easiest way to turn it off is to right-click on the Windows desktop and select Personalize. This opens the Personalization control panel.

Scroll to the bottom and pick one of the basic themes (Windows 7 Basic or Windows Classic work best). By default, Windows 7 Basic displays a Windows logo, but you can click on Desktop Background in the bottom pane to change to a different background. You can also point to a folder of images so the background changes at specified intervals.

Change Performance Settings

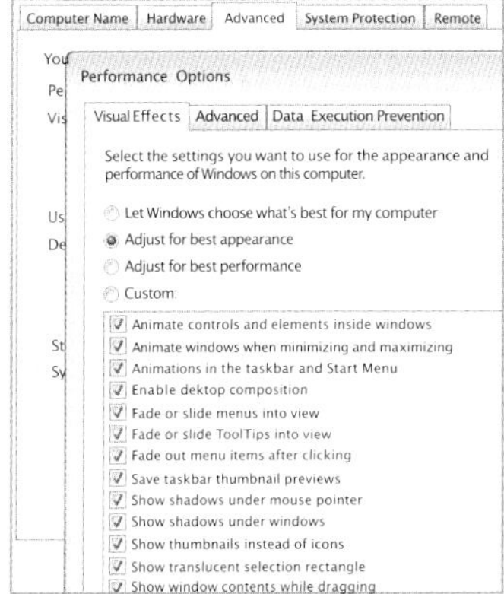

You can gain an additional speed boost by adjusting settings in the Performance Options panel.

01. Go to Start > Control Panel > System to open the System Control Panel.
02. Choose Advanced System Settings and click on the Advanced tab. The first section is Performance.
03. Click on the Settings button to open the Performance Options panel, then click on the Visual Effects tab.

Here you'll see a long list of effects. By default, they're all checked. To turn them all off, click on the Adjust for Best Performance button; the interface will then resemble Windows XP.

Additional Steps

To learn more about improving performance, type "Optimize Windows 7 for better performance" in the Windows help system. You can get additional advice from books such as Joli Ballew's *Degunking Windows 7* or David Pogue's *Windows 7 The Missing Manual.*

Disable Unneeded Start-up Items

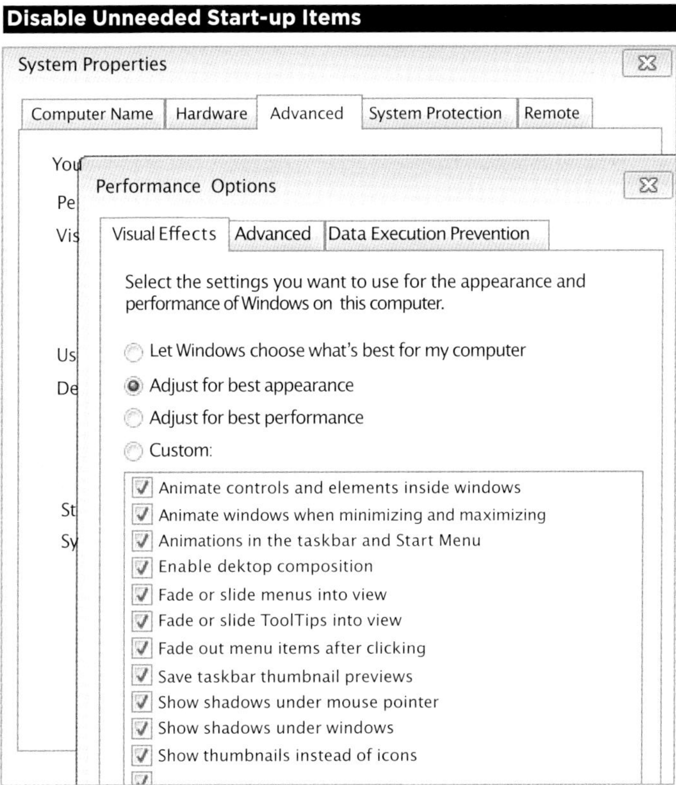

Many programs automatically install software components that launch whenever you boot up Windows. Some of these start-up items are necessary for the smooth operation of your system. Others needlessly slow down the start-up process and consume system resources while running in the background. You can use the Windows System Configuration utility to prevent these items from starting up.

01. Open the Start menu and enter "msconfig" in the search field. This opens the configuration utility.
02. Click on the utility's Startup tab. You should see a list of start-up items with checkboxes.
03. If a box is checked, click on it to uncheck that item and prevent the program from starting up at launch.

The trick is figuring out which start-up items are necessary and which ones are not. Several websites maintain databases of start-up items that include advice about whether or not you should disable them. Two good ones are at Bleeping Computer (http://www.bleepingcomputer.com/startups/) and Pacman's Portal (http://www.pacs-portal.co.uk/startup_content.php). You can also try Googling the name of the start-up item to learn about its function.

Quick Shortcuts

Managing Fonts

You will work more efficiently by activating only the fonts you need, when you need them. Mac OS X and Windows both include built-in font-management features, but designers who work frequently with type may want to opt for a third-party solution.

Font Book

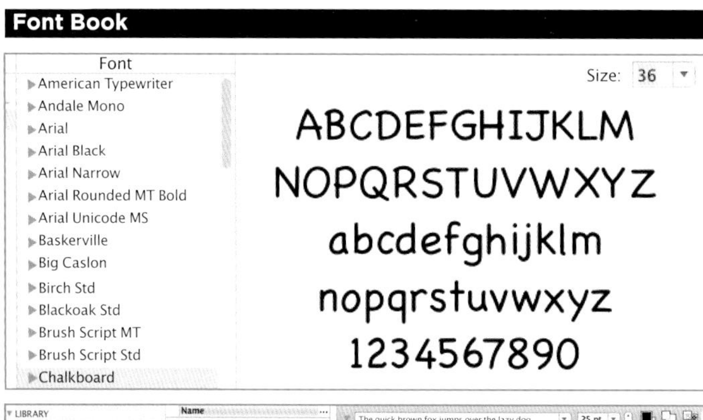

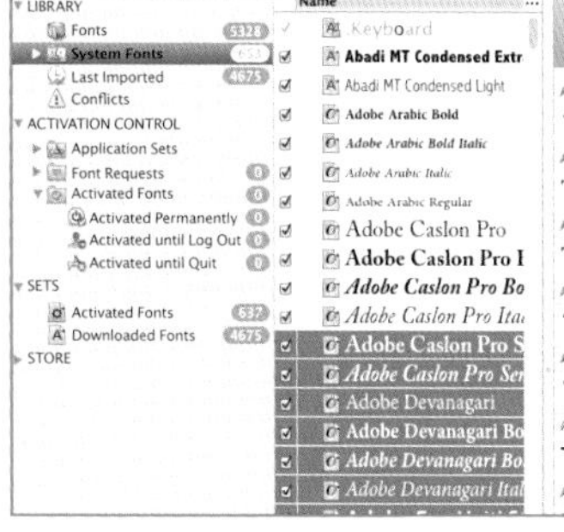

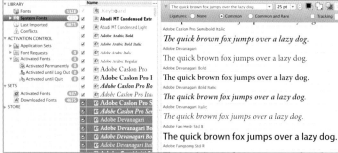

Font Book is Mac OS X's built-in font-management utility. You can use it to install, remove, disable, or preview fonts. You can also organize fonts into Collections or Libraries, and validate fonts to ensure that they work properly within the applications.

- To install a font, click on the plus sign in the Font panel or choose File > Add Fonts.
- To view information about a font, select it and click on the Info button (OS X 10.7) in the toolbar. You can also choose Preview > Show Font Info (OS X 10.6 and earlier).
- To add a Collection, click on the plus sign in the Collection panel or choose File > New Collection. Collections are useful for organizing fonts based on their design, language, etc.
- To add a Library, choose File > New Library or right-click in the Collection panel. A library can include fonts that are not installed in one of Mac OS X's built-in font libraries. This is a good way to manage fonts that you might use periodically on specific projects.
- To disable a font or a collection, select it and choose Edit > Disable, or right-click on the font. The font remains installed, but will not appear in font menus.
- Font Book automatically activates fonts that are not installed if they're present in your system. To enable this, click on Automatic font activation in Font Book > Preferences.
- For more advanced font-management functions, consider a third-party utility, such as Linotype's FontExplorer X Pro or Extensis Suitcase Fusion.

Managing Fonts in Windows

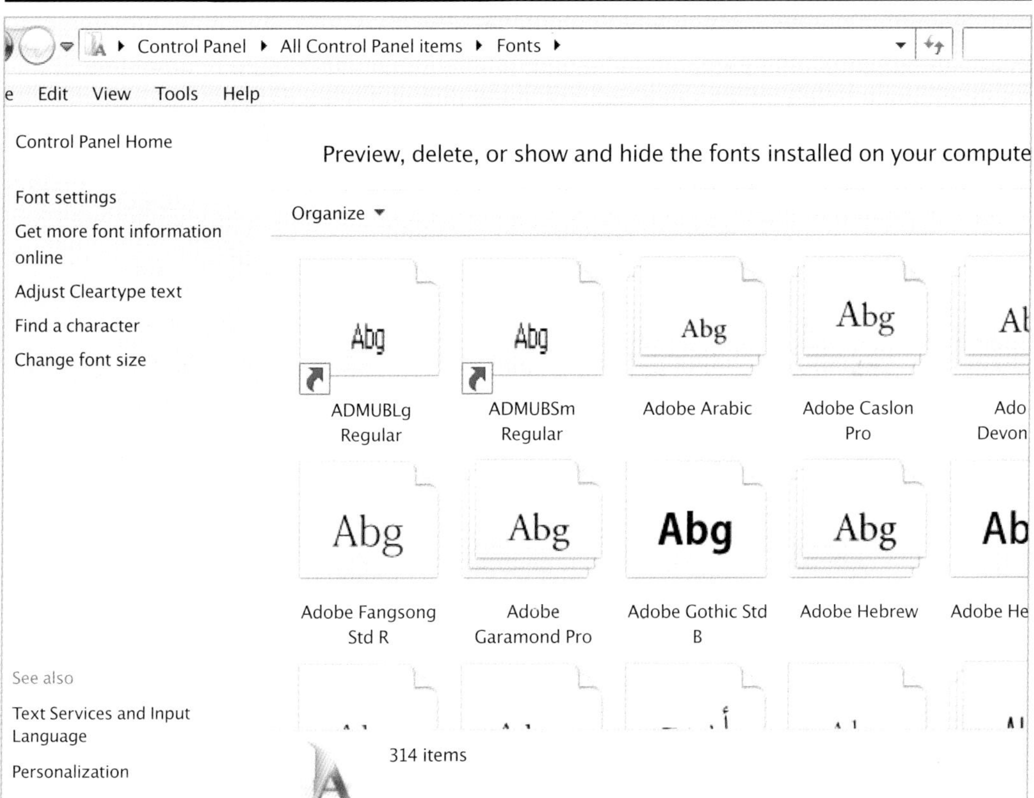

Windows offers limited font management functions via the Fonts Control Panel (Start menu > Control Panel > Fonts). Here you'll find a list of every font installed in the system. You can do the following:

- To install a font, drag it to the window.
- To delete a font, select it in the window and hit Delete, or right-click and select Delete from the menu.
- You can hide a font so it remains in the system, but doesn't appear in font menus: Right-click on the font and choose Hide from the context menu.
- To see a few sample characters in each font, change the view setting to Large Icons, Medium Icons, or Tiles.
- To see a more extensive font sample, right-click on the font and choose Preview from the context menu. This opens a new window showing a complete character set in multiple sizes. You can also print the sample from this window. On the left side of the window, you'll see a few options for changing the way Windows displays type on screen.

For more advanced font-management functions in OS X or Windows, consider a third-party utility, such as Linotype's FontExplorer X Pro or Extensis Suitcae Fusion.

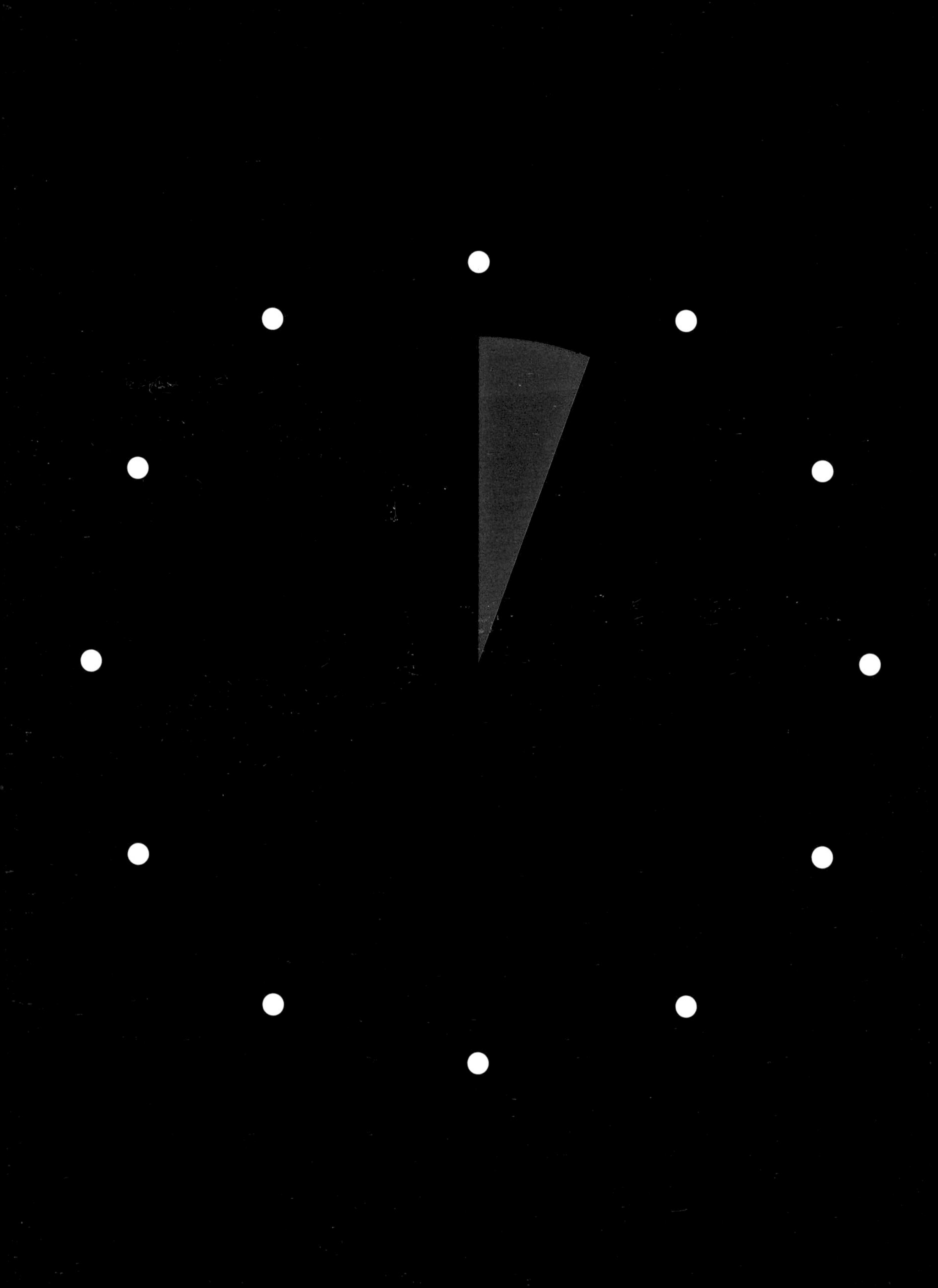

Creative Suite 6
Photoshop
Illustrator
InDesign
Dreamweaver
Flash Professional
Edge
Fireworks
Muse
Acrobat Professional
Bridge
Kuler
Online
Mac
Windows

Chapter Two. Fast Fixes

01→05 mins

Fast Fixes

InDesign Presets

You can save time when setting up or printing InDesign documents by defining presets for common design and production tasks.

Document Presets

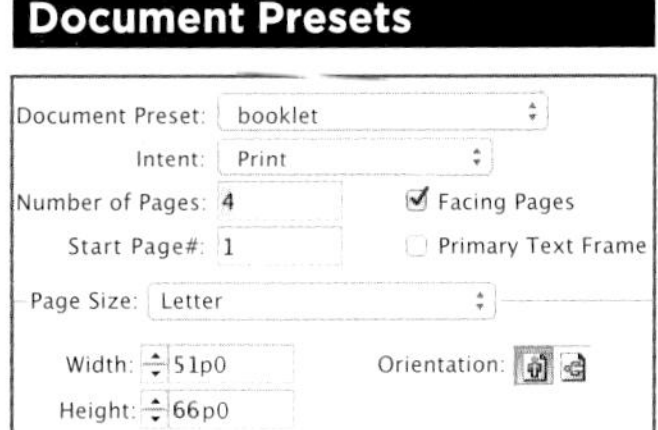

Create presets for frequently used document types so you don't have to keep reentering settings. Click "Save Preset" from the New Document dialog box (File > New) to make your settings available in the preset list.

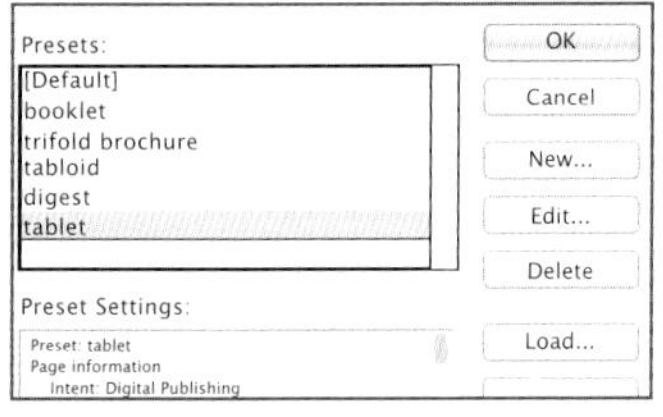

You can manage presets from the Document Presets dialog box (File > Document Presets > Define). Click the Save As and Load buttons to exchange presets with other users.

Print Presets

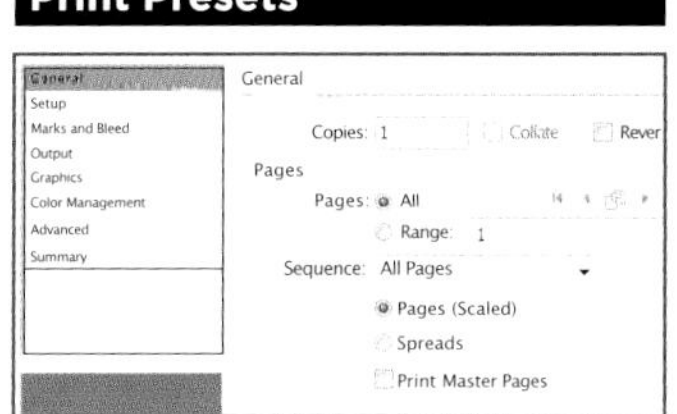

Save output settings such as crop marks, bleeds, and transparency flattener options so they're always accessible from the preset list.

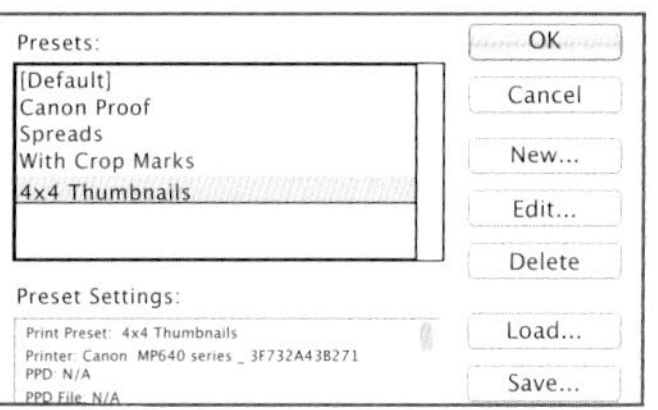

The Print Presets dialog box (File > Print Presets > Define) lets you create and edit print presets. As with document presets, you can exchange print presets with other users.

PDF Presets

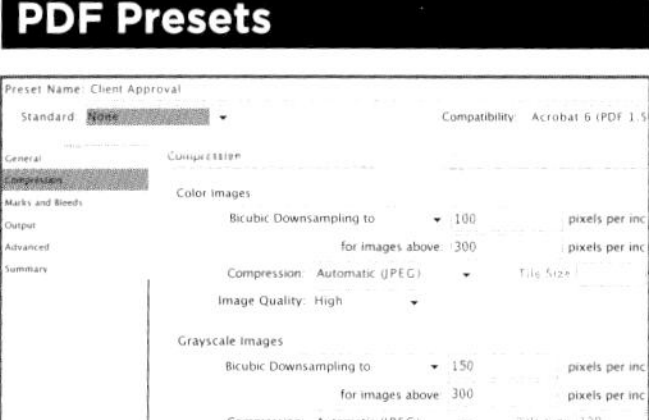

PDF Export Presets (File > Adobe PDF Presets > Define) are similar to print presets. InDesign ships with six presets for commonly used PDF settings, which you can use as the basis for your own.

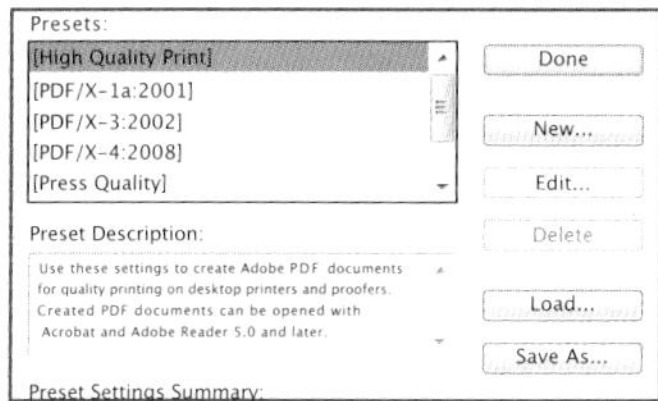

Select a built-in preset and click on the New button. InDesign will create a copy that you can modify to suit your needs.

Tip

InDesign also stores custom keyboard shortcuts, find/replace queries, color swatches, and many other items as presets that you can share with other users. You'll find them in these locations:

Mac: \Applications\Adobe InDesign CS6\Presets

Windows: C:\Program Files (x86)\Adobe\Adobe InDesign CS6\Presets

Fast Fixes

Illustrator Presets

Illustrator's presets can save time with tasks such as printing documents, exporting PDF files, or creating Perspective Grids.

Print and PDF Presets

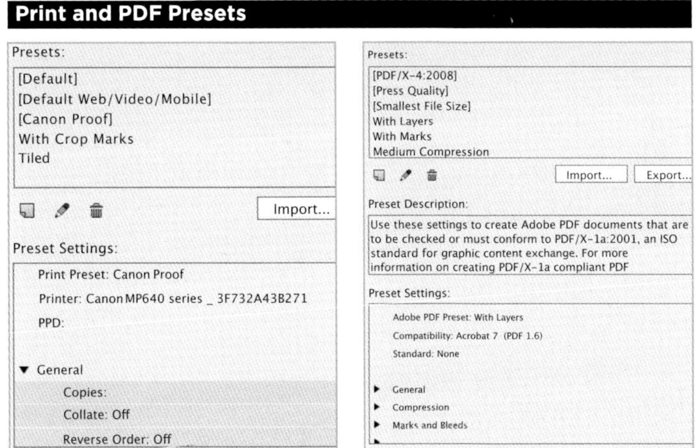

Print and PDF presets in Illustrator are similar to the ones in InDesign. To manage print presets, go to Edit > Print Presets. To manage PDF presets, choose Edit > Adobe PDF Presets.

Illustrator and InDesign can exchange PDF presets via the Import and Export options. However, they can't exchange print settings.

Illustrator doesn't have document presets like the ones in InDesign, but it does let you create Document Profiles, which are similar.

▶ **See Also page** 150

Perspective Grid Presets

Name: [3P-Normal View]copy
Perspective Grid Settings
Type: Three Point Perspective
Units: Points
Scale: 1:1
Gridline Every: 30 pt
At True Height Line, 1 pt on the Artboard represents 1 pt.
Viewing Angle: 45°
Viewing Distance: 480 pt
Horizon Height: 250 pt
Third Vanishing Point: X: 0 pt Y: -500 pt
Grid Color & Opacity
Left Grid: Custom...
Right Grid: Custom...
Horizontal Grid: Custom...
Opacity: 50%

These presets define the appearance of Perspective Grids. To manage these presets, go to Edit > Perspective Grid Presets.

Illustrator ships with presets for 1-, 2-, and 3-point perspective grids that you can use as the basis for your own. Choose an existing preset, and click the New button. This creates a copy that you can edit and save.

Tip

They're not labeled as such, but Actions, Brushes, Graphic Styles, Swatches, Symbols, and other items are Illustrator presets. It's generally best to manage these through their panels, but you can find them in these locations:

Mac: Applications\Adobe InDesign CS6\Presets
Windows: C:\Program Files\Adobe\Adobe Illustrator CS6\Presets

Fast Fixes

Photoshop Presets

In Photoshop, options for almost any tool or image adjustment can be stored as a preset and reused with a few mouse clicks. The program also provides handy features for managing presets.

Tool Presets

You can manage tool presets using these features:

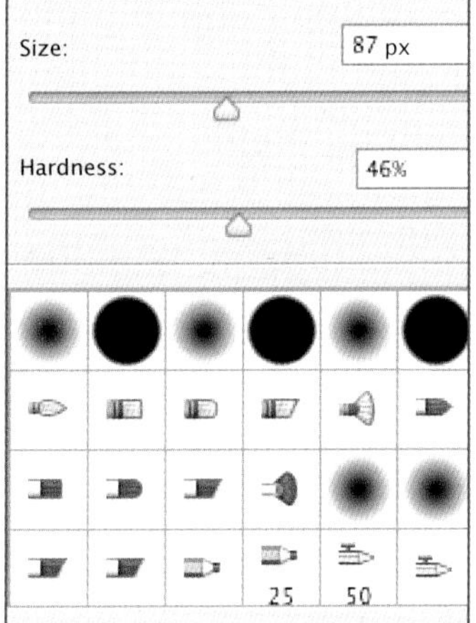

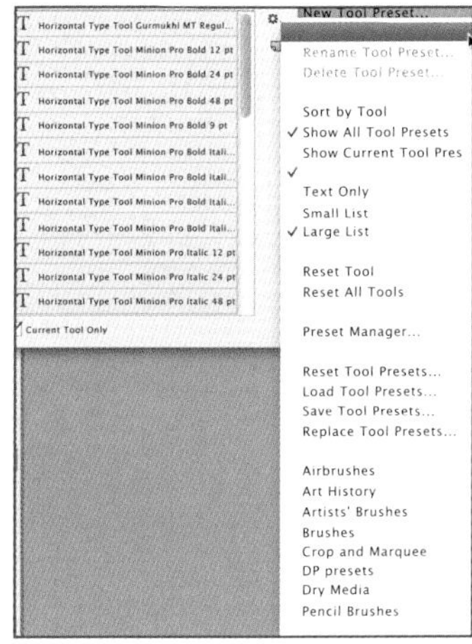

The Tool Preset Picker

This appears as a menu on the left side of the tool options bar when any tool is selected. The same options are available from the Tool Presets panel (Window > Tool Presets). Click the Current Tool Only checkbox if you just want to see presets for the currently selected tool.

The Brush Preset Picker

This appears next to the Tool Preset picker when any Brush tool is selected.

To Create a Preset

Select the tool and set the desired options in the options bar.

Open the Tool Preset picker, Brush Preset picker, or Tool Presets panel.

Click on the New Preset button, or open the panel menu and choose New Tool Preset. In the Tool Preset picker and Brush Preset picker, you can open the panel menu by clicking on the gear icon.

Give the preset a name and click OK.

Preset Manager

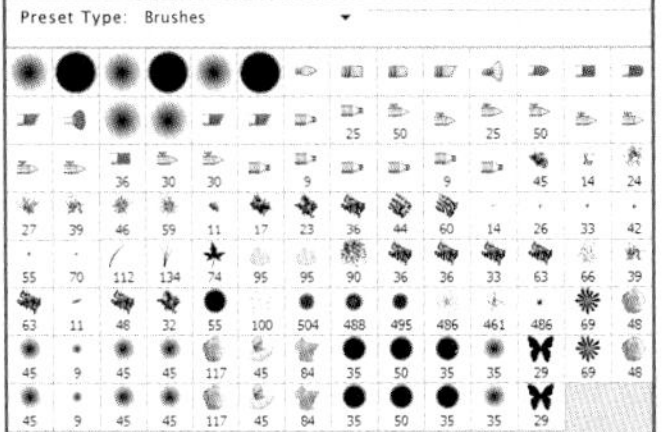

The Preset Manager (Edit > Preset Manager) provides a single location for managing presets for brush and tool presets as well as swatches, gradients, styles, patterns, bevel contours, and custom shapes.

Use the Preset Type menu to choose a category of presets.

Use the Load command to import presets you've obtained from other sources. See page 204 for a list of websites that offer free downloadable brushes, patterns, styles, and other elements that you can import.

Use the Save Set command to export presets. Shift-click on a range of presets to select them for export, or ⌘-click (Ctrl-click) to select discontiguous presets.

You can also create presets for the selection and type tools. For example, you can create Type tool presets with specified character formats.

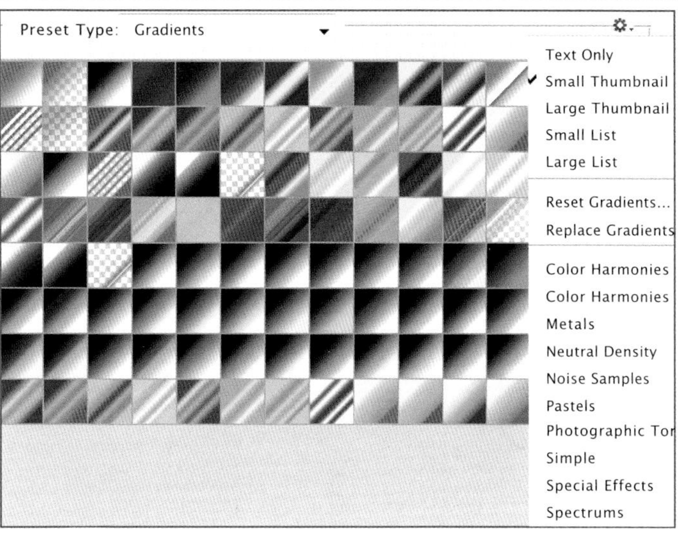

Click on the gear icon to open the panel menu. This provides access to libraries of presets grouped by theme, such as the gradient collections shown above. These libraries are built into Photoshop, but you still need to select them to make them available. You can also add these libraries from the tool's panel or brush picker.

Tip

Options for Levels, Curves, Exposure, Hue/Saturation, Black & White, Channel Mixer and Selective Color can all be saved as presets. In CS6, use the Save Preset command in the Properties panel for those adjustments. In CS5, the same command is available in the Adjustments panel.

Fast Fixes

Photoshop Layers

Mastering layers is one of the keys to working in Photoshop. Here are some tips to help you use them more productively.

The Layers Panel

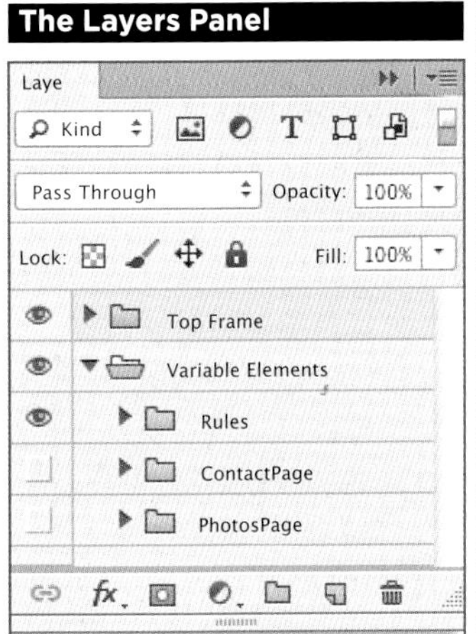

Get to know this panel and its options—this is where you'll be doing most of your work with layers.

Layer Filters: This is a new feature in CS6. Click on the right-most button to enable or disable. See the next section for details.

Blend mode/Opacity: These controls and options determine how a layer blends with the those layers below.

Lock: You can lock transparency, image pixels, position or all layer attributes.

Visibility Icons: Click on these to hide or reveal a layer.

Frequently-used Options: Click on these buttons to create a new layer, layer styles, layer masks, adjustment layers, etc.

Layer Filters

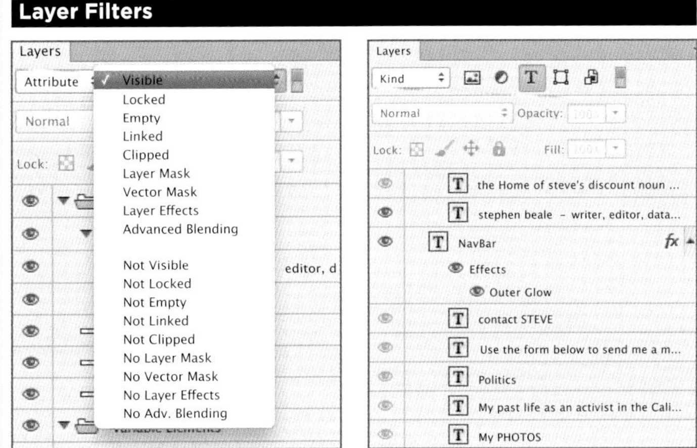

CS6 introduces a small but important enhancement to the Layers panel—a set of filters that limit the display to specific kinds of layers. This can be useful in documents with lots of layers. You can filter by:

Kind: Show only pixel layers, adjustment layers, type layers, etc.

Name: Show layers matching a text value that you enter.

Effect: Show layers with specific effects such as Bevel & Emboss or Drop Shadow.

Mode: Filter by blend modes such as Darken, Lighten, Color, or Luminance.

Attribute: Show layers that are Visible/Not Visible, Locked/Not Locked, with or without Layer Masks or Layer Effects, etc.

Color: Show layers assigned with color labels.

Smart Layer Management

- If the number of layers becomes unmanageable, organize them into Layer Groups. A group can contain individual layers or other groups. Move layers in or out of groups by dragging on them.
- Give your layers and groups descriptive names. Double-click on the item's name to rename it.
- You can increase the thumbnail size to make it easier to see the contents of each layer, though it may also reduce the number of layers you can see without scrolling. This setting is available via the Panel Options dialog in the panel menu.
- Right-click on a layer to open a contextual menu.
- Use the Duplicate Layer command in the panel menu to copy a layer to another open document or to save it as a new file. To copy to another document, choose that document in the Destination menu. Choose New to save it to a new file.
- Double-click on the background in the Layers panel to convert it to a layer.

Layer Shortcuts

Action	Shortcut
Open Layers Panel	F7
Create New Layer	Shift-⌘-N (Shift+Ctrl+N)
Create new layer below selected layer	⌘-click (Ctrl-click) on New Layer button in Layers panel.
Copy Selection to New Layer	⌘-J (Ctrl+J)
Cut Selection to New Layer	Shift-⌘-J (Shift+Ctrl+J)
Select/deselect contiguous layers	Shift-click
Select/deselect discontiguous layers	⌘-click (Shift+click)
Select all layers	⌘-Option+A (Ctrl+Alt+A)
Select top layer	Option+. (Alt+.)
Select bottom layer	Option+, (Alt+,)
Select next layer down/up	Option-[(Alt+[) down; Option-] (Alt+]) up
Move Selected Layer(s) Up	⌘-] (Ctrl+])
Move Selected Layer(s) to Top	Shift-⌘-] (Shift+Ctrl+])
Move Selected Layer(s)	⌘-[(Ctrl+[)
Move Selected Layer(s) to Bottom	Shift-⌘-[(Shift+Ctrl+[)
Merge Selected Layers	⌘-F (Ctrl+E) If only one layer is selected, it's merged with layer below it.
Merge Visible Layers	Shift-⌘-E (Shift+Ctrl+E)
Show/hide other visible layers	Option-click (Alt-Click) on eye. Useful if you want to view one layer in isolation from others.
Group Selected Layers	⌘-G (Ctrl+G)
Ungroup Layers	Shift-⌘-G (Shift+Ctrl+G)

Fast Fixes

Layer Comps

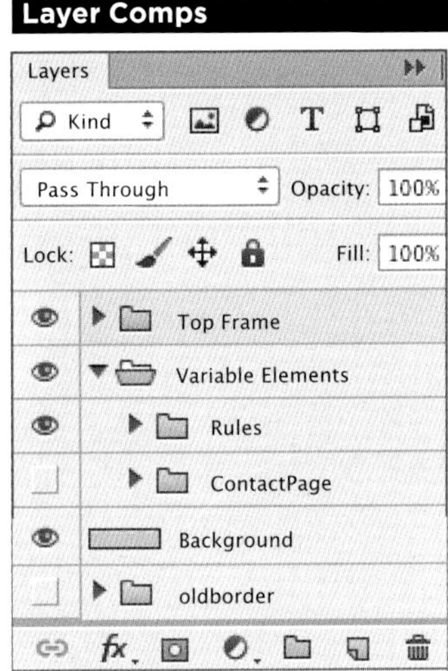

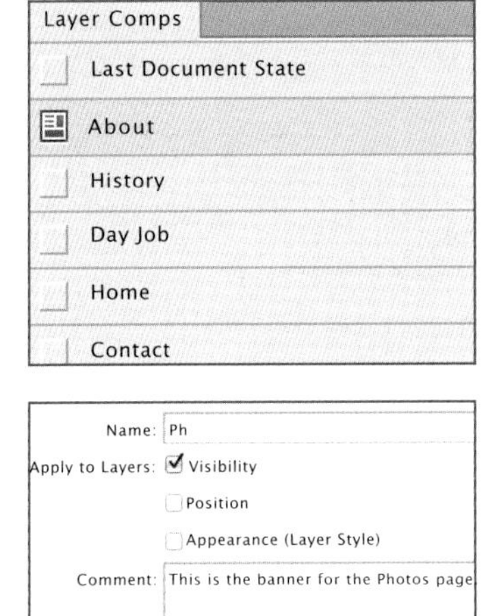

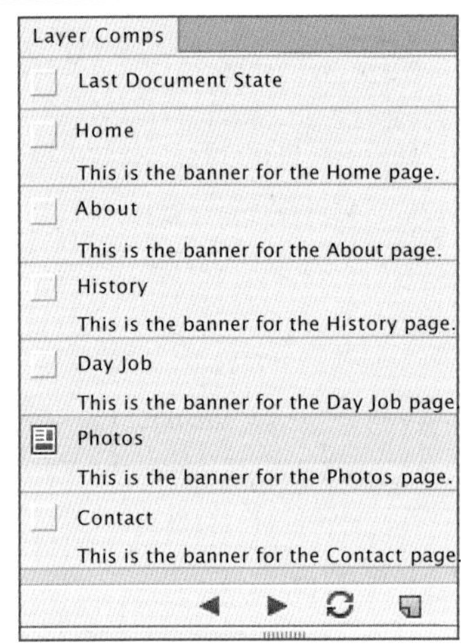

This panel lets you save any combination of layers or layer groups as comps, and then recall them with a single click. For example, you can mock up a website, with some layers visible only on specific pages, and use the panel to define a separate comp for each page.

To create a layer comp:

01. Open the Layers panel (Window > Layers) and Layer Comps (Window > Layer Comps).

02. In the Layers panel, click on the Visibility icons (the eyes) to show the layers you want to include in a comp.

03. In the Layer Comps panel, create a new layer comp. You can click on the Create New Layer Comp icon at the bottom of the panel or choose New Layer Comp from the panel menu.

04. Give it a name and a description. Click OK.

Repeat the process for each comp you'd like to create.

Once you've set up your layer comps, you can recall them by clicking in the box next to the name. You can export each layer comp using the File > Save As or File > Save for Web options, or use the Photoshop file itself for client presentations. Click on the Next or Previous buttons at the bottom of the panel to cycle through the comps.

To add or remove layers from a layer comp:

01. Click in the box next to the layer comp you want to change.

02. Show or hide layers in the Layers panel by clicking on the visibility icons.

03. Click on the Update Layer Comp button (the recycle symbol) at the bottom of the panel.

Fast Fixes

Selections, Masks, and Channels

Photoshop gets much of its power from the ability to work on selected regions of an image. Mastering the selection and masking tools will go a long way toward improving your productivity.

The Quick Selection Tool

This tool, which is grouped with the Magic Wand, is often the quickest way to create selections. It works like the Brush tool—you can even use the same keyboard shortcuts to increase or decrease the brush size. On the Mac, press Ctrl-Option and drag left or right. On Windows, press Alt and right-click. Or press the right or left bracket keys.

Paint inside the area you want to select and Photoshop will automatically expand the selection to the borders. If the selection extends too far, hold down the Option (Alt) key and paint over the area you want to deselect.

Color Range

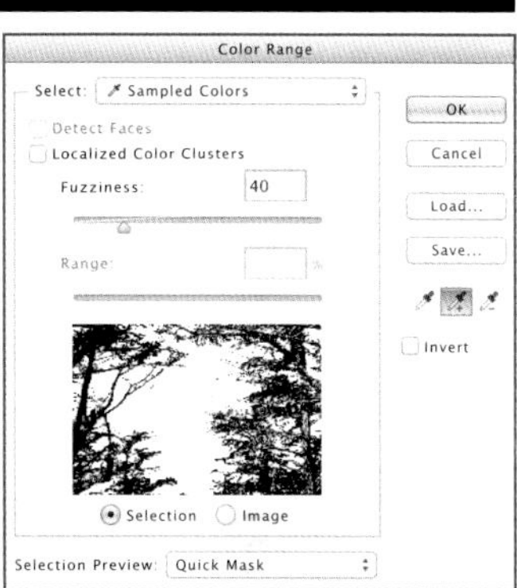

Use this command (Select › Color Range) to select or deselect areas of an image matching a specified range of color values. Unlike the Magic Wand tool, selections made with this feature can have varying opacity. For example, if you select Reds, orange pixels will be partially selected because red is part of the color mix.

The feature typically works best with the Sampled Colors option. When you mouse over the image, the cursor becomes an eyedropper. When you click on a color, Photoshop selects pixels with similar color values.

The Fuzziness control determines the range of color values you select. A lower setting selects fewer colors.

To add color ranges to the selection, Shift-click with the eyedropper, or use the Add to Sample eyedropper (the one with a plus sign). Use the Localized Color Clusters option to prevent Photoshop from including intermediate color ranges in your selection.

To subtract a color range from the selection, Option-click (Alt-click) or use the Subtract From eyedropper.

Fast Fixes

Refine Edge

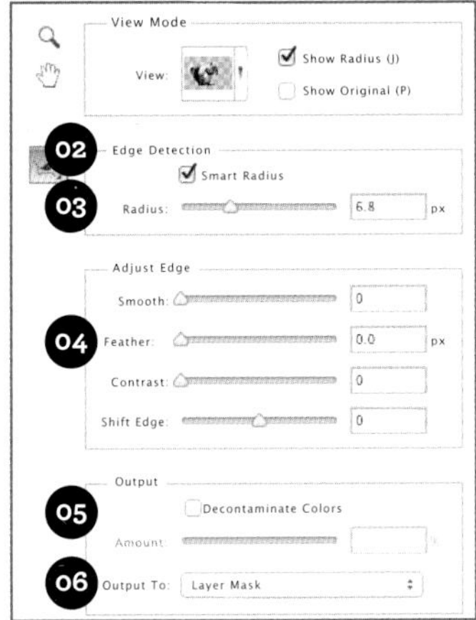

This dialog box provides a host of features for fine-tuning selections. Its Edge Detection function is especially useful for difficult selections involving hair or fur. You specify a radius beyond the original selection border, and Photoshop automatically finds the edges within that area.

Use any of the selection tools to make a selection. Open the dialog box by clicking on the Refine Edge button in the tool options bar, or choose Select > Refine Edge.

01. **View Menu:** Lets you choose how Photoshop displays the selection. Check Show Radius to view the radius.

02. **Edge Detection:** If you check Smart Radius, Photoshop will automatically look for hard or soft edges (such as fur) in the border area. Use this if the border area has a mix of hard and soft edges.

03. **Radius Slider:** This sets the radius width. It should be wide enough to include the edges in your selection.

04. **Adjust Edge:** Use the Feather adjustment to blur the selection edge.

05. **Output Options:** Check Decontaminate Colors to reduce color fringing around the edges of your selection. The selection will be copied to a new layer or document, depending on which option you choose in the Output menu.

06. **Output To:** For the most efficient workflow, choose Layer Mask or New Layer with Layer Mask (see page 70).

07. **Radius tools:** The Refine Radius and Erase Refinement tools let you manually adjust the border. Refine Radius works like the Brush tool, expanding the border area used for edge detection. Use it to paint over soft areas such as hair that you want to include in the selection. Use the Erase Refinement tool to reduce the border area. Press Shift-E to toggle between the tools. Press Option (Alt) to switch temporarily from one tool to the other.

Masks

Masks are often an easier way to make selections because you can modify them using Photoshop's painting tools. Unlike selections made with Photoshop's selection tools, masks can have varying degrees of opacity.

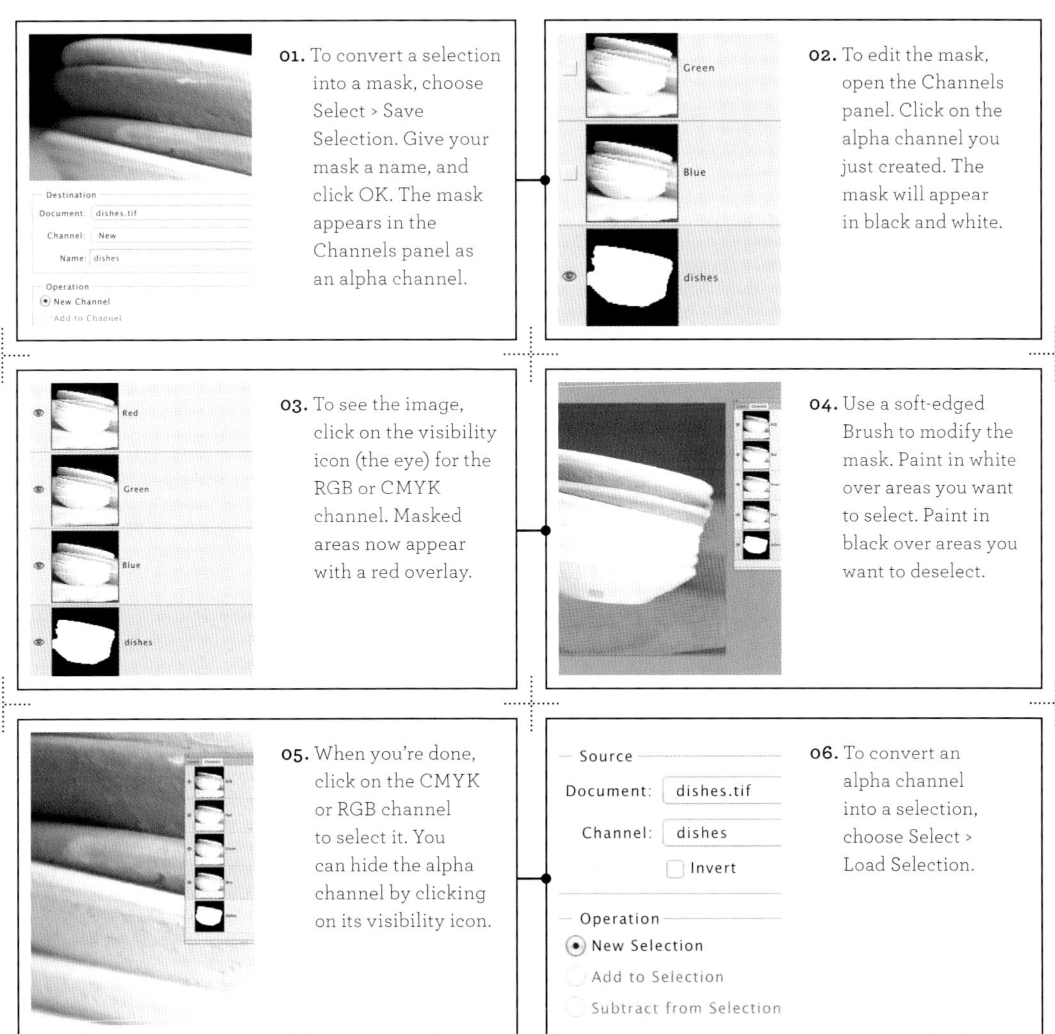

01. To convert a selection into a mask, choose Select > Save Selection. Give your mask a name, and click OK. The mask appears in the Channels panel as an alpha channel.

02. To edit the mask, open the Channels panel. Click on the alpha channel you just created. The mask will appear in black and white.

03. To see the image, click on the visibility icon (the eye) for the RGB or CMYK channel. Masked areas now appear with a red overlay.

04. Use a soft-edged Brush to modify the mask. Paint in white over areas you want to select. Paint in black over areas you want to deselect.

05. When you're done, click on the CMYK or RGB channel to select it. You can hide the alpha channel by clicking on its visibility icon.

06. To convert an alpha channel into a selection, choose Select > Load Selection.

Tip

When modifying the mask, you can press D to switch the foreground and background colors to black and white. While painting, press X to switch between white and black.

Fast Fixes

Layer Masks

Layer masks provide an easy way to make parts of a layer transparent. They're especially useful for compositing work, or if you just need to make a quick selection on a layer.

01. Open the Layers panel and click on the layer to which you want to apply the mask. Once you've added a layer mask, you can use the Brush tool to paint over areas you want to make transparent.

02. Click on the Add Layer Mask icon at the bottom of the Layers panel, or choose Layer > Layer Mask > Reveal All. The layer mask is represented as a white square next to the layer thumbnail.

03. Use the Brush or Pencil tool to paint the mask. Paint in black over the areas you want to mask. Paint in white over the areas you want to reveal. Masked areas will be transparent. Remember that you're not actually erasing the layer—you're just hiding parts of it.

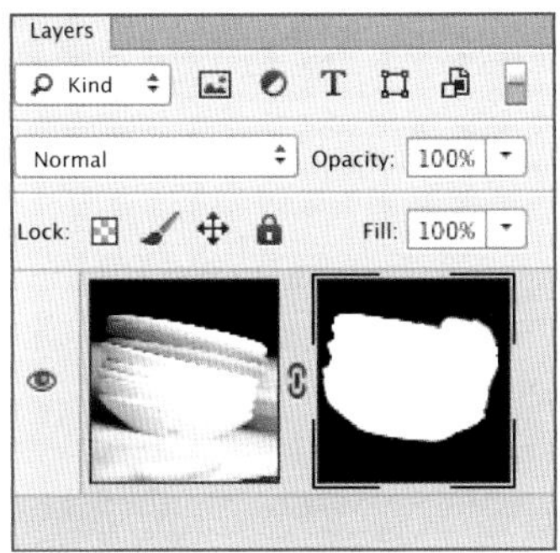

A border around the thumbnail indicates whether the mask or image is targeted by the painting tools. If the mask thumbnail has a border, painting tools will apply to the mask.

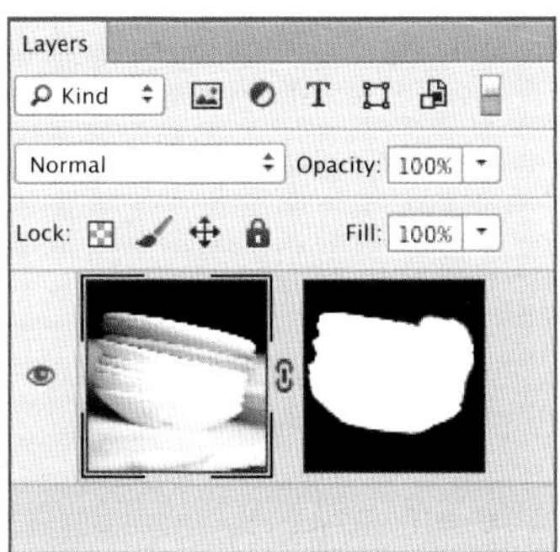

To work on the image, click on the layer thumbnail.

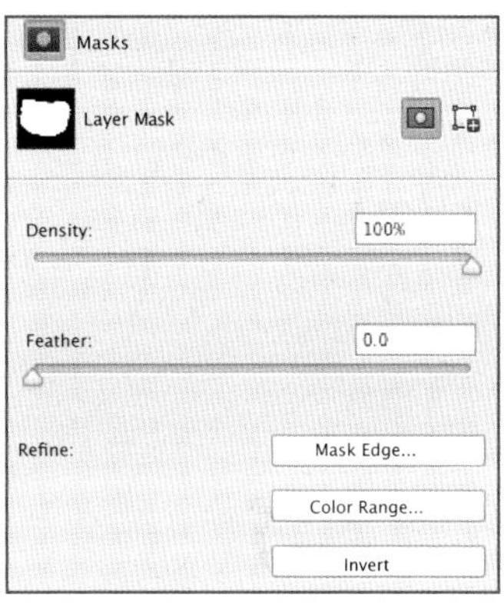

Use the Properties panel (CS6) or Masks panel (CS5) to adjust the mask's opacity or feathering. The panel also provides access to the Refine Edge and Color Range dialogs. Click the Invert button to invert the mask.

To temporarily remove the layer mask, right-click on the mask thumbnail and choose Disable Layer Mask. Masked portions of the layer are now revealed.

Quick Mask Mode

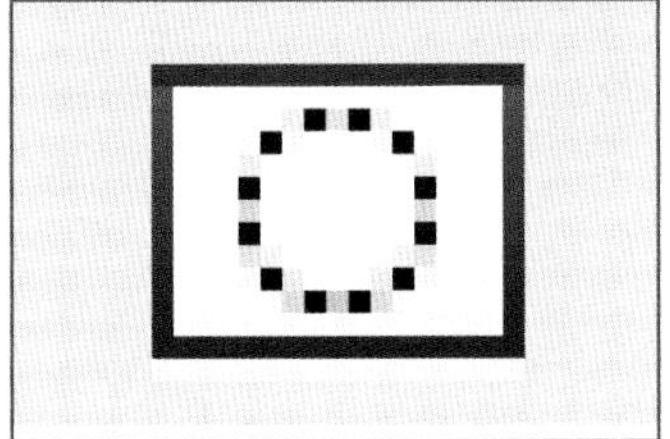

Use Quick Mask Mode to temporarily convert a selection into a mask. Click on the Edit in Quick Mask Mode button near the bottom of the toolbar, or press Q. Now you can use the Brush or Pencil tool to modify the mask. Press Q again (or click on the same button) to switch back to Standard Mode. The mask becomes a selection with the familiar "marching ants."

Tip

You can use Photoshop's selection tools as a quick first step toward creating a layer mask. Create a rough selection around the area you want to preserve, click on the Add Layer Mask button. Areas outside your selection will be automatically masked. Then use the painting tools to refine the selection.

Fast Fixes

Clipping Masks

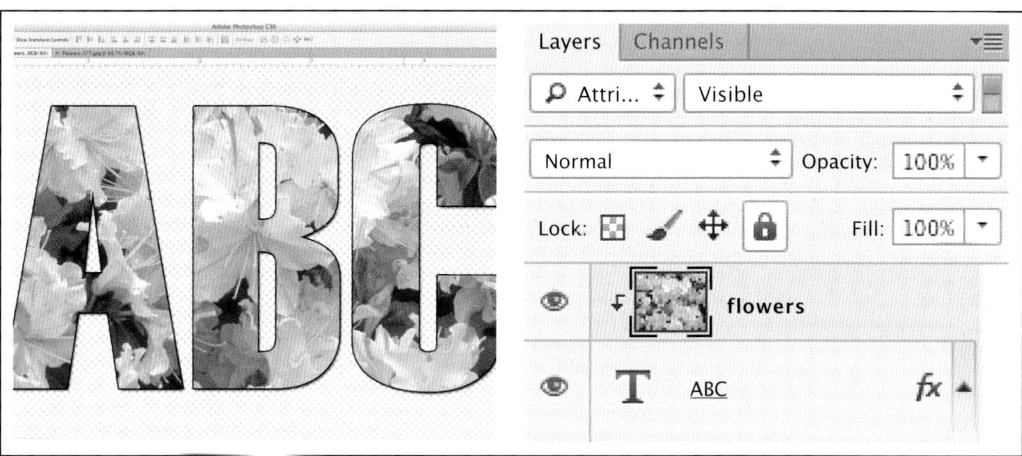

Clipping masks allow you to use a "base layer" to mask the contents of other layers. This is often used to create effects in which a photograph or other image appears inside a block of type.

01. Open a document containing the image you want to use as the interior for the type.

02. Open the Layers panel. If the image is on the background layer, double-click to unlock it.

03. Choose the Type tool and enter some text. The effect works best with headline fonts set to a large point size. The Type layer you created will be the base layer for the effect.

04. Drag the base layer underneath the image.

05. Select the image layer, and choose Layer > Create Clipping Mask.

You can enhance effects by applying layer styles, such as a drop shadow or stroke, to the base layer.

See Also page 112

Fast Fixes

InDesign Layers

Layers in InDesign are useful for organizing your project. The Layers panel also provides an easy way to select items and manage groups.

The Layers Panel

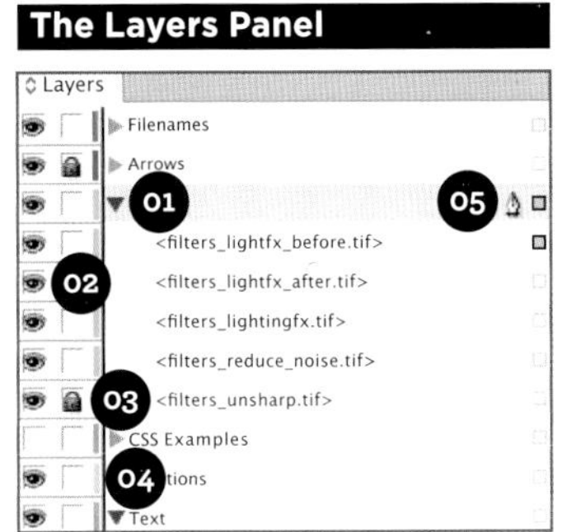

01. Disclosure Triangles: Click on these to show the objects on the layer.

02. Visibility Icons: Click here to hide or show layers or objects.

03. Lock Icons: Click here to lock or unlock a layer or object.

04. Selection Color: This shows the selection marks for items on the layer. When you select an item, the color of the bounding box will indicate which layer it's on.

05. Selection Icon: Click here to select an object, group or layer. Shift-click to add or remove items from the selection.

Layer Options

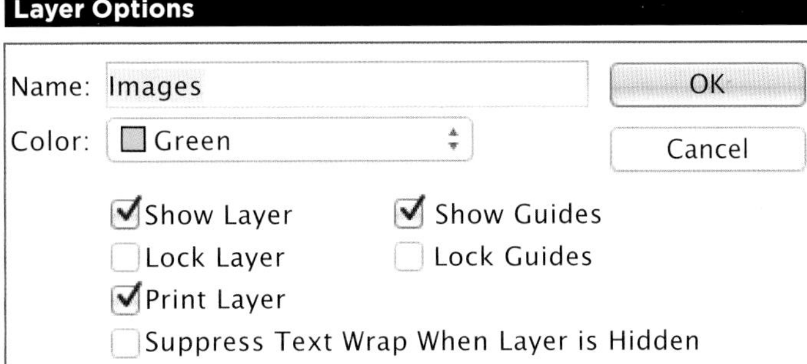

Open this dialog from the panel menu. You can do the following:

- Rename the layer
- Change the selection color
- Uncheck Print Layer if you don't want the layer to be printed
- Check Suppress Text Wrap When Layer is Hidden, so text doesn't wrap around it
- Hide or show guides on the layer.

Tips for Working with Layers

- It's good practice to separate artwork, text, and nonprinting elements such as guides or labels into different layers.
- The Layers panel can be the easiest way to select items within a stack. You can also change the stacking order by dragging objects up or down.
- Move objects in and out of groups by dragging on them. You can also drag objects from one layer to another.
- Give your layers descriptive names to make them easier to identify.

Tip

You can Option-click (Alt-click) on a layer's visibility icon to hide all other layers. Option-click (Alt-click) again to reveal the hidden layers. If you Option-click (Alt-click) on an object's visibility icon, all other objects within that layer will be hidden. The same shortcuts apply to the lock icons if you want to lock other layers or objects.

Fast Fixes

Illustrator Layers

Layers in Illustrator are useful for organizing your project as well as preparing artwork for export to Photoshop, Acrobat, and other programs. The Layers panel also provides an easy way to select and target objects.

The Layers Panel

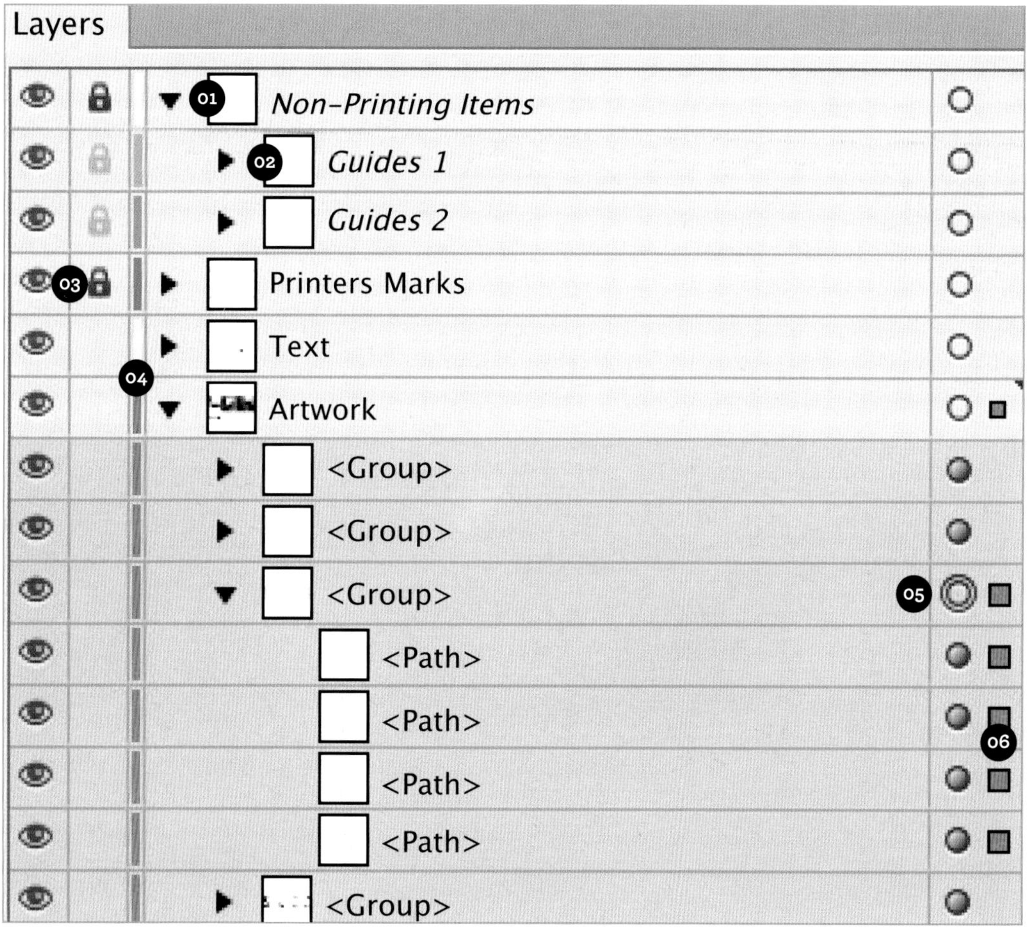

Layers

01 Non-Printing Items
02 Guides 1
Guides 2
03 Printers Marks
Text
04 Artwork
<Group>
<Group>
<Group> 05
<Path>
<Path> 06
<Path>
<Path>
<Group>

The panel behaves much like the one in InDesign, with a few key differences. For example a layer in Illustrator can have sublayers, and Illustrator's Layers panel includes a target icon that provides information about each object's appearance attributes.

01. Disclosure Triangles: Click on these to show sublayers, groups, and objects. Layers and sublayers have shaded backgrounds. Groups and objects have white backgrounds.

02. Visibility Icons: Click here to hide or show layers or sublayers. Option-click (Alt-click) to hide all other layers or sublayers. ⌘-click (Ctrl-click) on a layer's visibility icon to show other layers as outlines.

03. Lock Icons: These lock or unlock items. Option-click (Alt-click) to lock/unlock all other layers or sublayers.

04. Selection Color: This shows the selection color of objects on the layer. When you select an object, the color of the path and bounding box will indicate which layer it's on.

05. Target Icon: A hollow circle indicates that the object has a basic appearance—a single stroke and fill. A solid circle indicates a complex appearance, such as live effects or multiple strokes. A ring around the circle indicates that the item is a target for the Appearance menu.

06. Selection Icon: A large square indicates that an entire layer or group is selected. A small square indicates that items within the layer or group are selected.

Tips for Working with Layers

- Click on the Target or Selection icon to select an object, group, or layer. Shift-click to add or remove items from the selection. If you select a group, all objects within the group are selected, but you can also select or deselect those objects individually.
- Drag the Target icon from one object to another to move its appearance attributes. Option-drag (Alt-drag) to copy appearance attributes.
- You can rearrange objects, groups, layers, and sublayers by dragging them up or down. For example, you can move an object from one group to another, move it to a different layer, or change the stacking order.
- Use the Locate Object feature to find an object's location within the panel. First, select the object on the artboard. Then click on the magnifying glass at the bottom of the panel, or choose Locate Object from the panel menu.
- Use Panel Options in the panel menu to increase or decrease the row size. Increasing the row size will make it easier to see the contents of each layer or sublayer.

Fast Fixes

Illustrator Appearance Panel

The Appearance panel is one of Illustrator's most powerful productivity features. Use it in conjunction with the Layers panel to view and modify strokes, fills, live effects, and other attributes for targeted objects, groups, or layers.

The Appearance Panel

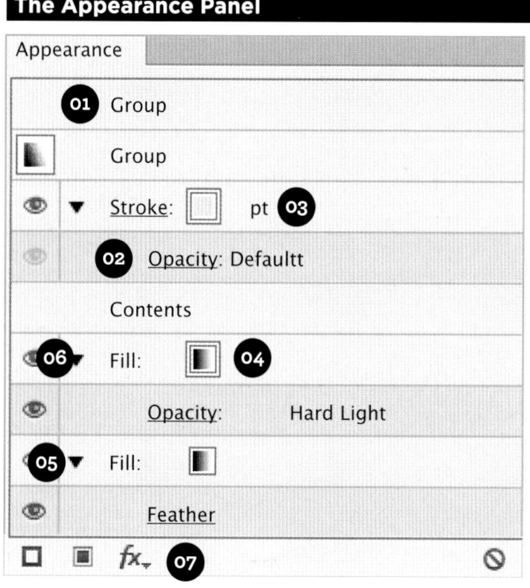

01. Thumbnail: Drag this to any object in the document window to copy attributes. You can also copy attributes via the Eyedropper tool (see page 77) or the Layers panel (see page 74).

02. Attributes: A blue underline indicates that you can open a panel or dialog box to modify an attribute.

03. Stroke Settings: Click to the right of strokes to change color or weight.

04. Fill Settings: Click to the right of fills to change color.

05. Visibility: Click on the visibility icons to hide or show an attribute. You can drag an attribute up or down to change its stacking order.

06. Disclosure Triangles: Click on these to see additional attribute settings.

07. Frequently Used Features: Click on these icons to create a new stroke, fill, or Live Effect.

Tips

- You can target objects or groups by selecting them with the Selection or Direct Selection tool, but for complex projects, you may find it easier to use the Layers panel.
- Regardless of how you select an object, pay attention to the target icon in the Layers panel—this will make it clear which item's appearance is currently targeted.
- If no objects are selected, the Appearance panel shows the current stroke and fill attributes that will be applied to new objects.

The Eyedropper

Illustrator's Eyedropper tool provides a quick way to apply attributes from one object to another. It not only samples colors, but also stroke weights, dash patterns, and other attributes. It can even sample character and paragraph styles.

01→05 mins

Applying Attributes to a Selected Object

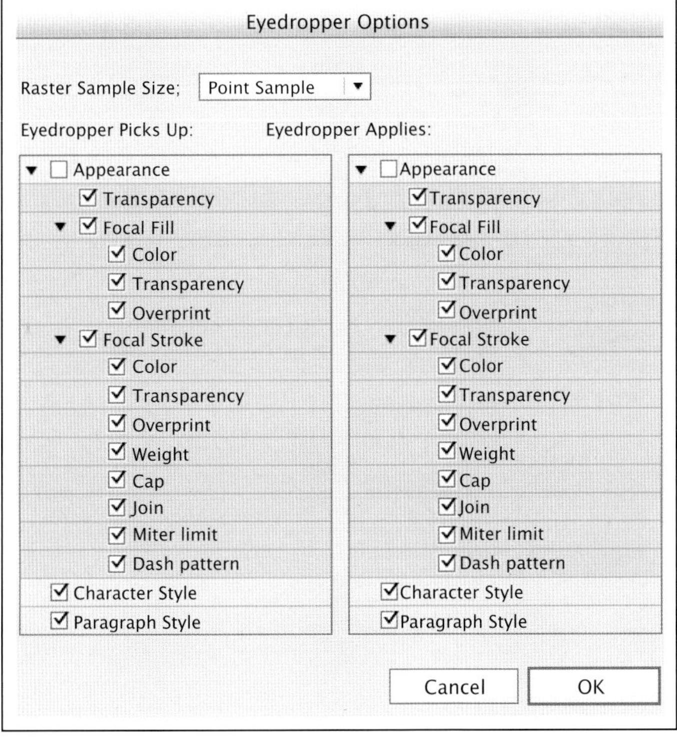

Double-click on the Eyedropper tool to choose which attributes you want to pick up and apply.

01. Select the object you want to target using the Selection or Direct Selection tool, or use the Layers panel.
02. Choose the Eyedropper tool. The default keyboard shortcut is "I."
03. Click on the object whose attributes you want to sample. The targeted object will automatically match its appearance. Shift-click to sample the color only, as in Photoshop. This will work with raster images in addition to vector objects.

Applying attributes with no objects selected:

01. Click in an empty area with the Selection tool to deselect all objects.
02. Choose the Eyedropper tool.
03. Click once on an object whose attributes you want to pick up.
04. Option-click (Alt-click) on other objects to apply those attributes.

Fast Fixes

Illustrator Brushes

Creating artwork with vector tools isn't always intuitive. However, Illustrator provides brush tools that enable the kinds of effects you'd otherwise have to create in a paint program.

The Brushes Panel

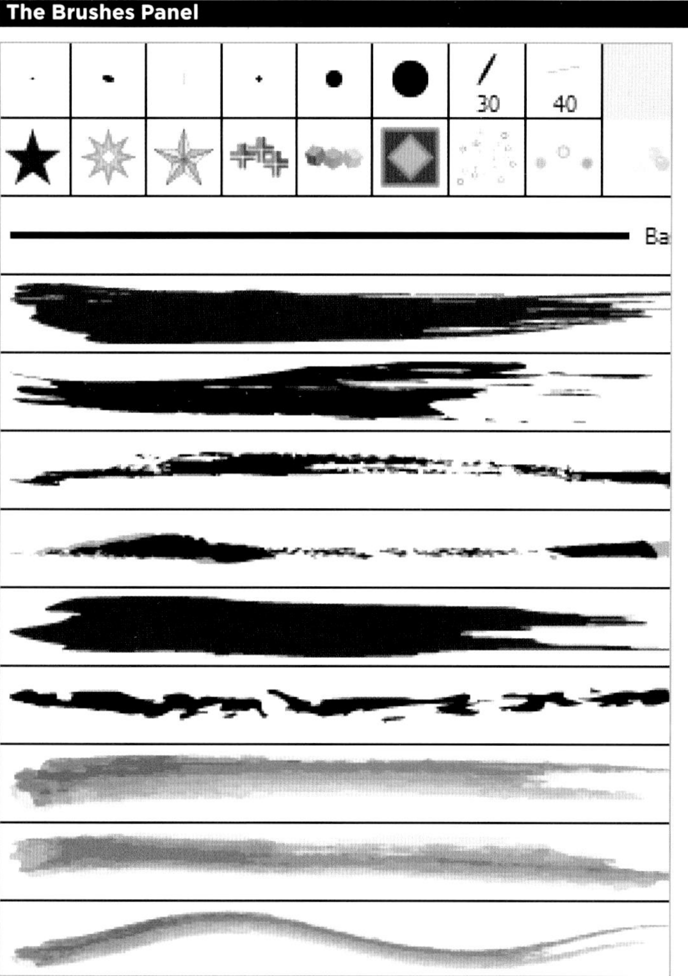

The Brushes panel (Window > Brushes) provides access to five kinds of brushes. You can use the built-in brushes, create your own, or install brushes you've downloaded from the web. You can apply brushes to paths you've already drawn, or use the Paintbrush tool to paint from scratch.

- To apply a brush to an existing path, select the path and click on the brush in the Brushes panel.
- To add a brush from one of the built-in libraries, choose Open Brush Library from the panel menu. Choose Open Brush Library > Other Library to add a library you've downloaded from the web.
- To create a new brush, choose New Brush from the panel menu and select which kind you want to create. To create a Scatter, Art, or Pattern brush, you'll need to specify an existing piece of artwork as a basis.
- To modify an existing brush, select it in the Brushes panel and choose Brush Options from the panel menu.
- To convert brush strokes into editable paths, select the object and choose Object > Expand Appearance.

The Blob Brush

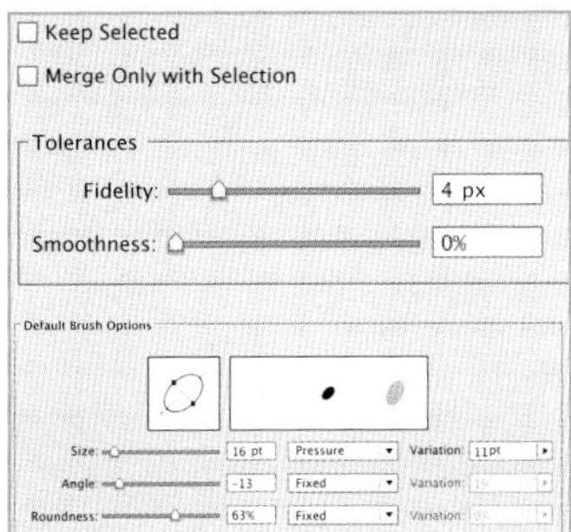

This is another tool that mimics a paintbrush, but in a different way. As you paint, it creates filled paths matching the current stroke color. If paths with the same color overlap, they're merged into a single object.

- Double-click on the tool to set the brush size, angle, and roundness.
- Use a pressure-sensitive tablet to vary the brush size or other attributes as you paint. Increase or decrease the brush size by pressing the left and right bracket keys.
- Press the Option (Alt) key to temporarily switch to the Smooth tool. This modifies edges to make them smoother with fewer anchor points.

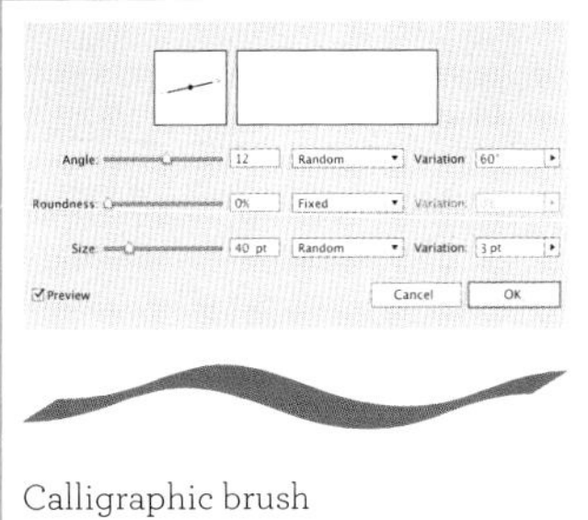

Calligraphic brush

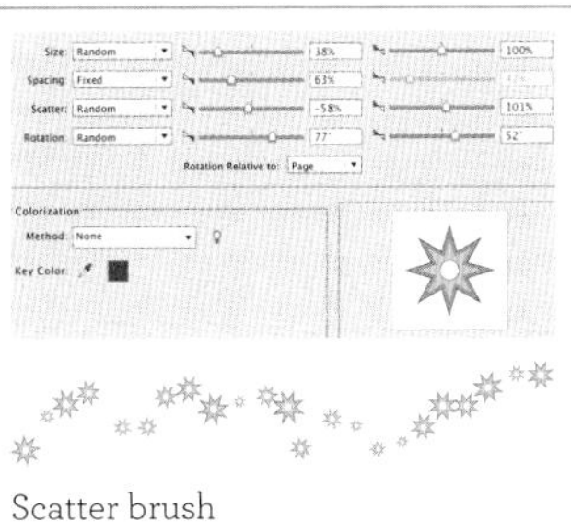

Scatter brush

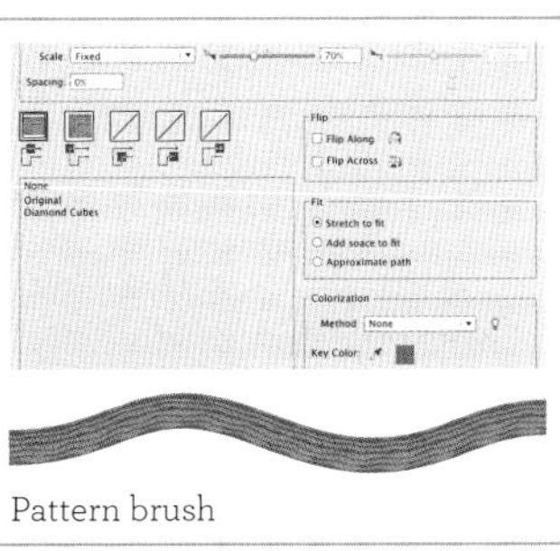

Pattern brush

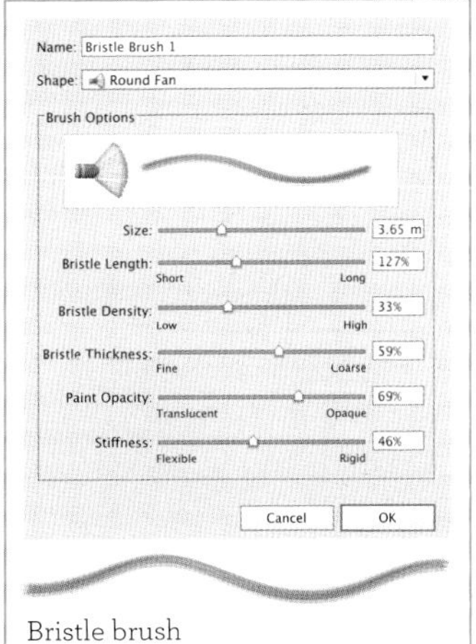

Bristle brush

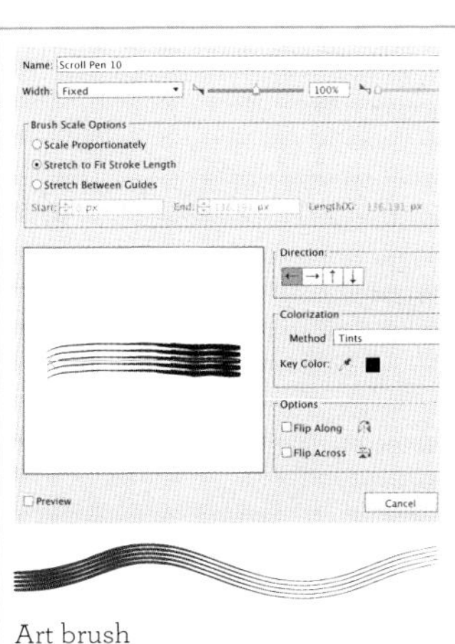

Art brush

The Eraser

This tool mimics the Eraser tool in Photoshop, removing any parts of an object you paint over. The objects remain in vector form with editable paths. As with the Blob brush, you can double-click on the tool to set the brush size and other attributes.

- If no objects are selected, the tool will erase anything below it except for layers or objects that are locked. You can limit its actions to specific objects by selecting them before you choose the tool. Press the ⌘ (Ctrl) key to temporarily switch to the Selection tool and select other objects as you're erasing.
- Option-drag (Alt-drag) to erase large rectangular areas.
- The opposite end of a Wacom pressure-sensitive stylus will automatically apply the Eraser tool as you're applying other tools. For example, you can paint with the Blob brush, and then flip the stylus to erase.

Fast Fixes

Converting Bitmaps to Vectors

Often, the fastest way to create a vector illustration is to begin with a bit-mapped image and convert it using Illustrator's tracing function, which underwent a major overhaul in CS6.

The Image Trace Panel

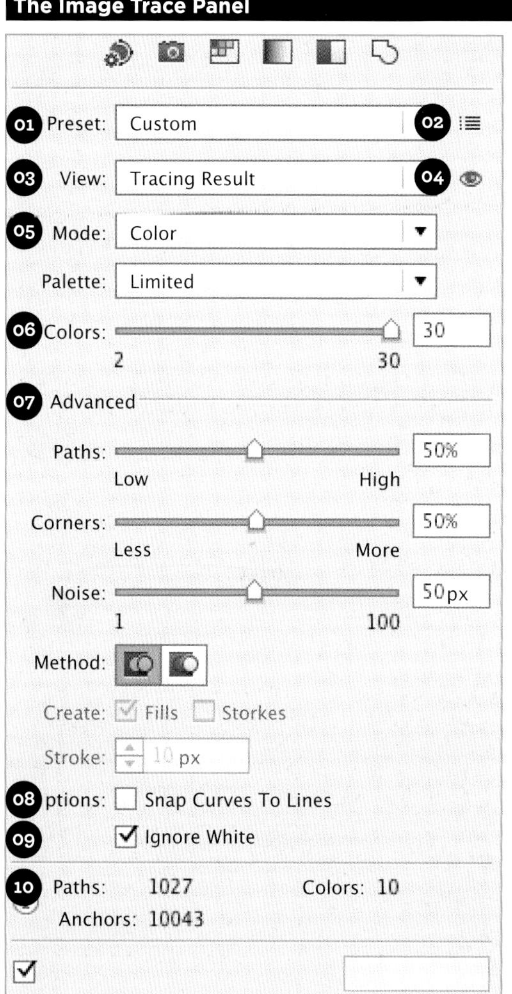

The new Image Trace panel (Window > Image Trace) replaces the Live Trace Options dialog in CS5. Begin by selecting the raster image you want to trace.

01. **Preset:** Choose a preset from the list or the buttons on top. Illustrator will perform an initial trace, but you can tweak the settings to get the results you want.
02. **Save:** Click here to save custom settings as a preset.
03. **View:** Choose whether you want to view the tracing result, source image, or outlines.
04. **Temporary View:** Click here to temporarily view the source image.
05. **Mode:** Use the Mode menu to choose from a Color, Grayscale, or Black & White trace.
06. **Colors:** You can set the number of colors or use any of the custom libraries in the Swatches panel.
07. **Advanced Settings:** Use these to determine how Illustrator traces the paths.
    - **Paths:** Use a higher setting for a closer fit with the source image. Use a lower setting if you want paths with fewer anchor points.
    - **Corners:** A higher value produces paths with more corners. A lower value yields smoother paths.
    - **Noise:** The trace will ignore areas below the specified pixel size. A higher value reduces noise and yields illustrations with fewer anchor points.
08. **Snap Curves to Lines:** Creates paths that are more angular.
09. **Ignore White:** If this is checked, white areas in the original image are made transparent.
10. **Paths, Colors, Anchors:** Shows the number of paths, colors, and anchor points based on the current settings.

11. **Black and White Mode:** Use the Threshold slider to determine which pixels are converted to black or white. A higher threshold turns more colors black.
12. **Fills and Strokes:** Choose whether you want paths to include fills, strokes, or both.
13. **Strokes:** If you choose strokes, this setting determines the maximum stroke width. Areas of the image above this threshold are traced as outlines.

You can also trace images by clicking on the Image Trace button in the Control Panel, or by choosing Object > Image Trace > Make. However, you'll still have to open the Image Trace panel to adjust the settings.

To edit the paths in the traced image, click on the Expand button in the Control Panel, or choose Object > Expand.

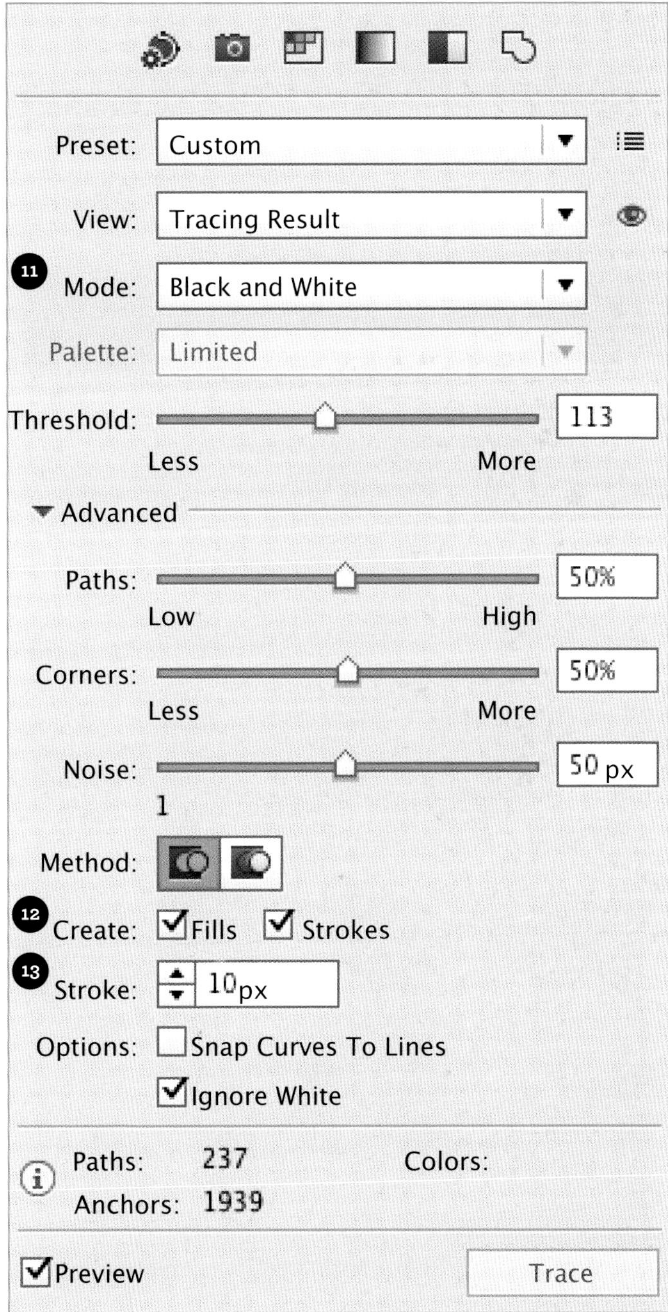

01→05 mins

Fast Fixes

Modifying Colors in Photoshop

Use these tools to modify colors in Photoshop.

Hue/Saturation Adjustment

The Hue/Saturation dialog makes it easy to modify the hue, saturation, and brightness in an image or selection. In this example, we'll recolor the flower petals.

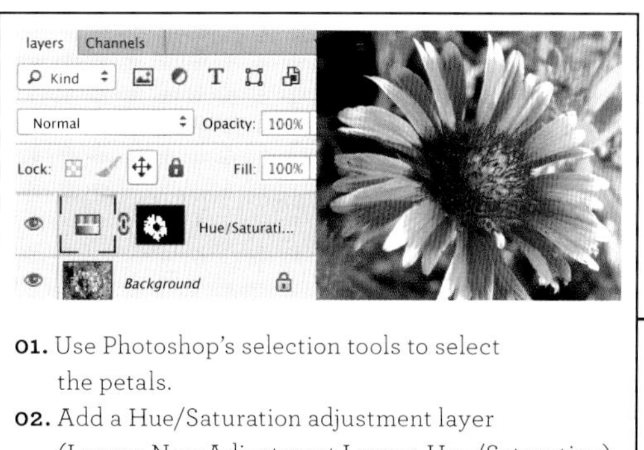

01. Use Photoshop's selection tools to select the petals.

02. Add a Hue/Saturation adjustment layer (Layer › New Adjustment Layer › Hue/Saturation). Photoshop will apply a layer mask, which confines the recoloring to the petals.

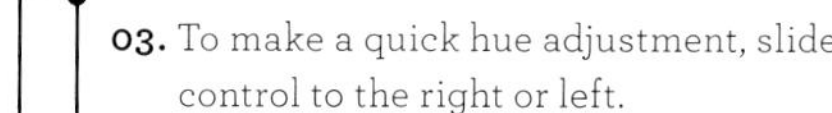

03. To make a quick hue adjustment, slide the Hue control to the right or left.

04. To limit the adjustment to a specific range of colors in the image, choose a color from the drop-down menu under the Preset menu. The default value is Master, which means the changes will apply to all colors. If you choose Reds, the hue adjustment is limited to the red parts of the flower, leaving the yellows untouched. Orange areas are partially changed, because they contain red and yellow.

The On-image Adjustment tool provides another way to choose which colors will be affected:

01. Click on the hand next to the color menu.
02. Mouse over the image. The cursor becomes an eyedropper.
03. Click on the color you want to adjust. Drag left or right to decrease or increase saturation. ⌘-drag (Ctrl-drag) to change the hue. Use the eyedroppers for even greater control. The one with a plus sign (+) adds to the color range. The one with a minus sign (-) subtracts colors.

For even greater control over the affected color range, use the eyedroppers on the bottom of the panel. The eyedropper with a plus sign (+) adds to the color range. The one with a minus sign (-) subtracts colors.

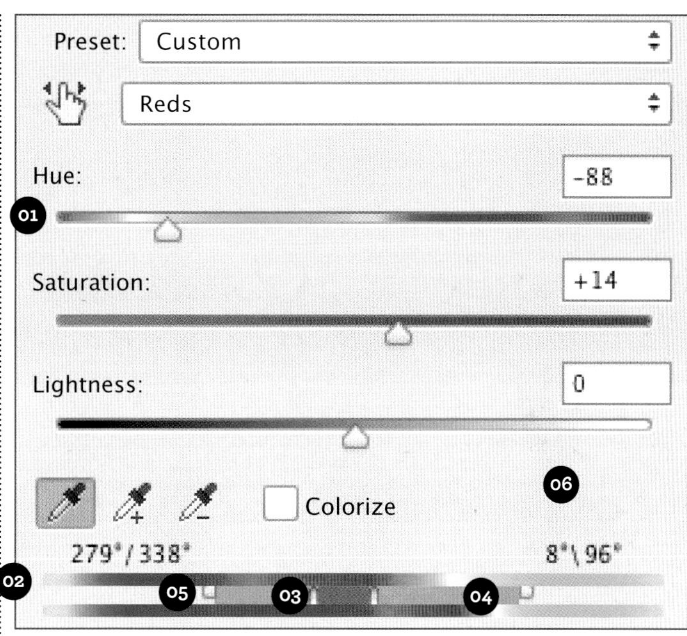

You can also use the gray slider to modify the color range:

01. This color bar indicates the original hues.
02. This color bar indicates the new hues.
03. The dark gray area of the slider determines the range of colors that are affected. Drag here to move the slider.
04. The light gray area indicates the "fall-off"—colors that are only partially affected. Drag here to increase or decrease the color range without affecting the fall-off.
05. Drag these handles to change the fall-off without affecting the color range.
06. Drag these handles to adjust the color range and fall-off.

Fast Fixes

Blend Modes

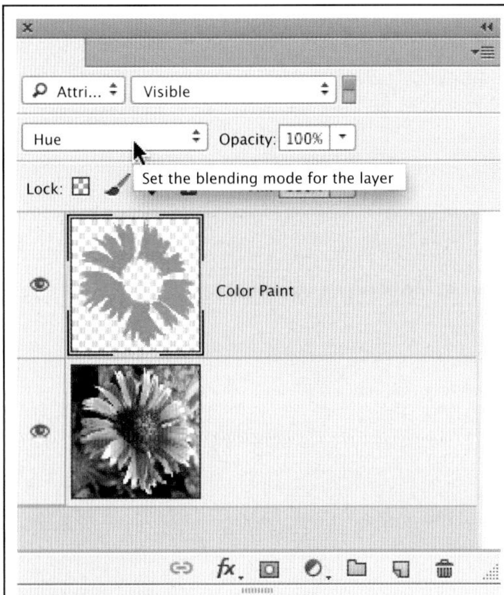

The Hue and Color blend modes allow you to modify colors using the Brush tool.

01. Select the part of the image you want to recolor.
02. Open the Layers panel.
03. Create a new layer above the one you want to recolor (Layer > New Layer or click the Create a new layer icon at the bottom of the Layers panel.)
04. Choose Hue from the new layer's Blend Mode drop-down.
05. Choose the foreground color you'd like to use.
06. Press B to select the Brush tool and paint over the image. The image will be recolored to match the hue of the foreground color, while retaining its original luminosity and saturation.

Choose Color as the blend mode if you want to match the foreground color's hue and saturation. This will tend to make the recoloring more vivid, but less realistic.

Match Color

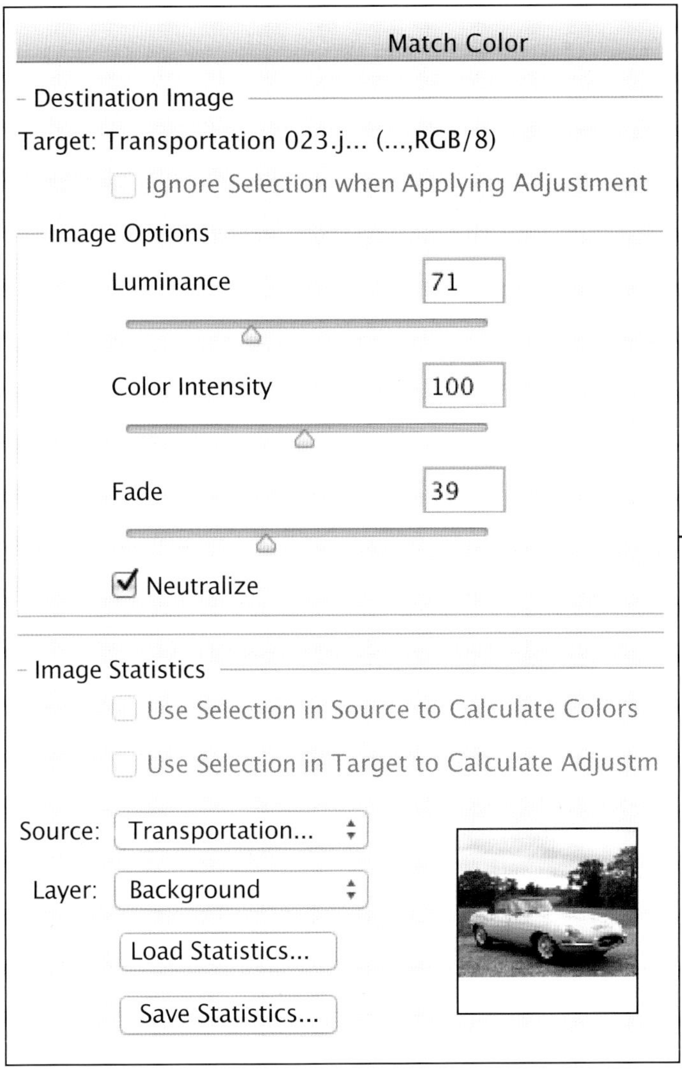

Match Color

Destination Image

Target: Transportation 023.j... (...,RGB/8)

Ignore Selection when Applying Adjustment

Image Options

Luminance 71

Color Intensity 100

Fade 39

Neutralize

Image Statistics

Use Selection in Source to Calculate Colors

Use Selection in Target to Calculate Adjustm

Source: Transportation...

Layer: Background

Load Statistics...

Save Statistics...

This feature adjusts colors in your artwork so they match the color scheme in a source image. You can also use it to match colors between layers. It works only in RGB mode.

01. Open the image you want to use as a source. The feature works best with images that have similar composition.

02. Open the image you want to modify. You can't apply Match Color as an adjustment layer, so it's a good idea to work on a duplicate.

03. Choose Image > Adjustments > Match Color.

04. In the Source drop-down, choose the source image.

05. Use the Luminance, Color Intensity, and Fade controls to modify the effect. Fade restores the original colors. The Neutralize option reduces color casts. You can get a quick before-and-after view by clicking and unclicking in the Preview checkbox.

06. Click OK when you're done.

Fast Fixes

Modifying Colors in Illustrator

Illustrator's Edit Colors/Recolor Artwork dialog box provides a single location for adjusting colors. Use it to edit color groups or to quickly modify colors in selected objects.

Editing Colors

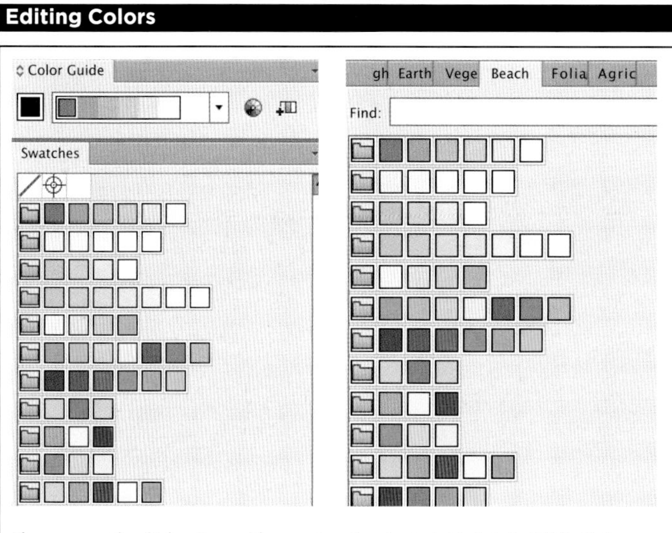

If you open the dialog box with no artwork selected, it's labeled Edit Colors and provides an extensive array of tools for modifying color groups in the current document.

The first step is to load the swatch library (or libraries) you want to use in the document. Skip this step if you've already created the color groups you want to modify.

01. Open the Swatches panel.

02. Open a Swatch library. You can do this via the Window > Swatch Libraries submenu, or the Swatch Libraries Menu on the bottom of the Swatches panel. Each library contains a series of color groups, each with a folder on the left.

03. To add a color group to the Swatches panel, click on the group's folder. To add multiple color groups, Shift-click or ⌘-click (Ctrl-click) on the folders, and choose Add to Swatches from the library's panel menu.

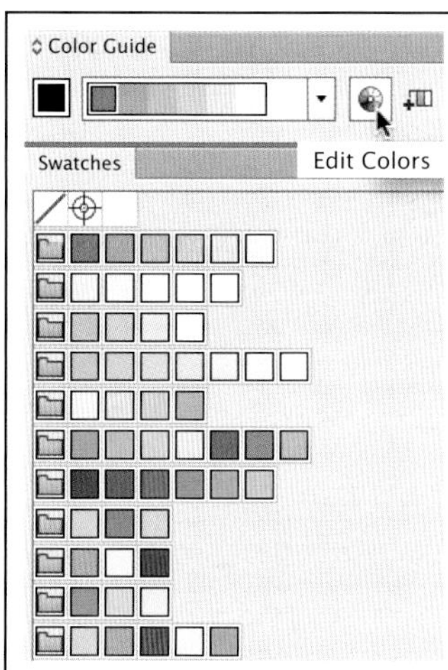

Now you can use the Edit Colors dialog box to adjust the colors. From the Color Guide panel (Window > Color Guide), click on the Edit Colors button.

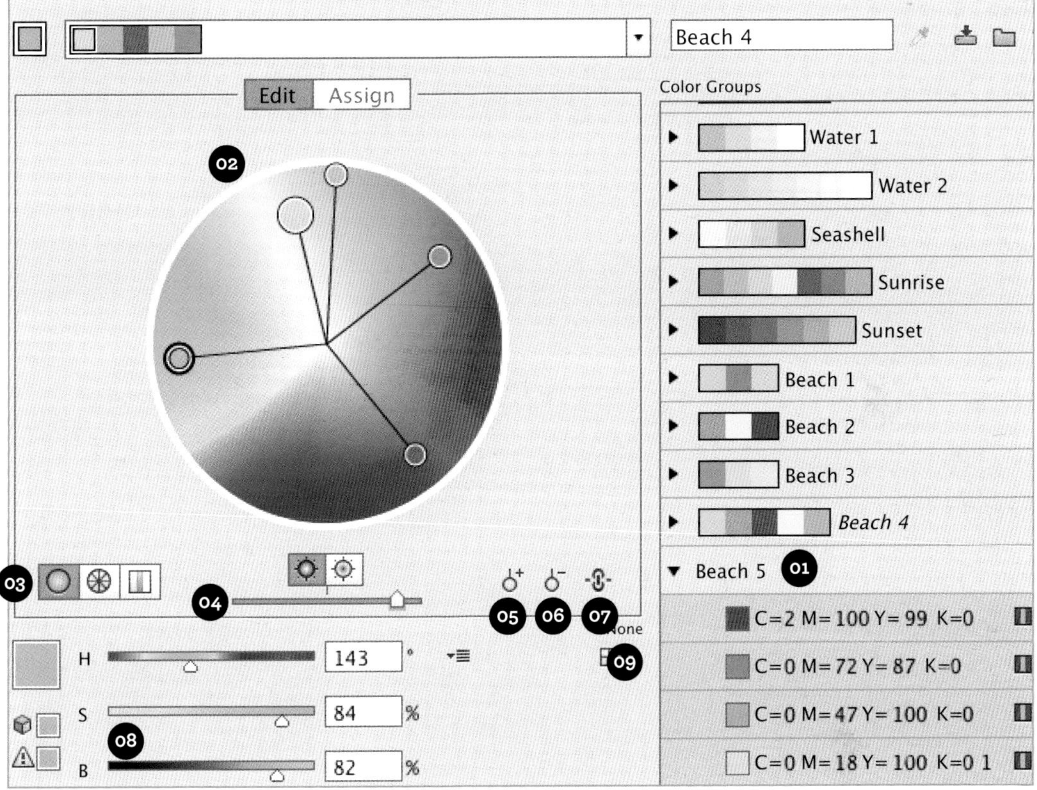

01. Color Groups: Click on a group to modify it. Click on the disclosure triangles to see individual swatches.

02. Color Wheel: Each swatch appears as a small circle. Drag swatches around the wheel to change the hue. Drag them in or out to change brightness or saturation. Double-click on a swatch to open the Color Picker.

03. Color Wheel Display: These buttons control how colors in the wheel are displayed: smooth, segmented or as color bars.

04. Saturation and Brightness Buttons: If the first button is clicked, hue and saturation appear in the color wheel, and the slider controls brightness. If the second button is clicked, hue and brightness appear in the color wheel, and the slider controls saturation.

05. Add: Add a color to the wheel.

06. Delete: Delete a color from the wheel.

07. Harmony Colors: If these are linked, moving one swatch around the wheel causes the others to move along with it, so their harmony is maintained. If they're unlinked, you can adjust each swatch independently. A solid line indicates that the swatches are linked.

08. Color Values: These sliders provide more precise control over the color values for the selected swatch.

09. Color Mode: Open this menu to choose the color mode for the sliders. The default is HSB but you can choose RGB, CMYK, Lab, or Global Adjust.

Fast Fixes

Recoloring Artwork

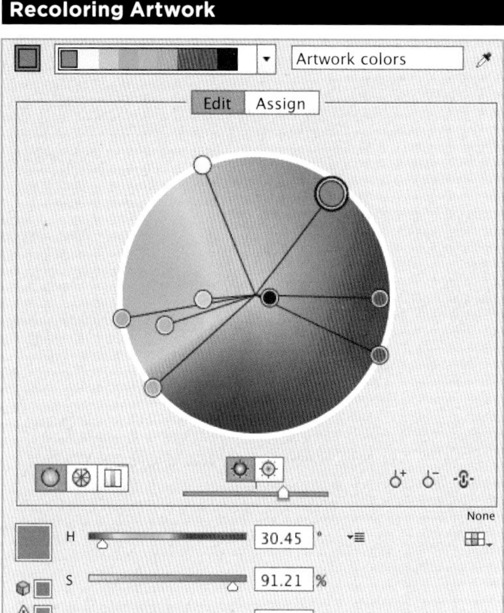

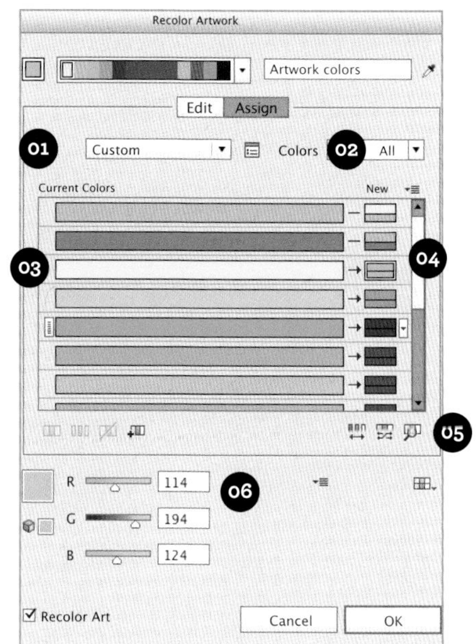

The same dialog box you use to edit color groups can also recolor selected artwork. In this context, it becomes the Recolor Artwork dialog box.

01. Select the artwork you want to recolor and choose Edit > Edit Colors > Recolor Artwork. The Edit tab is nearly identical to the one on the previous page. However, instead of modifying a color group, you can edit the colors in the selected artwork.

02. Click on the Assign tab to reassign specified colors in your artwork. The current colors are shown on the left. New colors are shown on the right.

01. Preset: Specify a preset for recoloring the artwork.

02. Color Reduction Options: See next page.

03. New Color: To assign a new color, click on the box in the New column. Make your changes using the slider controls on the bottom. Double-click on the box to open a color picker.

04. Arrow: If you don't want to reassign a particular color, click on this arrow.

05. Magnifying Glass: This helps you locate the selected color in your artwork. All colors except the one you select will be dimmed.

06. Slider Controls: These work the same way they do in the Edit tab. You can choose RGB, HSL, CMYK, Lab, or Global Adjust.

Reducing Colors

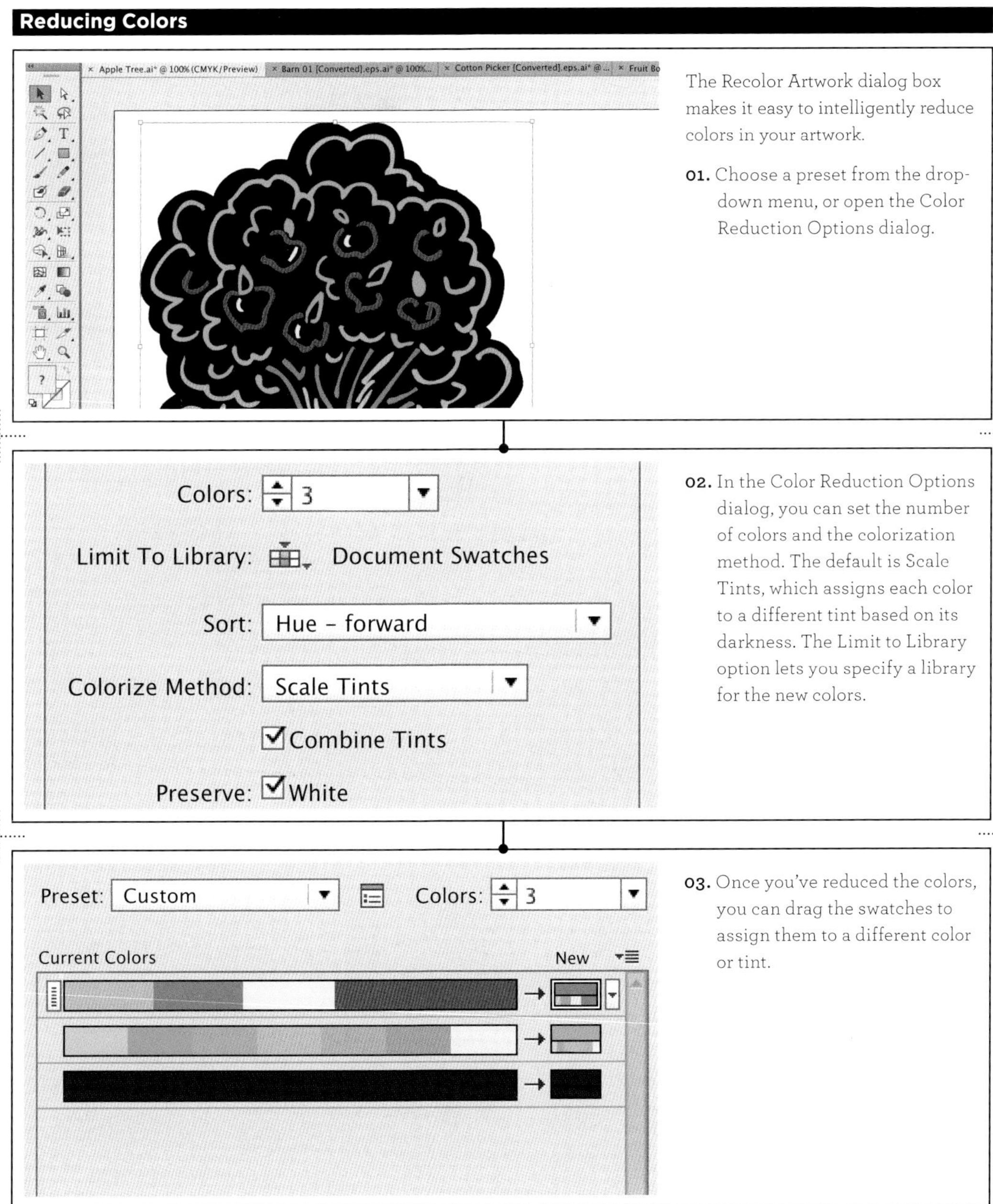

The Recolor Artwork dialog box makes it easy to intelligently reduce colors in your artwork.

01. Choose a preset from the drop-down menu, or open the Color Reduction Options dialog.

02. In the Color Reduction Options dialog, you can set the number of colors and the colorization method. The default is Scale Tints, which assigns each color to a different tint based on its darkness. The Limit to Library option lets you specify a library for the new colors.

03. Once you've reduced the colors, you can drag the swatches to assign them to a different color or tint.

Fast Fixes

Using Kuler

Kuler provides a fun and easy way to create, share, and download harmonized color themes. It's available as a website, tablet app and panel in Photoshop, InDesign, and other programs.

Kuler Themes

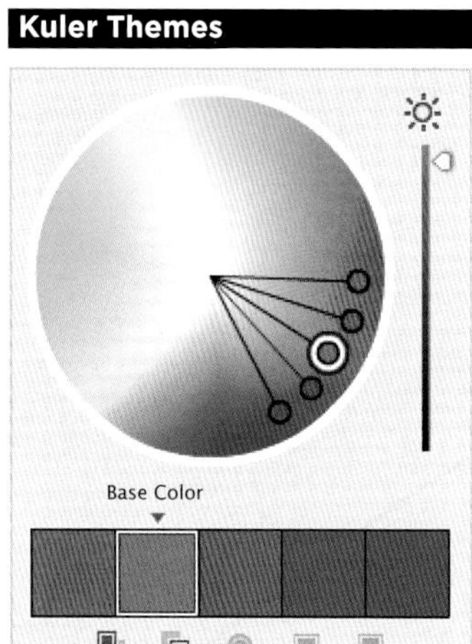

Analogous

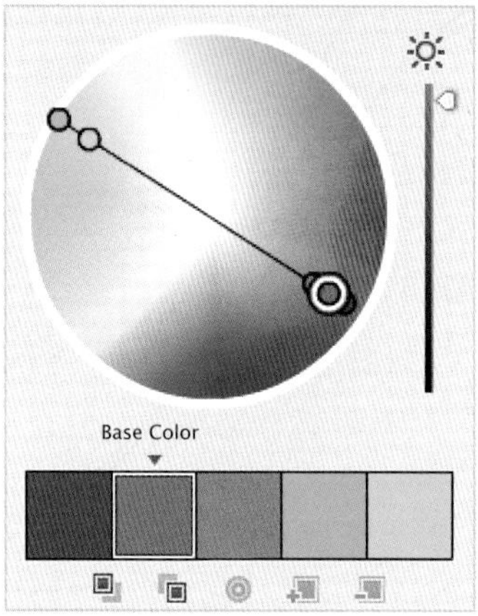

Complementary

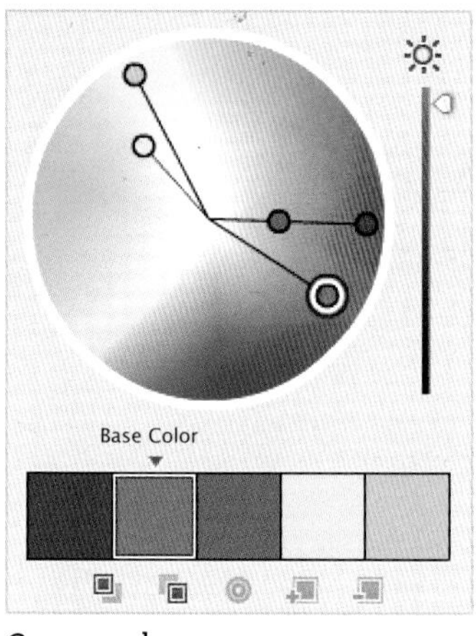

Compound

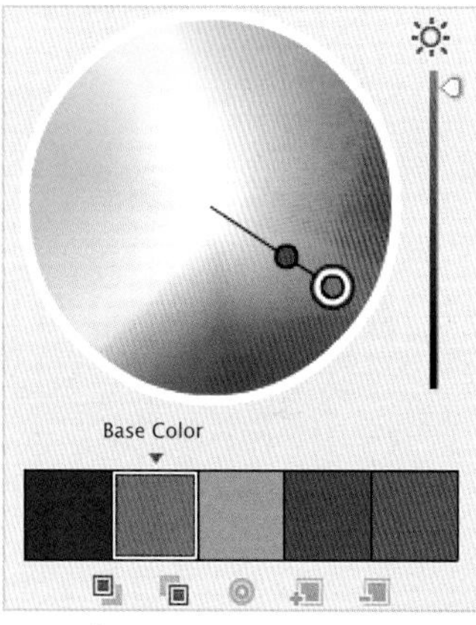

Monochromatic

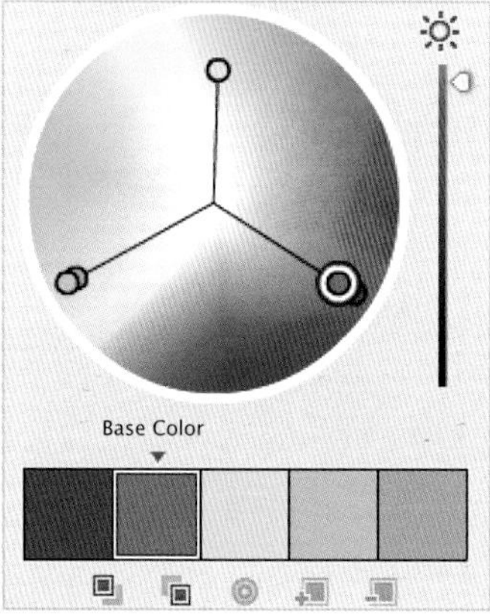

Triad

Each theme consists of one base color and four related colors. The color relationships are determined by one of six harmony rules: Analogous, Monochromatic, Triad, Complementary, Compound, and Shades. If you'd rather not follow one of these rules, you can choose the Custom option and include any colors you'd like.

Each Kuler app has two main sections: A theme browser, where you can view and download themes, and Create, where you can build your own.

The Website

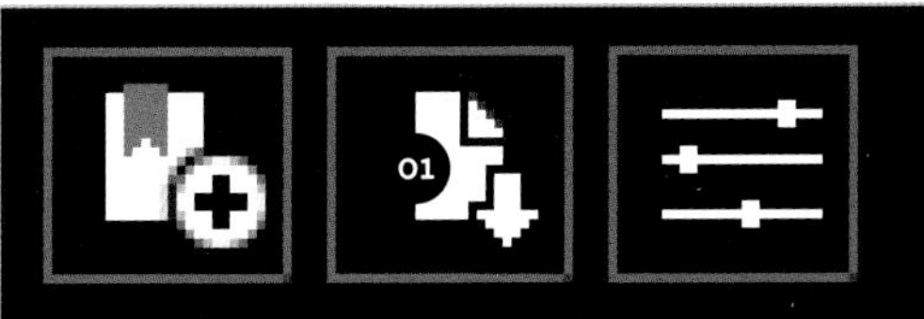

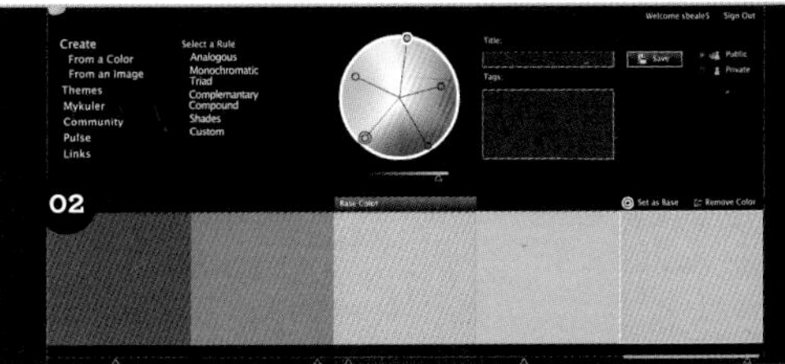

To join the Kuler community (http://kuler.adobe.com), you'll need to sign in with an Adobe Live ID. You can view the most popular themes, or search by tag, title, or creator.

01. **Download:** Click on this icon to download a theme. It will be saved in the Adobe Swatch Exchange format, which can be opened in most Creative Suite programs.
02. **Create:** This section lets you build your own themes. You can modify colors using the wheel or slider controls. As you change one color, values for the others shift according to the harmony rule you've selected.
03. **Color Theme:** Another option is to create a color theme from an image. Upload the image and select a mood (Colorful, Bright, Muted, Deep or Dark), and Kuler will sample five colors indicated by the circles. Customize the theme by dragging the circles to different parts of the image.

The Panel

The Kuler panel is available by choosing Window > Extensions > Kuler in Illustrator, Photoshop, InDesign, Fireworks, or Flash Professional. One benefit of running Kuler in these programs is that you can save themes directly to the Swatches panels.

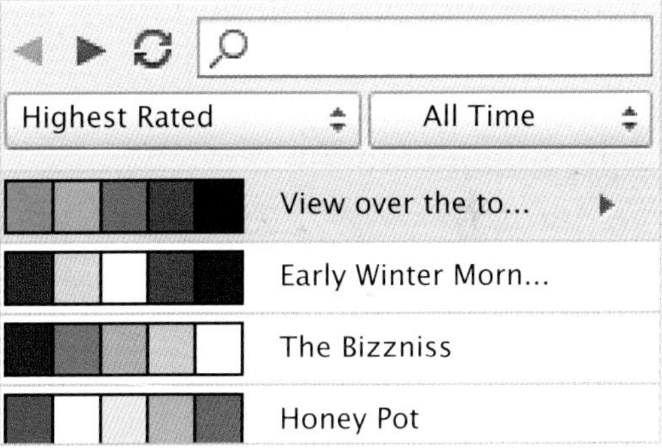

Browse Tab: The panel links to themes on the Kuler website. Click the Browse tab to view the themes based on criteria you select in the menus on top. To edit a theme or add it to the Swatches panel, select it and click once on the arrow. You can also double-click on a theme to modify it.

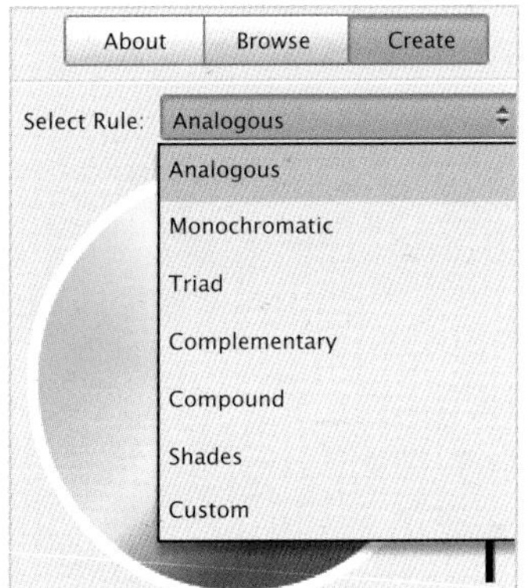

Create Tab: This section lets you build or modify a theme. The controls are similar to those on the website.

Fast Fixes

Quick Photo Fixes

Photoshop offers many time-saving features for fixing color casts, over- or under-exposure, and other common photo mishaps.

Camera Raw

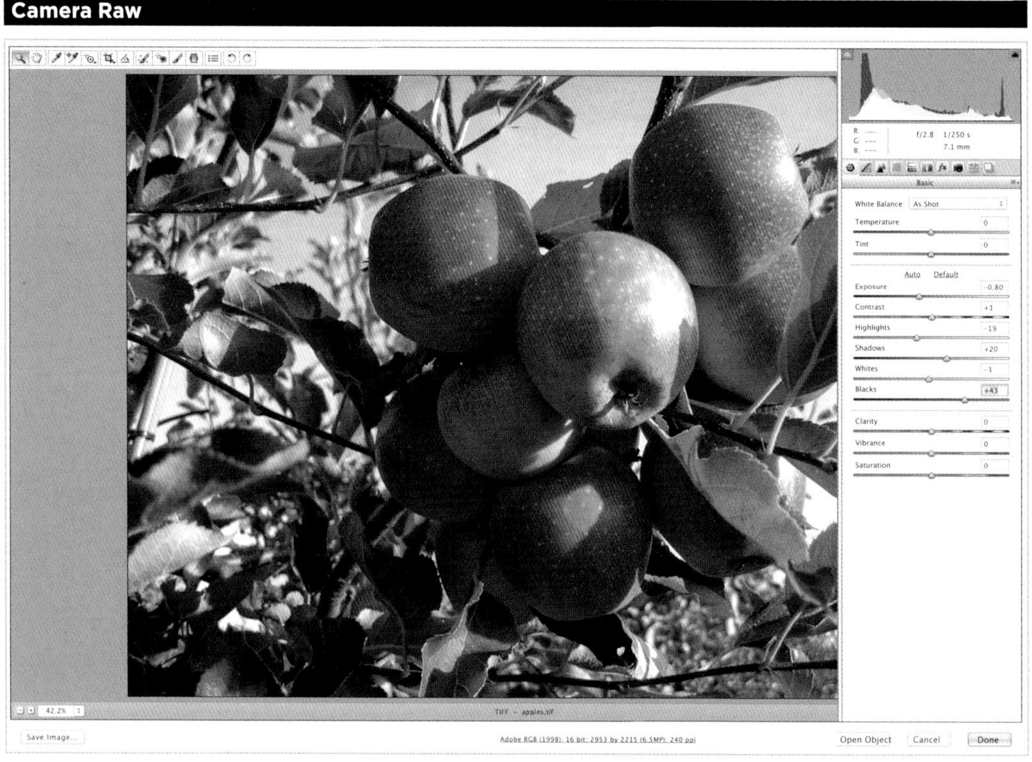

This plug-in should generally be your first stop if you're working with raw images captured with a digital camera. It launches from Photoshop or Bridge when you open an image in a raw format. A common workflow is to use Camera Raw to adjust white balance and tonal settings, and then open the image in Photoshop for additional enhancements. However, you can apply a wide range of image adjustments and save them as presets. In CS6, the new Highlights, Shadows, and Whites controls effectively replace the Recovery, Fill Light, and Brightness sliders, respectively, of previous versions. Double-click on a slider to restore the original value. Press Shift and double-click to apply automatic modifications.

The Adjustments Panel

When correcting images in Photoshop, you'll work more efficiently by using adjustment layers rather than the equivalent Image > Adjust commands. Even better, use this Photoshop panel (Windows > Adjustments) to quickly add adjustment layers and modify their settings.

In CS5, you apply settings for each adjustment within the panel. In CS6, you apply settings in the new Properties panel.

- The Levels adjustment is a good place to start. You can try an Auto adjustment, use a preset or manually reset the sliders. The Auto adjustments in CS6 provides much better results than in previous versions. It consults an image database to apply adjustments based on the unique characteristics of each photo
- Use the Curves adjustment for more-challenging images where you want to selectively fine-tune highlights, midtones, or shadows.

Content-Aware Fill

This feature removes defects or unwanted objects from images by sampling pixels from the surrounding area. It's available in several ways:

- Choose the Spot Healing Brush and click on Content-Aware in the options bar. Paint over the object you want to remove.
- Use Photoshop's selection tools to select the part of the image you want to remove. Open the Fill dialog (Edit > Fill or Shift-F5). Choose Content-Aware in the Use menu and click OK. For optimal results, extend the selection slightly beyond the area you want to remove.
- In CS6, you can also use the new Content-Aware option for the Patch tool. This option modifies the patch to match the surrounding area. Try different Adaptation settings to determine how much of the patch is modified.
- The new Content-Aware Move tool in CS6 lets you move a selection from one part of the image to another. Then it fills in the empty area with a pattern sampled from the surrounding pixels. It works best if the source and destination areas are similar. The tool is grouped with the Spot Healing Brush. Choose the Move mode in the options bar and move the selection to the new location.

Fast Fixes

Fix Crooked Photos

Photoshop's Ruler and Crop tools provide a nice hidden time-saver for fixing crooked photos. It works best if the photo includes an element such as a horizon line that you can use as a reference.

Ruler: This tool is grouped with the Eyedropper. Choose it and draw a line across the image to indicate the desired rotation angle. Click on Straighten (CS5) or Straighten Layer (CS6). In CS5, Photoshop straightens the image and crops it to remove transparent areas. In CS6, Photoshop rotates the target layer, but does not crop the image.

Crop: In CS6, the new and vastly improved Crop tool provides a more flexible way to straighten images. Choose the tool and click on Straighten in the Options bar. Then draw a line on the canvas as you do with the Ruler tool. As you draw, a tool tip will show the rotation angle. Rotate the image by dragging outside the corners of the crop box.

Cropping Images

Photoshop's Crop tool got a major facelift in CS6. The changes may seem jarring at first, but provide greater flexibility—and productivity—if you need to crop images.

01. **Crop Handles:** When you choose the tool, crop handles automatically appear at the edges of the canvas. Drag on any handle to increase or decrease the crop area.
02. **Aspect Ratio:** Use this menu to specify an aspect ratio or rotate the crop box.
03. **Size & Resolution:** Use this option in the menu to create your own preset.
04. **View:** Use this menu to change the overlay. You can select classic composition guidelines such as Golden Spiral and Golden Ratio in addition to the previous Rule of Thirds.

Leave Delete Cropped Pixels unchecked to preserve the area outside the crop box.

✓ Unconstrained
Original Ratio
1 x 1 (Square)
4 x 5 (8 x 1
8.5 x 11
4 x 3
5 x 7
2 x 3 (4 x 6)
1c.tif @ 25
02

Crop Image Size & Resolution
Source: Current Image...
Width: 6.827 Inches
Height: 5.12 Inches
Resolution: 300 Pixels/Inch
Save as Crop Preset
03

04

01→05 mins

Fast Fixes

Photoshop Filters

Photoshop ships with more than 100 filters that allow you to make quick changes to photos and other artwork. Here are some tips for using them productively.

Use the Filters...	To...
Artistic, Brush Stroke, and Sketch filters	Transform photos into simulated color paintings and sketches.
Blur > Gaussian Blur	Soften overly sharp details; smooth wrinkles and blemishes in portraits. Best used with masks or selections to preserve detail in masked areas.
Blur > Field Blur	Opens the new Blur Gallery, which makes it easier to create photographic "bokeh" effects with blurred backgrounds.
Lens Correction	Fix geometric distortions, chromatic aberration, vignetting, and other problems specific to popular camera lenses.
Noise > Add Noise	Add static to overly smooth areas.
Noise > Median	Soften dots in scanned halftones to reduce or remove Moiré patterns. Best used on high-res images that can be scaled down and sharpened after the filter is applied.
Noise > Reduce Noise	Remove or reduce JPEG artifacts and other pixel defects. Best used with masks or selections to preserve detail in masked areas.
Render	Add simulated clouds, fibers or lens flares to photos or illustrations.
Render > Lighting Effects	Add realistic highlights and shadows to photos or illustrations.
Sharpen > Unsharp Mask or Smart Sharpen	Sharpen details in soft or blurry images prior to output. Can also be used to prepare photos before converting them to sketches or line art.
Texture > Texturizer	Simulate textured backgrounds such as canvas, burlap, or brick.

Working with Smart Filters

Most Photoshop filters can be run as Smart Filters, and this is generally a good option. Smart Filters are nondestructive, so you can always go back to the image's original state if things don't work out. You can apply as many filters as you like and easily change their settings.

- Go to Filter > Convert for Smart Filters. This converts the layer into a Smart Object.
- Run a filter and choose its settings. When you're done, the filter appears in the Layers panel.
- Apply any other filters you'd like. Filter effects are cumulative—the filter on top modifies the filter below it, and so on. Drag filter names up or down the stack to change the order in which they're applied.
- Double-click on a filter name to change its settings.
- Click on the visibility (eye) icon to hide or show each filter effect.
- Double-click on the icon to the right of the filter name to choose a different blend mode.
- Right-click on the filter name to delete or disable it.
- When you apply a Smart Filter, Photoshop automatically adds a Filter Mask to the Channels panel. Use the mask to confine filter effects to selected parts of the image.

See Also page 67

01→05 mins

Unsharp Mask

Unsharp Mask is often the last step in preparing an image for output. It uses sophisticated algorithms to sharpen edge detail and reduce blurring. The best settings to use depend on the subject matter and sharpness of the original photo. The following should work for most situations:

Amount: Between 65 and 200 percent. The lower end of this range generally works best.

Radius: Between 1 and 4 pixels

Threshold: Between 0 and 20 levels.

Keep the following in mind:

- Higher Amount and Radius values increase the sharpening effect. Higher Threshold values decrease it.
- You can click the Preview checkbox on and off for a quick before-and-after view. Halos in edge areas indicate too much sharpening.
- In most cases, you should apply the filter after the image has been scaled to its final size. However, a heavy Unsharp Mask can be a good first step to enhance edge detail if you want to use one of Photoshop's Sketch effects.
- You can try the Smart Sharpen filter for even more control over sharpening.

Fast Fixes

Layout Tools in InDesign

You could be wasting hours on print and interactive layouts if you're not taking advantage of these productivity boosters in InDesign.

Working with Containers

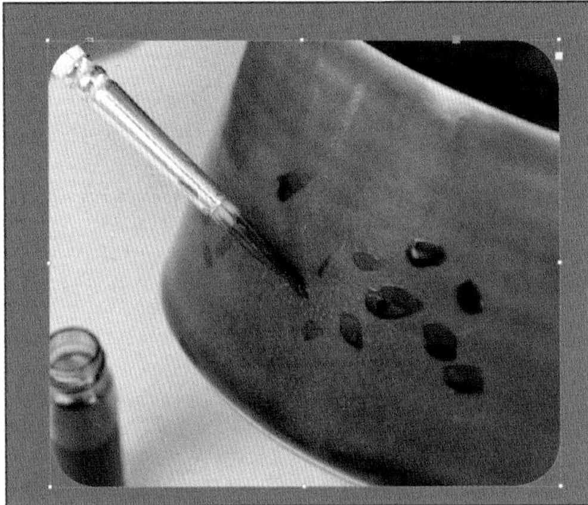

Beginning with CS5, InDesign introduced a streamlined approach to working with text and graphic containers—and the content within them.

If you click inside a container with the Selection tool, you can do the following:

- Drag the container to reposition it.
- Drag on the selection handles to resize the container (press Shift to constrain to the original aspect ratio).

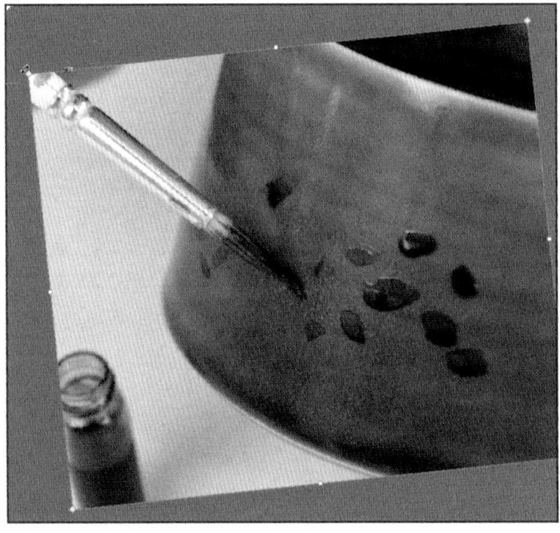

- Drag outside the corners to rotate the container.

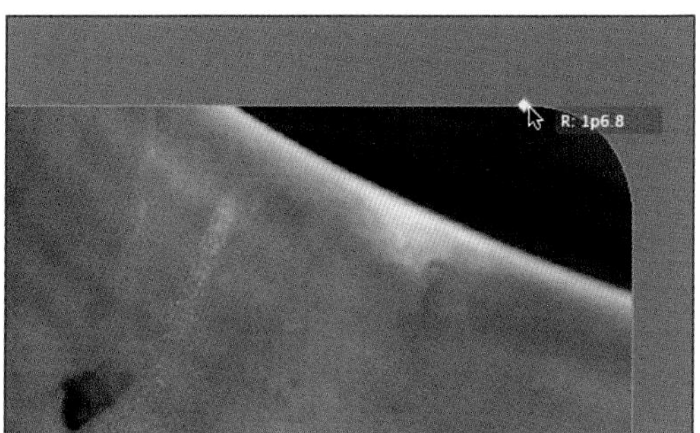

- Click on the yellow square to create rounded corners.
- If you double-click inside a text container, InDesign automatically switches to the Type tool, allowing you to edit the text.

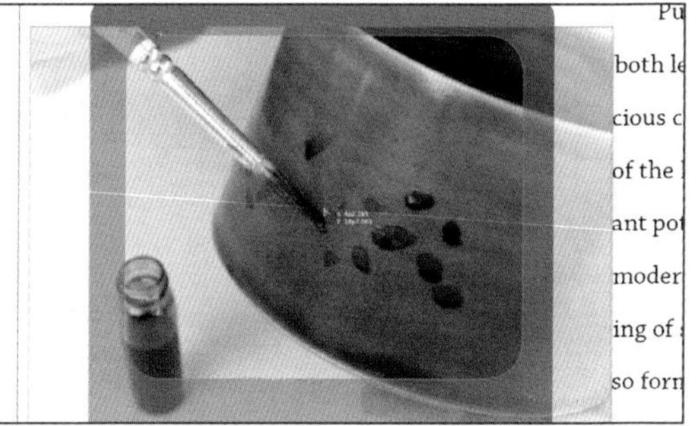

If you double-click inside a graphic container, the artwork within the container is selected, and you can do the following:

- Drag the image to reposition it within the container.
- Drag on the selection handles to resize the image (press Shift to constrain to the original aspect ratio).
- Drag outside the corners to rotate the image.

Double-click again, or press Esc, to re-select the container.

Tip

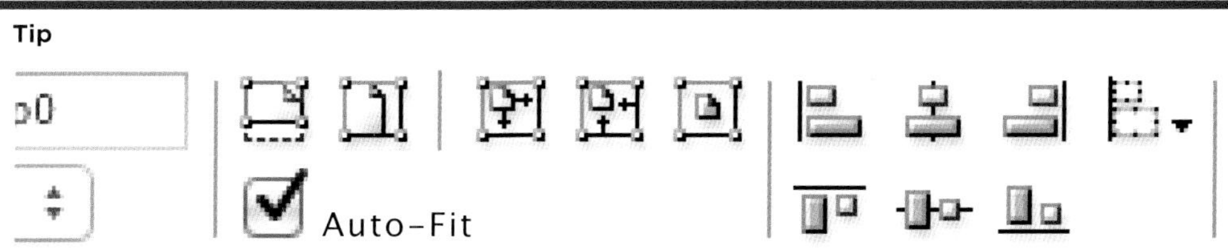

- Use fitting options in the Control panel to determine how the content fits into the frame. The options are Fill Frame Proportionally, Fit Content Proportionally, Fit Content To Frame, Fit Frame To Content and Center Content.
- Double-click on a corner handle to fit the frame to the content.
- To resize the container and the content, click Auto-Fit in the Control panel, or go to Object > Fitting > Frame Fitting Options and drag on a selection handle.
- If you lose track of whether you've selected the container or the contents, look at the bounding box. The container's bounding box will match the layer color, and it will have a yellow corner-editing box in the upper right. The content's bounding box will have a different color.

Fast Fixes

The Content Grabber

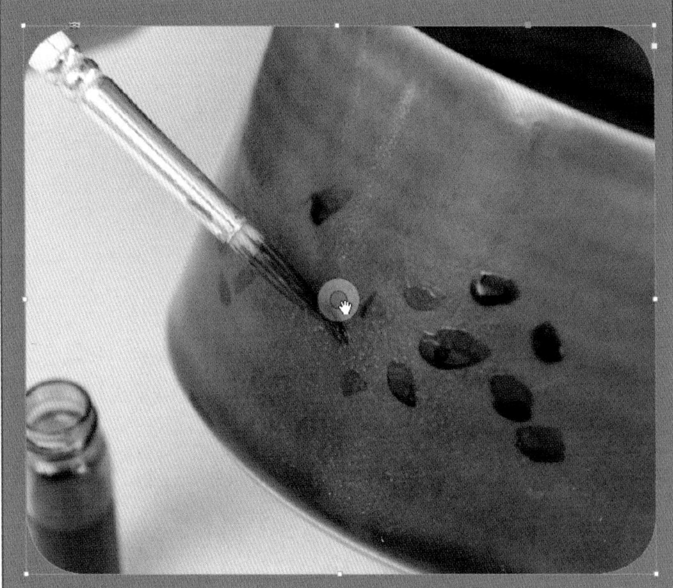

When you mouse over a graphic container with the Selection tool, a donut-shaped object known as a Content Grabber appears in the middle. If you click inside the grabber, the cursor changes to a hand, and you can reposition the image within the container.

Placing Multiple Items

When importing text or graphics with the Place command, you can select multiple files and place them in the layout in a single operation.

01. If you're importing graphics, open the Links panel. This isn't a requirement, but will make it easier to see which files you're placing.

02. Choose File > Place or press ⌘-D (Ctrl-D).

03. Select the files you'd like to import. Click on the Show Import Options checkbox if you want to choose import options for text or graphics.

04. The "place gun" should be loaded with thumbnails of each imported file. You can then place each file at any desired location in the layout. Click and drag to draw a new frame, or click once where you want the upper-left corner to be.

Tip

- You can also import multiple files by dragging them from Bridge, Mini Bridge, the Mac OS X Finder, or the Microsoft Windows Explorer. However, you won't be able to choose import options.
- As you place the files, the place gun will indicate the number of files remaining.
- Graphics files you're placing will be listed in the Links panel. An "LP" next to the file name indicates the current file being placed.
- You can cycle through the files in the place gun by pressing the right and left arrow keys.
- Press Esc to remove a file from the place gun.

Placing Graphics in a Grid

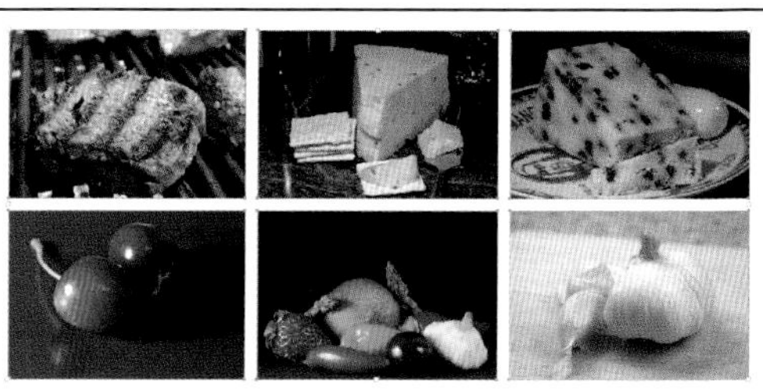

When importing multiple graphics, you also have the option to place them into a grid. You can use this feature to create simple contact sheets.

01. Follow steps 1–3 in Placing Multiple Items.
02. Click and drag to create the boundaries of the grid. Do not release the mouse button.
03. Press the right arrow key to create columns. Press the up arrow to create rows. Press the left and down arrow keys to reduce the number of columns and rows, respectively.
04. Release the mouse button. Each graphic will appear in a cell within the grid.

The Gap Tool

Introduced in CS5, this tool adjusts the gaps between objects.

As you drag, the tool moves the gap and resizes the objects.

⌘-drag (Ctrl-drag) to resize the gap. This also resizes the objects.

⌘-Option-drag (Ctrl-Alt-drag) to move the objects as you're resizing the gap.

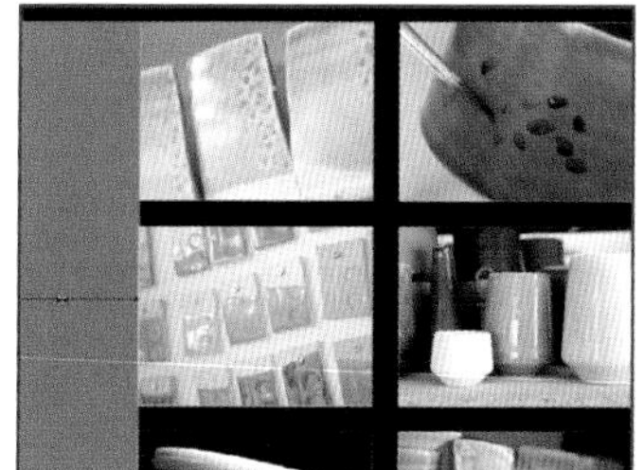

Option-drag (Alt+drag) to move the gap and objects in unison. If you Option-drag from the side, as shown here, the gap resizes and the objects move.

Press Shift with any of these actions to adjust only the nearest objects.

Fast Fixes

Smart Guides

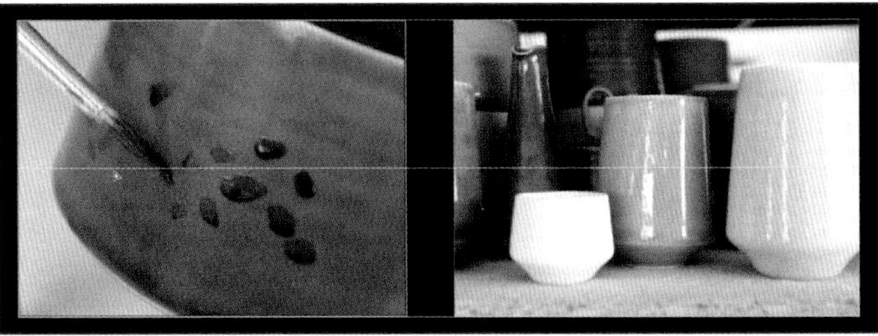

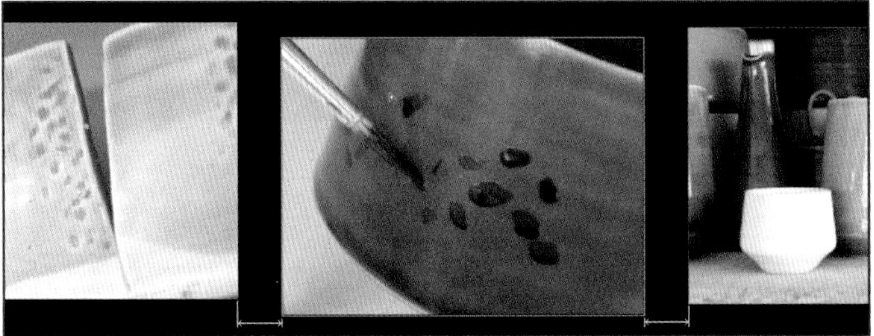

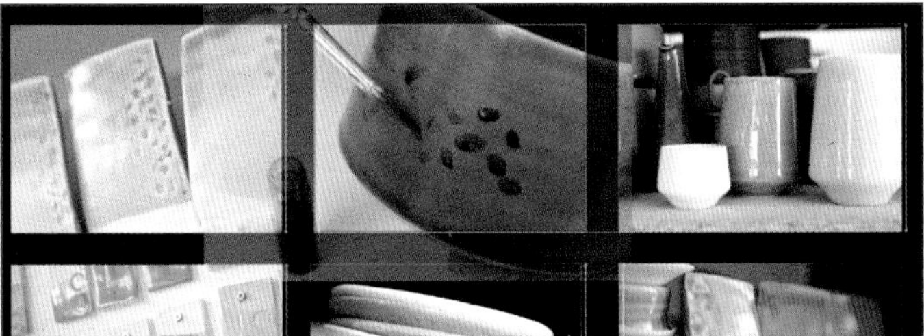

InDesign's Smart Guides enable you to quickly align or adjust objects even if you're not working in a grid. They're activated by default, but you can turn them on (or off) by choosing View > Grids & Guides > Smart Guides or pressing ⌘-U (Ctrl+U).

Smart Alignment causes guides to appear when an object is aligned with neighboring ones (top).

Smart Spacing causes guides to appear when the gap on the left matches the one on the right (middle).

Smart Dimensions shows guides when a resized object matches the dimensions or rotation angle of neighboring objects (bottom).

Roundtrip Editing

This is a big time-saver when working with graphics imported from Photoshop, Illustrator, or other programs. If you find that an imported image or illustration needs more work, select the graphic and choose Edit > Edit Original. The artwork will open in the program that created it. Make the desired changes and save the file. The version in the InDesign layout will be updated automatically.

You can also choose Edit > Edit With to modify the artwork in a different program.

Mini Bridge

InDesign's Mini Bridge panel provides some of the functionality of Bridge from within the program. You can use it to quickly locate and import text, graphics and other assets and drag them into your InDesign layout. As with the Place command, you can place multiple files, though you can't apply import options.

Mini Bridge (and Bridge) can show you images linked to other InDesign documents, in case you'd like to use those assets in your current layout:

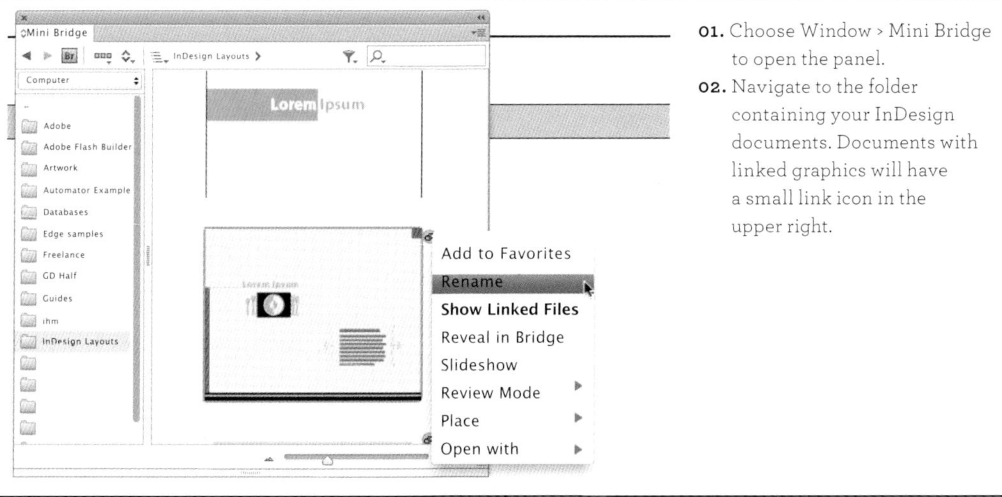

01. Choose Window > Mini Bridge to open the panel.

02. Navigate to the folder containing your InDesign documents. Documents with linked graphics will have a small link icon in the upper right.

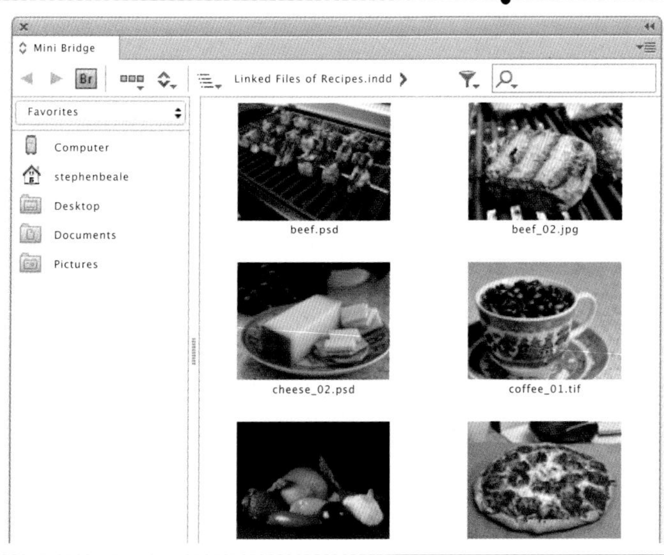

03. Right-click on the link icon to open the contextual menu.

04. Choose Show Linked Files. Mini Bridge will open a panel containing the linked files.

05. Select the files you want to import and drag them into the layout.

Fast Fixes

Create an Acrobat Portfolio

Acrobat Portfolios provide an easy way to create mood boards, client presentations, and catalogs of your projects. Unlike regular PDF files, an Acrobat Portfolio can embed files in their native formats.

Make a Portfolio

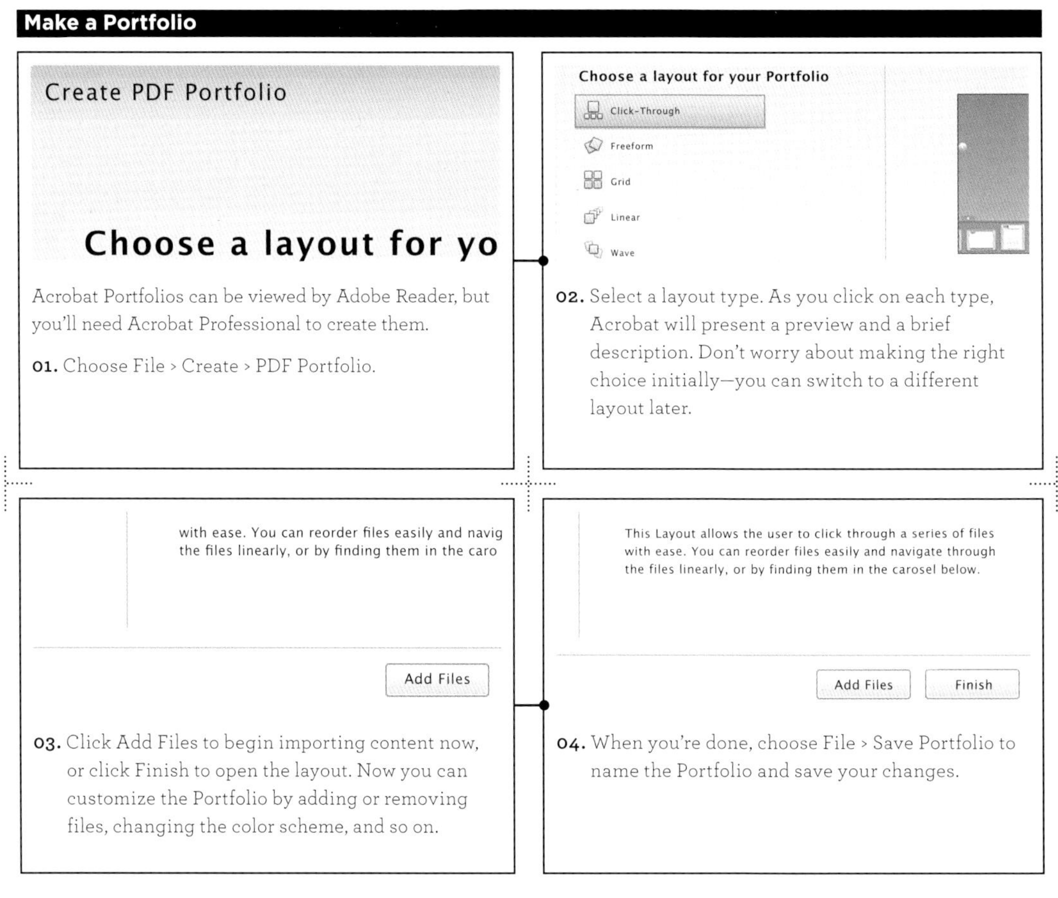

Acrobat Portfolios can be viewed by Adobe Reader, but you'll need Acrobat Professional to create them.

01. Choose File > Create > PDF Portfolio.

02. Select a layout type. As you click on each type, Acrobat will present a preview and a brief description. Don't worry about making the right choice initially—you can switch to a different layout later.

03. Click Add Files to begin importing content now, or click Finish to open the layout. Now you can customize the Portfolio by adding or removing files, changing the color scheme, and so on.

04. When you're done, choose File > Save Portfolio to name the Portfolio and save your changes.

Layout View

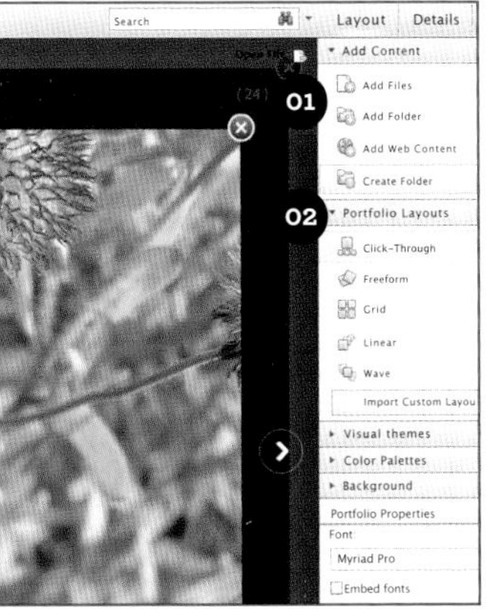

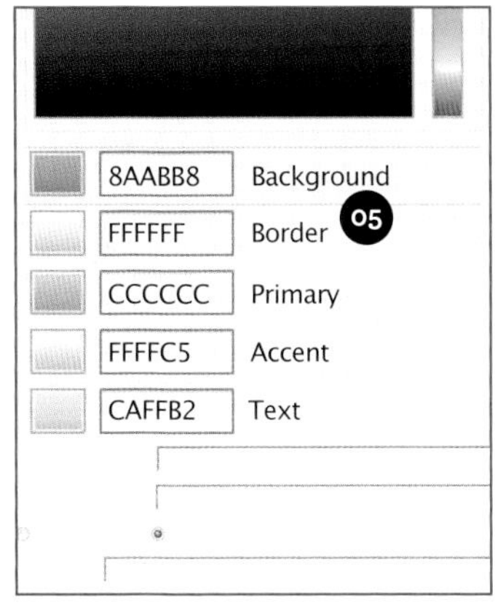

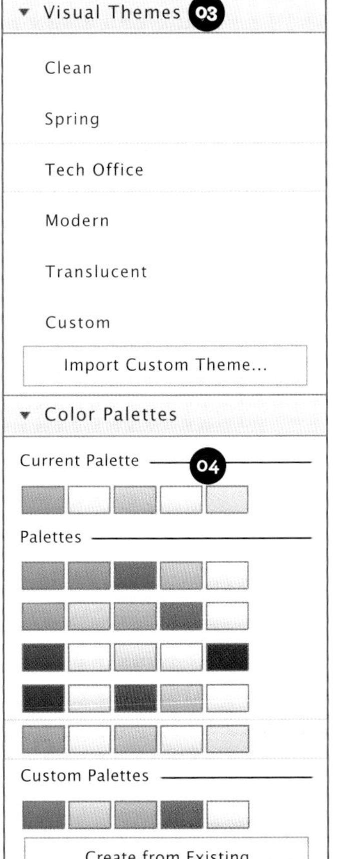

01. Add Content: Use these options to add files, folders, or web content.

02. Portfolio layouts: Click here to change the layout type.

03. Visual Theme: Each theme has its own color palette and background, which you can customize in the panes below.

04. Color Palettes: These panels contain five alternative palettes you can choose from, or click Create from Existing to make your own palette.

05. Background Dialog: Here you can further customize the layout by choosing a background color or image.

Navigating the Layout

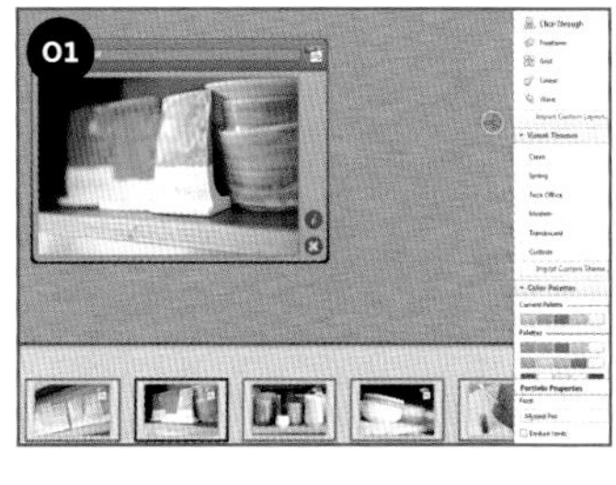

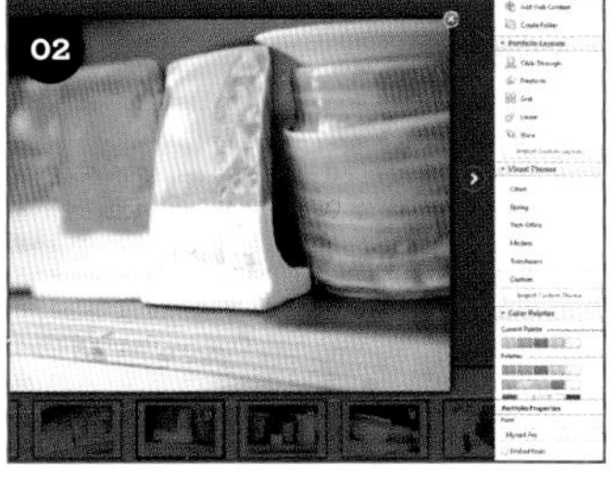

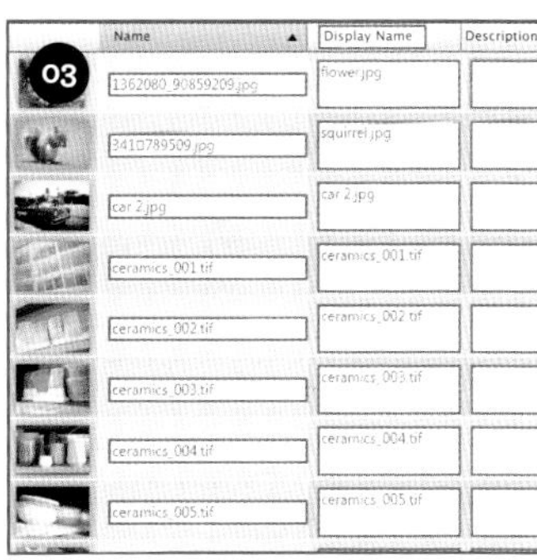

01. Card: Each file in a Portfolio layout is displayed as a "card." Depending on the file format, this could be a thumbnail image or an icon representing the file type.

02. Preview: Double-click on a card to see a full-screen preview. Double-click on the preview to open the file in its native application.

03. Details View: Displays the files in a list format.

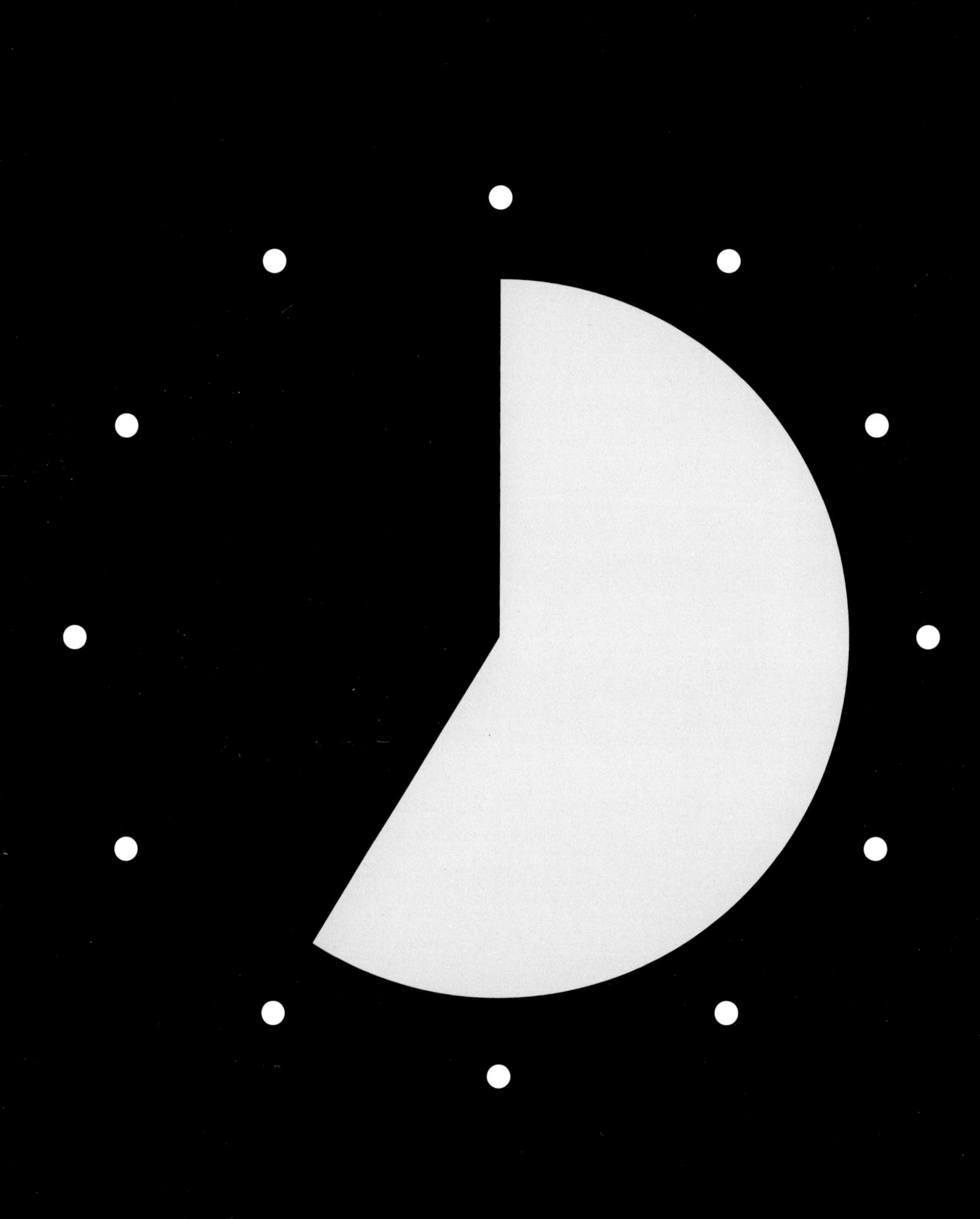

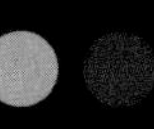

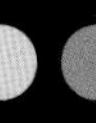
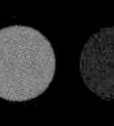
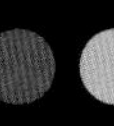
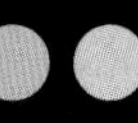
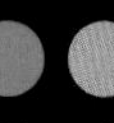

Creative Suite 6
Photoshop
Illustrator
InDesign
Dreamweaver
Flash Professional
Edge
Fireworks
Muse
Acrobat Professional
Bridge
Kuler
Online
Mac
Windows

Chapter Three. Medium Savers

10→60 mins

Medium Savers

Managing Assets in Bridge

Bridge can be an indispensable tool for any designer who works with large collections of photos, illustrations, videos, or other media assets. Here's a quick look at some of its most useful features.

The Bridge Interface

01. **Application Bar:** Provides quick access to common functions.
02. **Path Bar:** Lets you quickly navigate up the folder hierarchy.
03. **Workspace:** Choose a workspace, or click on the arrow to define your own.
04. **Search Bar**
05. **Sort Files:** Choose how you want to sort the files. Click on the arrow to toggle between ascending and descending.
06. **Favorites Panel**
07. **Folders Panel:** Use this to navigate the file system.
08. **Content Panel:** Files appear as thumbnails. Press the Spacebar to view the files in full screen mode. Double-click to open the file in its associated program, or right-click to open with a different program.
09. **Change Thumbnail Size**
10. **Grid View**
11. **Details View**
12. **List View**

Keywords

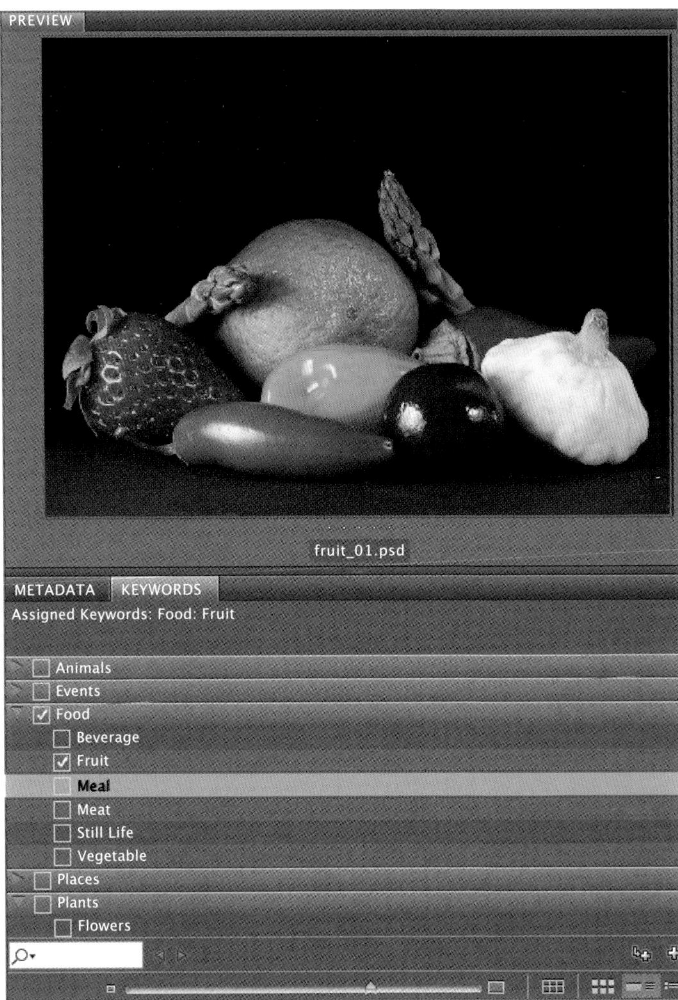

Use the Keywords panel to create keywords and sub keywords that you can assign to images and other assets. Once you've assigned keywords, you can include them in file searches, filters, or Smart Collections.

- To create a keyword, choose New Keyword from the panel menu, click on the New Keyword button or right-click to open a context menu.
- To create a sub keyword, click on a keyword group. Choose New Sub Keyword from the panel menu, click on the New Sub Keyword button, or right-click to open a context menu.
- To convert a keyword to a sub keyword, drag it over the keyword group you want to assign it to.
- To convert a sub keyword to a keyword, drag it to the bottom.
- To assign a keyword, select one or more files and click in the checkbox for the keyword. Shift-click to assign a sub keyword and its parent keyword. Go to Preferences > Keywords to automatically assign parent keywords when clicking on a sub keyword.

Tip

You can quickly create a set of keywords by importing them from a text file. Using any text editor, enter each keyword on a separate line. Place each sub keyword on a separate line underneath the keyword, preceded by a tab indent. Save the file, and choose Import from the panel menu to add the new keywords to the existing ones. Choose Clear and Import to replace the existing keywords.

Medium Savers

Labels and Ratings

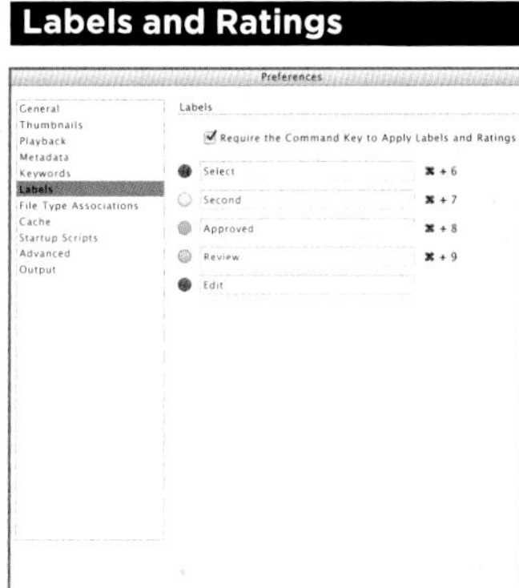

You can assign color-coded labels to determine what action to take with different files. The default labels are Select, Second, Approved, Review, and To Do. To assign a label, select the file(s) and make a choice from the Label menu. You can also use a keyboard shortcut or right-click to open a context menu. To remove labels, select the files from which you want to remove the labels and choose Label > No Label.

You can define your own labels via Preferences > Labels. In the screen grab above, we changed the last label from "To Do" to "Edit." You can also choose whether to include the Command key (Mac) or Ctrl (Windows) in the keyboard shortcut.

In addition to applying labels, you can use the Label menu to assign ratings of one to five stars, or tag a file as a reject.

Find Files

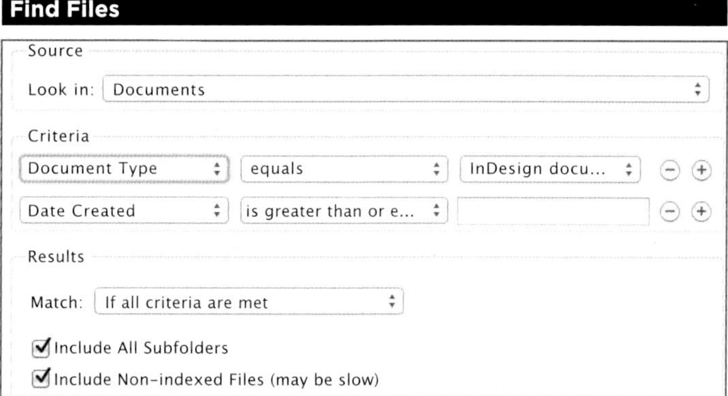

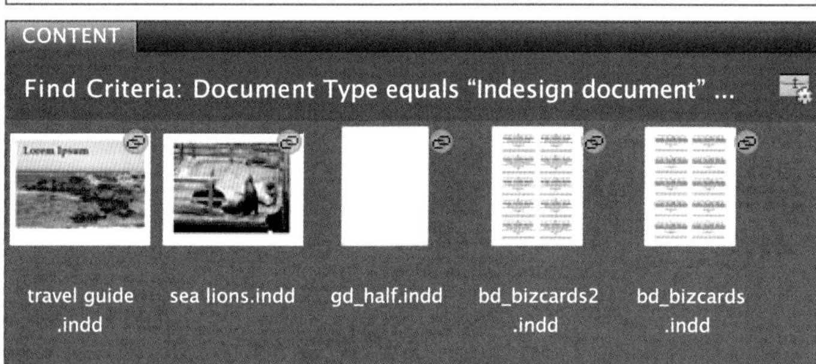

Choose Edit > Find or press ⌘-F (Ctrl+F) to open the Find dialog. You can determine which locations to search and add multiple search criteria, including the filename, file type, created date, keywords, labels, and ratings. In the search results window, click on the Save as Smart Collection button to save your search.

Collections

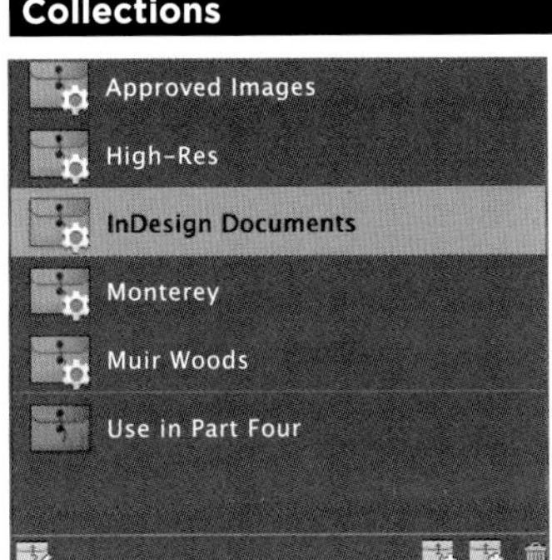

Collections (bottom, in brown) contain files dragged from the content window. Smart Collections (top, in blue) consist of files matching specified search criteria.

Collections and Smart Collections allow you to create groups of similar files regardless of their locations. In the Collections panel, click on the New Collection or New Smart Collection button, or right-click to open a context menu.

To add a file or folder to a Collection, drag it from the Content pane. When you create a Smart Collection, Bridge opens a dialog box that's identical to the Find dialog. Choose the search criteria you want to assign to the collection. Files matching those attributes will appear in the Content panel whenever you choose that Smart Collection.

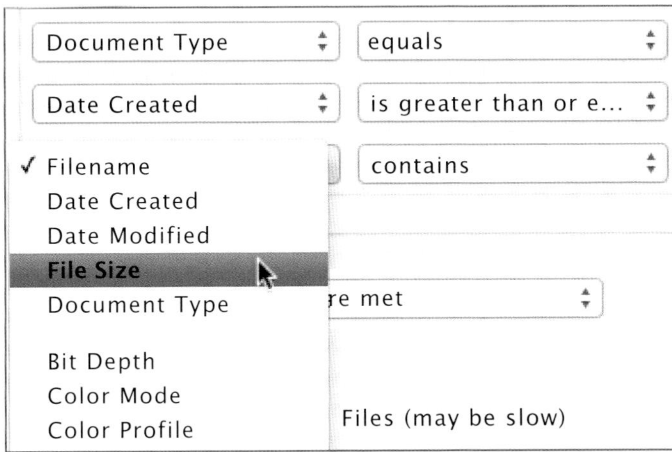

Filters

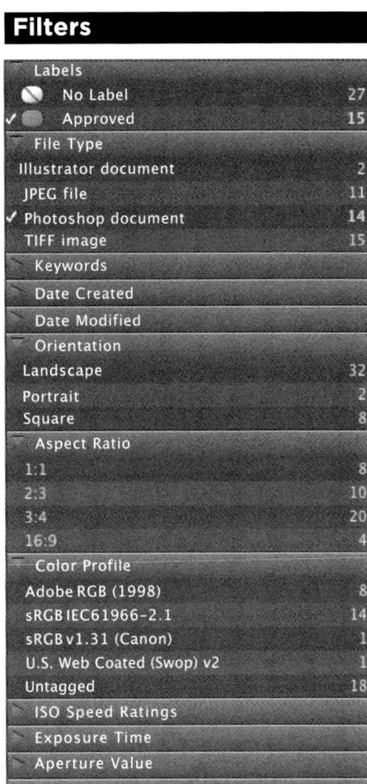

Use the Filter panel to limit the display to files matching specified criteria. You can filter by file type, keywords, ratings, labels, aspect ratio, orientation, and many other attributes.

Click on the Pushpin icon at the bottom of the Filters panel to keep the same filters in place as you browse other folders. Click on the Clear Filter button to clear all filters, or press ⌘-Option-A (Ctrl+Alt+A).

Medium Savers

Photoshop Layer Styles

Layer Styles let you quickly add drop shadows, bevels, strokes, overlays, and other effects to Photoshop layers. They're especially useful for creating type effects and website navigation elements.

Creating Layer Styles

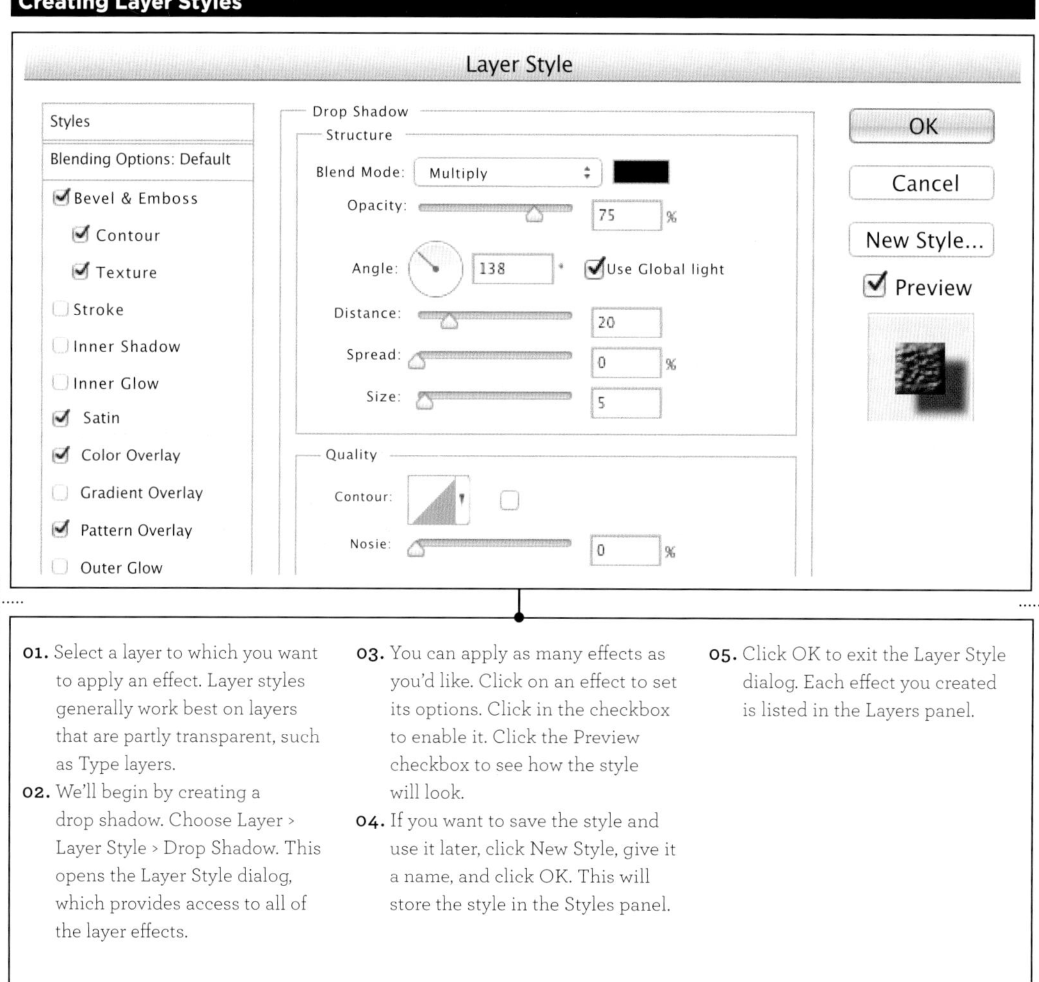

01. Select a layer to which you want to apply an effect. Layer styles generally work best on layers that are partly transparent, such as Type layers.

02. We'll begin by creating a drop shadow. Choose Layer > Layer Style > Drop Shadow. This opens the Layer Style dialog, which provides access to all of the layer effects.

03. You can apply as many effects as you'd like. Click on an effect to set its options. Click in the checkbox to enable it. Click the Preview checkbox to see how the style will look.

04. If you want to save the style and use it later, click New Style, give it a name, and click OK. This will store the style in the Styles panel.

05. Click OK to exit the Layer Style dialog. Each effect you created is listed in the Layers panel.

Working with Layer Styles

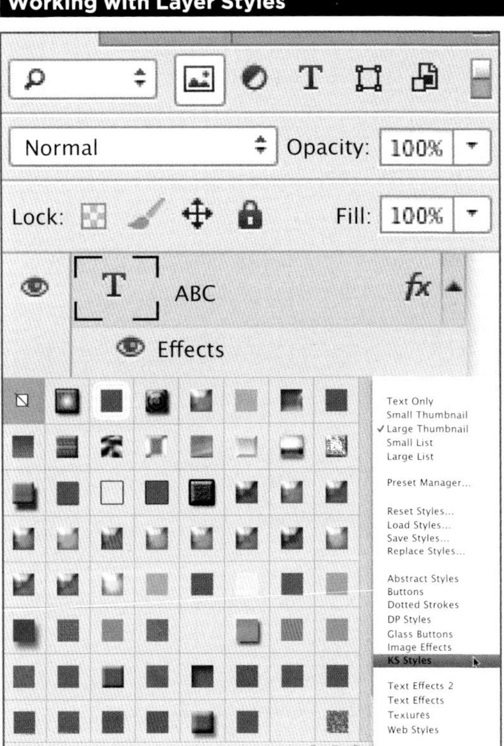

- To apply a layer style, select a layer and choose a style from the Styles panel.
- To copy a style from one layer to another, open the Layers panel and Option-drag (Alt-drag) the effect. Dragging the effect moves it to another layer without making a copy.
- Another way to copy a layer style is to right-click on a layer and choose Copy Layer Style from the context menu. Then right-click on another layer and choose Paste Layer Style.
- To modify a layer effect, open the Layers panel and double-click on the effect. To hide all effects, click on the Effects visibility icon. You can hide individual effects by clicking on their visibility icons.

To hide all effects, click on the Effects visibility icon. You can hide individual effects by clicking on their visibility icons.

Tip

Photoshop ships with a large number of built-in layer styles. To see how they're built, apply one to a layer, and double-click on it. You can then navigate through the Layers Styles panel to learn more about how to create specific kinds of effects.

ABC	ABC	ABC	ABC
Bevel	Gradient Overlay	Stroke	Pattern Overlay
Inner Shadow	Outer Glow	Inner Glow	Drop Shadow
Satin	Star Glow	Brushed Metal	Wood
Woodgrain	Chromed Satin	Chiseled Sky	Color Overlay

Medium Savers

Photoshop Character and Paragraph Styles

With Photoshop CS6, Adobe introduced the ability to create character and paragraph styles similar to the ones in InDesign. This can save a lot of time if you frequently use Photoshop's type features.

Paragraph Styles

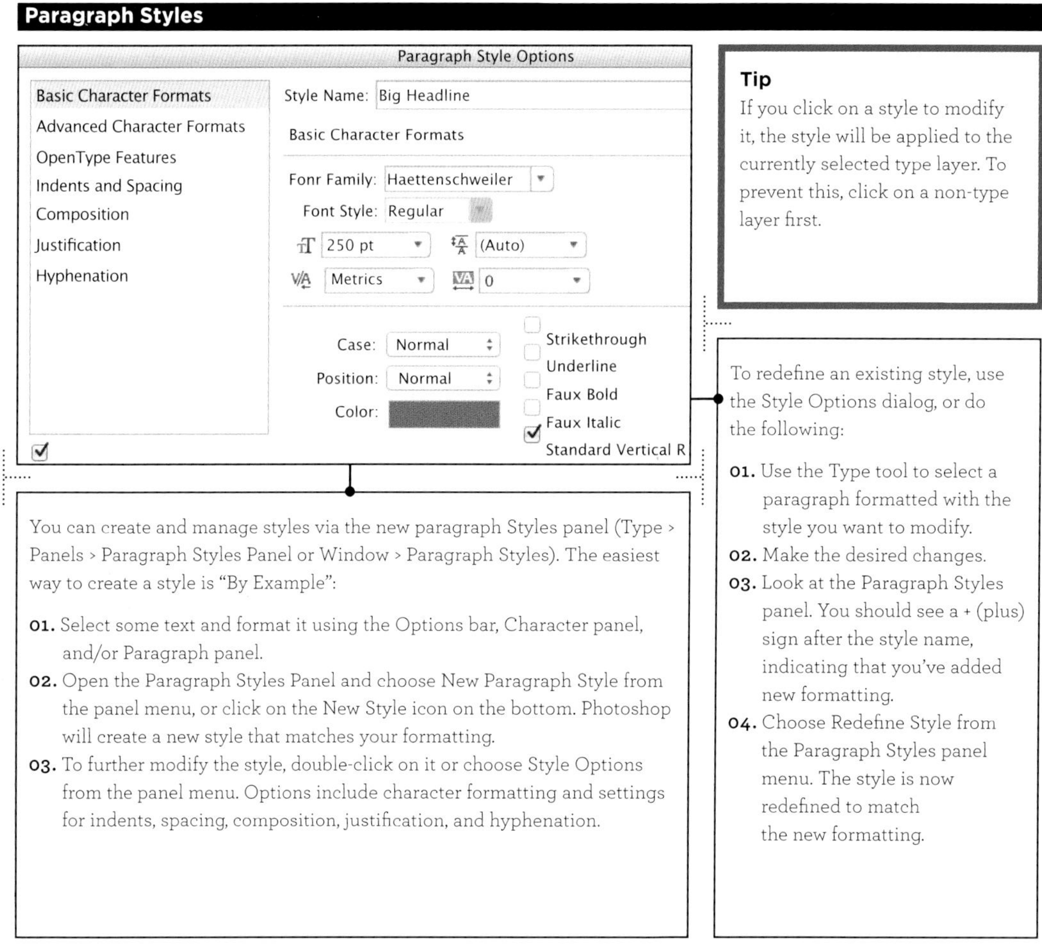

Tip
If you click on a style to modify it, the style will be applied to the currently selected type layer. To prevent this, click on a non-type layer first.

You can create and manage styles via the new paragraph Styles panel (Type > Panels > Paragraph Styles Panel or Window > Paragraph Styles). The easiest way to create a style is "By Example":

01. Select some text and format it using the Options bar, Character panel, and/or Paragraph panel.
02. Open the Paragraph Styles Panel and choose New Paragraph Style from the panel menu, or click on the New Style icon on the bottom. Photoshop will create a new style that matches your formatting.
03. To further modify the style, double-click on it or choose Style Options from the panel menu. Options include character formatting and settings for indents, spacing, composition, justification, and hyphenation.

To redefine an existing style, use the Style Options dialog, or do the following:

01. Use the Type tool to select a paragraph formatted with the style you want to modify.
02. Make the desired changes.
03. Look at the Paragraph Styles panel. You should see a + (plus) sign after the style name, indicating that you've added new formatting.
04. Choose Redefine Style from the Paragraph Styles panel menu. The style is now redefined to match the new formatting.

Tip
You can import styles from another Photoshop document by choosing Load Paragraph Styles from the panel menu.

Character Styles

Character Style Options

Style Name: Character Style 1

Basic Character Formats

Font Family: Abaddon™

Font Style: Regular

Case: Normal

Position: Normal

Color:

Strikethrough

Underline

Faux Bold

Faux Italic

Standard Vertical Roman Alignment

Character styles are similar to paragraph styles, but do not include paragraph-level attributes such as indents, spacing, or justification.

Keep in mind that character styles override paragraph styles. For example, if you apply a paragraph style that specifies Cambria as the font family, and then apply a character style that specifies Calibri, type will be formatted with the latter.

When you create a character style, values for font size, leading, or tracking can be left blank, and the paragraph style will determine those attributes. However, if you use the character style to specify values for font size, leading, or tracking, they will override those in the paragraph style.

To create or manage character styles, open the Character Styles panel (Type > Panels > Character Styles Panel or Window > Character Styles) and follow the same steps you used for Paragraph Styles.

Medium Savers

InDesign Styles

Over the course of a project, you'll save countless mouse clicks by using InDesign's paragraph and character styles instead of local formatting to define the appearance of text. Object styles are big time savers if you want a consistent look for frames, rules, and other graphic elements.

Paragraph Styles

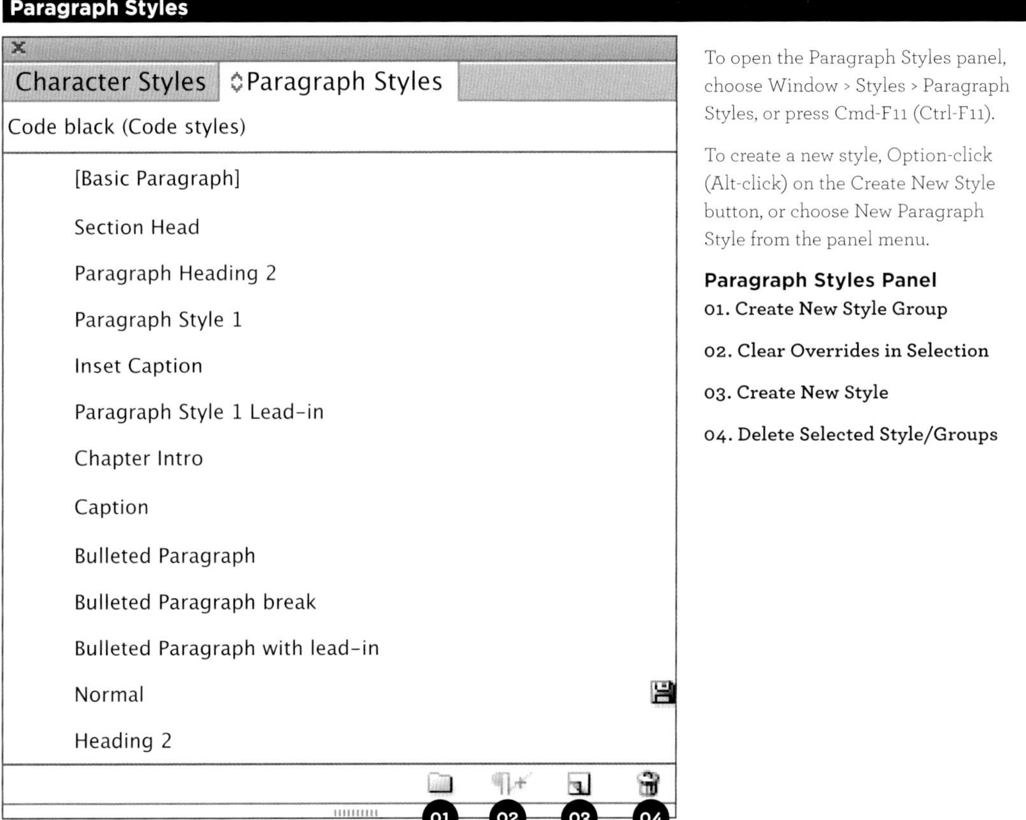

To open the Paragraph Styles panel, choose Window > Styles > Paragraph Styles, or press Cmd-F11 (Ctrl-F11).

To create a new style, Option-click (Alt-click) on the Create New Style button, or choose New Paragraph Style from the panel menu.

Paragraph Styles Panel

01. Create New Style Group

02. Clear Overrides in Selection

03. Create New Style

04. Delete Selected Style/Groups

Paragraph Style Options

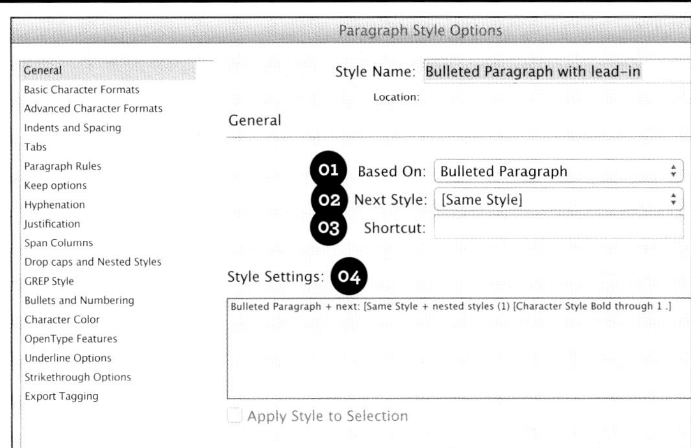

01. Based On Menu: Lets you link the new style to an existing "parent" style. Any changes to the parent style will be reflected in the new one. If you don't want your new style to have a parent, choose [No Paragraph Style].

02. Next Style: The style applied when you hit Enter. The default is [Same style], but you can choose a different one. For example, if you're defining a headline style, you can choose a style for the text that follows the headline.

03. Shortcut: Use this if you want to define a keyboard shortcut for the style.

04. Style Settings: This box provides a summary of the formats used in the style.

To apply a style, select the text, or place the cursor anywhere within it. Click on the style name, or press the keyboard shortcut you defined for that style.

To edit an existing style, double-click on it in the Paragraph Styles panel. Any changes you make will be reflected automatically in all paragraphs to which that style is applied. If it's a parent style, changes will also affect the styles that are linked to it.

Importing Styles

To import paragraph styles from another InDesign document, choose Load Paragraph Styles from the panel menu. Then choose Load All Text Styles to import paragraph and character styles.

Create by Example

You can build a style more quickly by using the Control panel to format some text in advance. Once you're happy with the look:

01. Place the cursor anywhere inside the text—you don't have to select the entire paragraph. Click on Create New Style. The previous formatting will be included in the new style.
02. Modify other format settings to create the desired look.
03. Click in the Preview checkbox to see the new style applied to the selected text.
04. If you use an existing style as the basis for the new one, you can still choose [No Paragraph Style] in the Based On menu if you don't want to create a parent-child relationship between the styles.

Overriding Local Formatting

If you apply a style to a paragraph and then add some local formatting, a plus sign will appear next to the style's name in the Paragraph Styles panel.

- To remove the local formatting, choose Clear Overrides in the panel menu, or click on the Clear Overrides button.
- To apply the changes to the style, choose Redefine Style from the panel menu, or press Shift-⌘-Option-R (Shift+Ctrl+Alt+R). The style will now match the formatting of the selected text, and all paragraphs tagged with that style will take on the new formatting.
- To break the link between the paragraph and the style, choose Break Link to Style from the panel menu. You can then use the paragraph as the basis for a new style.

Medium Savers

Character Styles

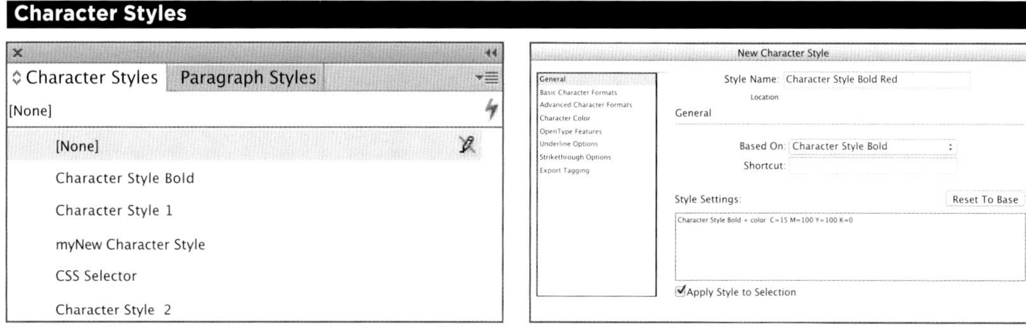

Character styles (Window > Styles > Character Styles) are similar to paragraph styles, except they apply to a portion of text within a paragraph.

Nested Styles

This powerful automation feature is an option when you create paragraph styles. It lets you define a character style that automatically appears at the beginning of a paragraph. A simple example is a paragraph style that includes a lead-in sentence in boldface. Rather than manually formatting the first sentence, use nested styles to do the work for you.

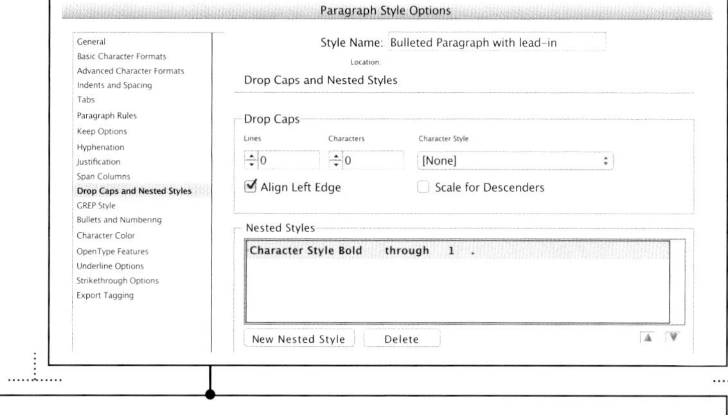

01. Create a character style for the lead-in.

02. Open the Paragraph Styles panel and create a new paragraph style.

03. Click on the Drop Caps and Nested Styles tab.

04. Click on the New Nested Style button.

05. Choose the character style you want to apply, or New Character Style to create one.

06. In the last column, choose a delimiter. You can enter a character, such as a period, or use one of the options in the menu. For example, if you choose Words and enter 5, the character style will be applied to the first five words in the paragraph.

07. In the second column, choose Up to if you want to apply the style to every character up to the delimiter, or Through if you want to include the delimiter.

Object Styles

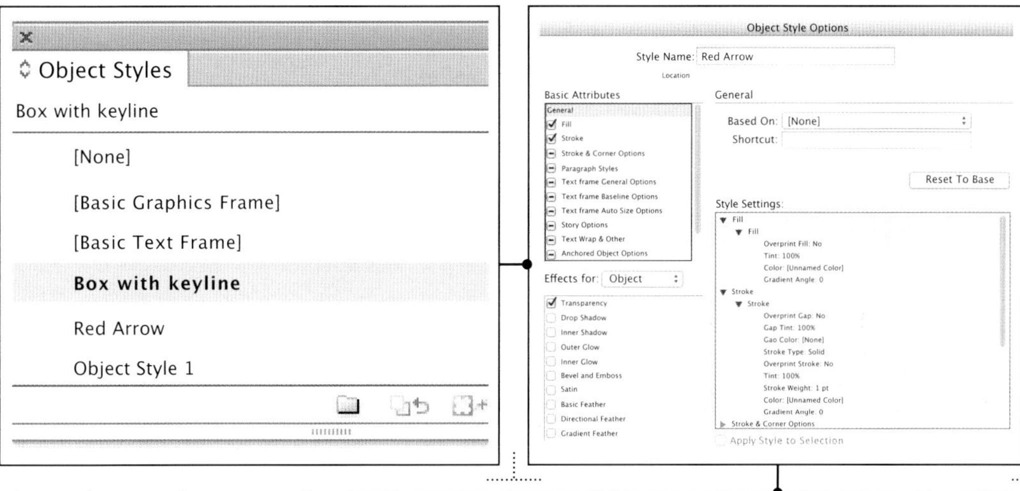

Object styles are similar to paragraph and character styles, except they apply to graphic elements such as frames, shapes, and lines. For example, you can create an object style that applies a certain kind of border or fill color to text or graphic frames, or one that adds a certain kind of arrowhead to a line.

Before you create an object style, it's a good idea to format an object in advance, or identify one that already has the style attributes you want.

01. Choose Window > Styles > Object Styles to open the Object Styles panel.
02. Select the object you want to use as the basis for the style. Option-click (Alt-click) on the Create New Style button, or choose New Object Style from the panel menu. This opens a dialog box similar to the ones used to define paragraph and character styles.
03. Give the style a name, and modify the attributes as desired. Uncheck any attributes that you don't want to be affected by the style.
04. Click OK. The style appears in the panel.

Tip

You can use the Object Styles panel to set the default style for a text or graphics frame. These are listed in the panel as [Basic Graphics Frame] and [Basic Text Frame]. Double-click on them to modify their attributes.

You can also set one of your own styles as the default. To do this, drag the "default" icon from [Basic Graphics Frame] and [Basic Text Frame] to a style that you've created. For example, dragging the icon from [Basic Graphics Frame] to the style Box with Keyline will make the latter the default style for graphics frames.

Medium Savers

Illustrator Styles

Use Illustrator's graphic styles to quickly apply appearances to multiple objects. As with character and paragraph styles in other programs, any changes to the style are instantly reflected in the objects to which they're applied.

Create a Graphic Style

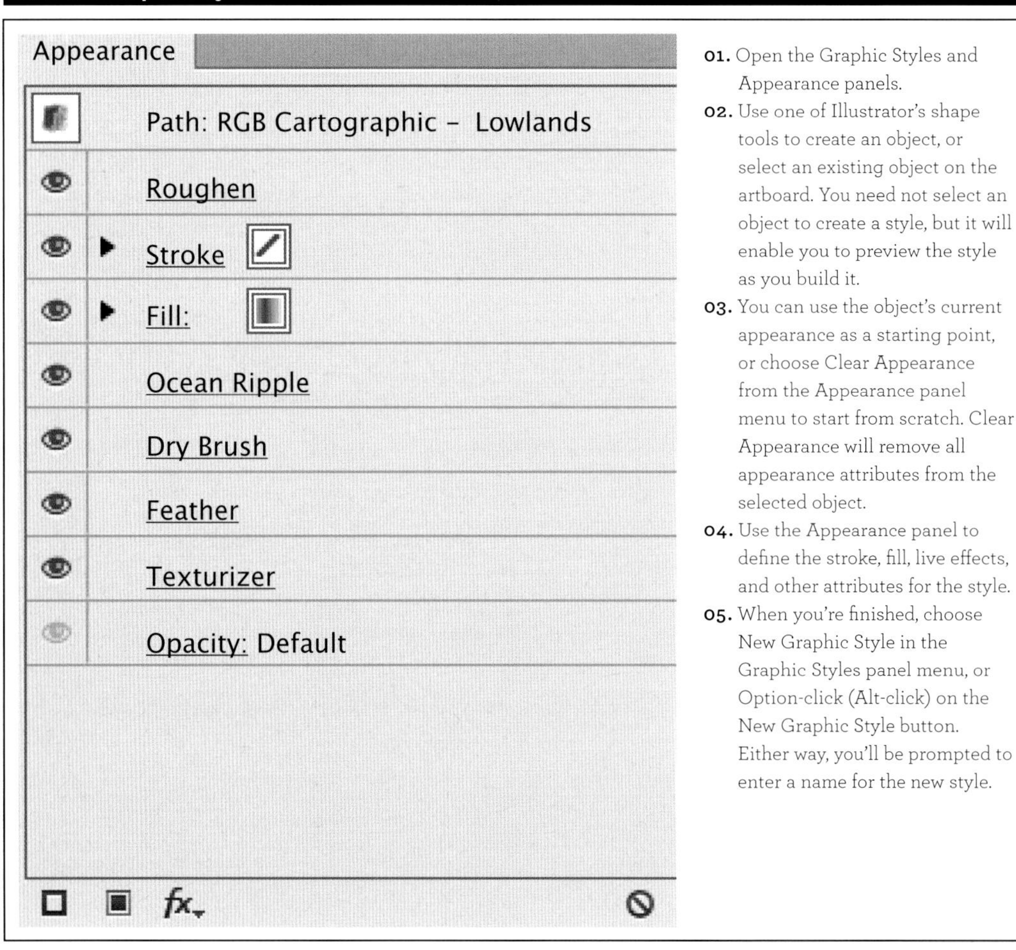

01. Open the Graphic Styles and Appearance panels.

02. Use one of Illustrator's shape tools to create an object, or select an existing object on the artboard. You need not select an object to create a style, but it will enable you to preview the style as you build it.

03. You can use the object's current appearance as a starting point, or choose Clear Appearance from the Appearance panel menu to start from scratch. Clear Appearance will remove all appearance attributes from the selected object.

04. Use the Appearance panel to define the stroke, fill, live effects, and other attributes for the style.

05. When you're finished, choose New Graphic Style in the Graphic Styles panel menu, or Option-click (Alt-click) on the New Graphic Style button. Either way, you'll be prompted to enter a name for the new style.

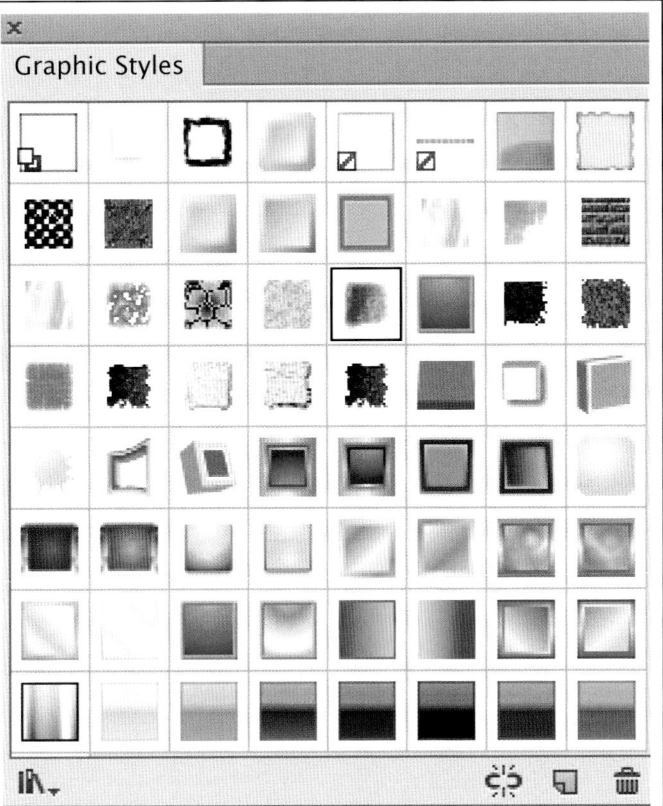

06. You can also drag the thumbnail from the Appearance panel, or click on the New Graphic Style button in the Graphic Styles panel. This will add an unnamed style to the Graphic Styles panel. You can name the style by double-clicking on it.

07. If you just want to create a new style from an existing object, you can skip steps 2, 3 and 4—just select the object and choose one of the options in step 5.

To apply a graphic style, select one or more objects and click on the style in the Graphic Styles panel. This will replace the objects' current attributes. To add a style to the objects' current attributes, Option-click (Alt-click) on the style.

Modifying Graphic Styles

01. Open the Graphic Styles panel and select the style you want to change.

02. Open the Appearance panel and make the desired changes.

03. Choose Redefine Graphic Style from the Appearance panel menu.

Tip

- Illustrator ships with 11 libraries of prebuilt styles (Window > Graphic Style Libraries) that you can use as starting points for creating your own. Used in conjunction with the Appearance panel, this can be a good way to explore Illustrator's styling features. You can also open these via the Graphics Style Library Menu button in the Graphic Styles panel.
- Two of these libraries, Additive and Additive for Blob Brush, provide examples of styles that work well on top of existing appearance attributes. Option-click (Alt-click) on the style to apply them.
- To import styles from external source—including websites—choose Window > Graphic Style Libraries > Other Library.
- Ctrl-click on the styles to see larger previews.
- The panel menu's Use Text for Preview option changes previews from squares to the letter "T."

Medium Savers

Troubleshooting Print Projects

Production errors at the prepress and printing stages can be a costly waste of time. InDesign's preflighting feature lets you spot and correct these problems early in the process—even as they happen.

Preflight Profiles

Many kinds of problems can prevent InDesign documents from printing correctly. InDesign knows which problems to check by referring to a preflight profile. The default "Basic" profile alerts you to the most common errors, such as missing fonts, broken image links, and overset text. But you can also create custom profiles that specify a much wider range of conditions, such as the presence of RGB images or style overrides.

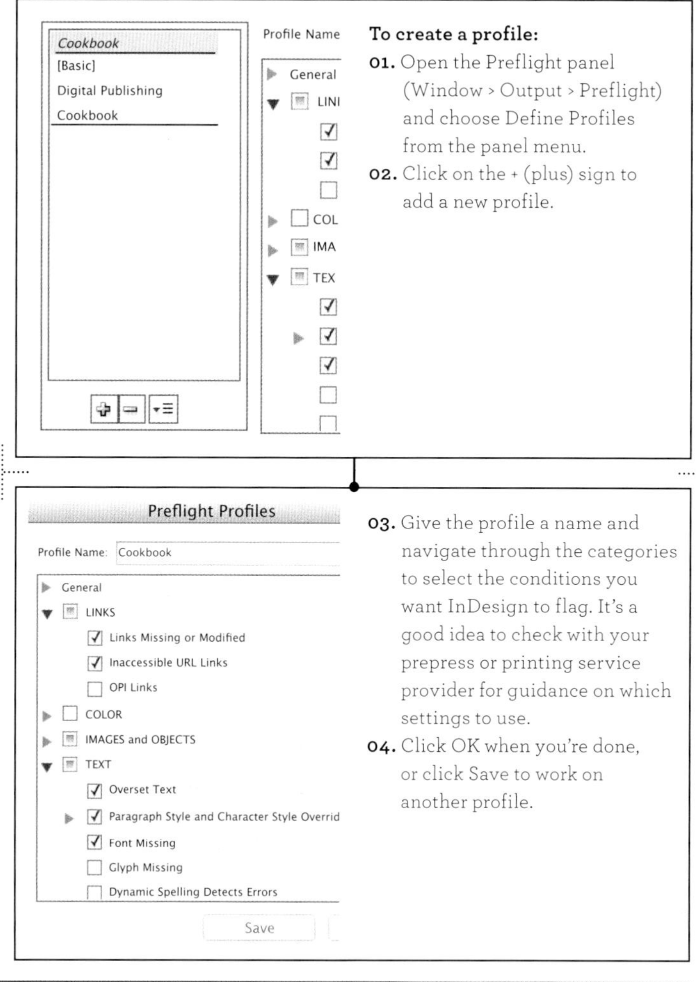

To create a profile:

01. Open the Preflight panel (Window > Output > Preflight) and choose Define Profiles from the panel menu.

02. Click on the + (plus) sign to add a new profile.

03. Give the profile a name and navigate through the categories to select the conditions you want InDesign to flag. It's a good idea to check with your prepress or printing service provider for guidance on which settings to use.

04. Click OK when you're done, or click Save to work on another profile.

Using the Preflight Panel

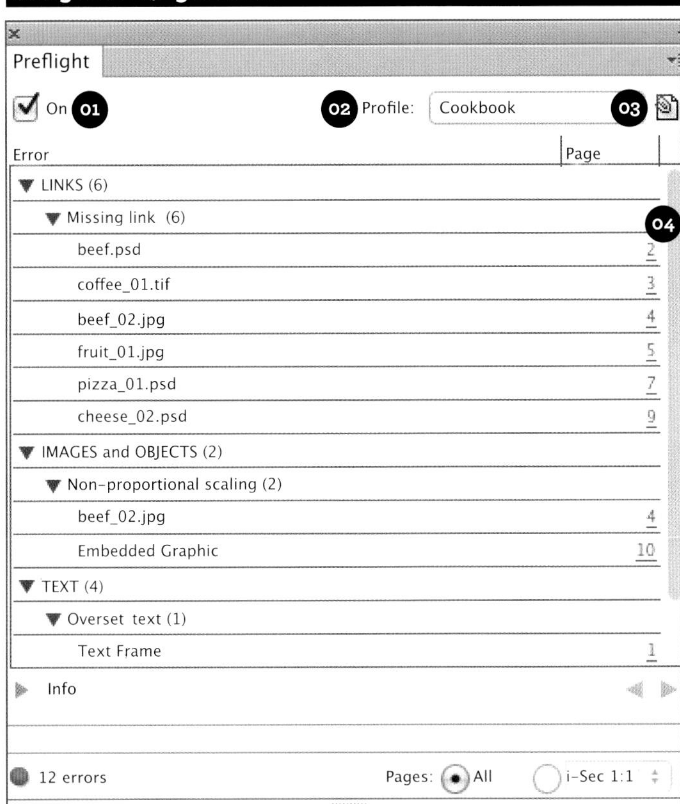

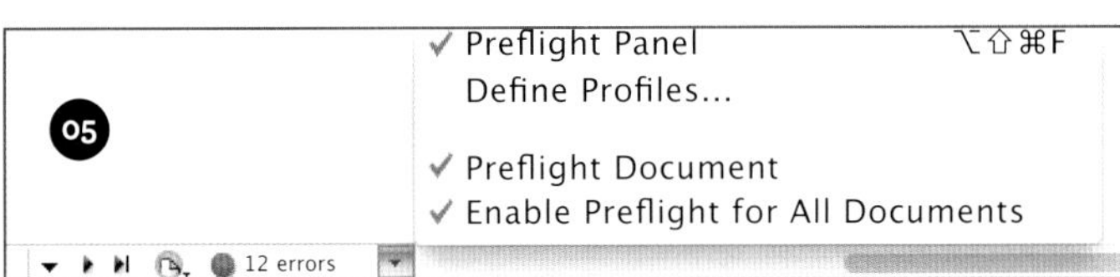

01. Preflight: Click here to turn on preflighting.
02. Profile: Click here to choose a profile.
03. Embed: Click here to embed the current profile in the document—a good step if you want to send it to another user.
04. Page Number: This indicates the page number containing the error. If you click on the link, InDesign will navigate to that item and select it.
05. Errors: At the bottom of the document window, InDesign will alert you to errors, even if the Preflight panel is closed.

The Links Panel

- The red question mark indicates a link is broken. To relink the image, double-click on the question mark, or choose Relink from the panel menu.
- If you've moved a group of images to a different folder, select them and choose Relink to Folder from the panel menu.
- If you've modified a linked image outside of InDesign, select it and choose Update Link from the panel menu. This is not necessary if you used InDesign's Edit Original command to make the changes.

Medium Savers

Save for Web

This module is an essential tool for any Photoshop or Illustrator user who produces graphics for the web. It lets you preview artwork and test various color settings to find the optimal balance between file size and image quality.

01. **Preview:** Use these tabs to choose how you want to preview your artwork. You can view the original image and up to three optimized versions.
02. **Preset:** Choose a preset.
03. **Save Preset:** Lets you save your choices as a preset.
04. **File Settings:** Choose the file format, maximum number of colors, reduction algorithm, and dithering options. Experiment with these to see the impact on file size and image quality. JPEG is the best choice for photos. Use GIF or PNG-8 for logos, type, line drawings, and other artwork with limited color palettes.
05. **Matte:** Use this to choose the background color of the web page. If the artwork includes transparency, the program will blend the edges against this color.
06. **Web Snap:** Converts colors to one of 216 "web-safe" colors. This palette is a vestige of the early days of the web when many computer displays were limited to 256 colors. You can leave this at 0%.
07. **Color Table:** This displays the current palette. It's disabled if you choose JPEG or PNG-24 as the image format.
08. **Transparent:** Click here to make selected colors transparent. You can select colors by clicking on them in the palette, or use the Eyedropper tool.
09. **Image Size:** Use these settings to scale the artwork.
10. **Animation:** These apply if you're creating an animated GIF file. You can preview the animation and determine how it loops.
11. **Eyedropper:** Shows the currently selected Eyedropper color.
12. **Slices:** Click here to toggle display of slices.
13. **File Info:** This shows the file format, file size, and download time at the specified speed. Use the panel menu to change the download speed.
14. **Zoom:** Click here to zoom in or out, or use the magnifying glass.
15. **Preview in Browser:** Click here to preview the artwork in a browser.
16. **Done and Save:** Click Done to close the dialog and remember the settings. Click Save to save the artwork with the currently selected settings. In the 4-Up layout, click on the panel with the settings you want to use before clicking Save.

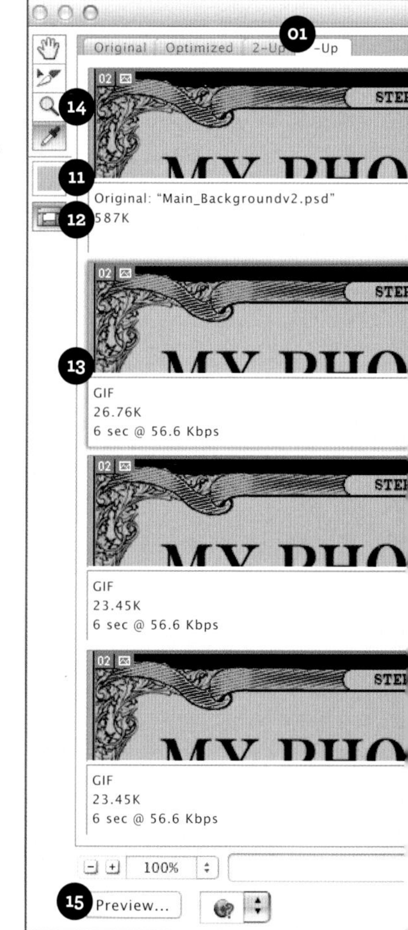

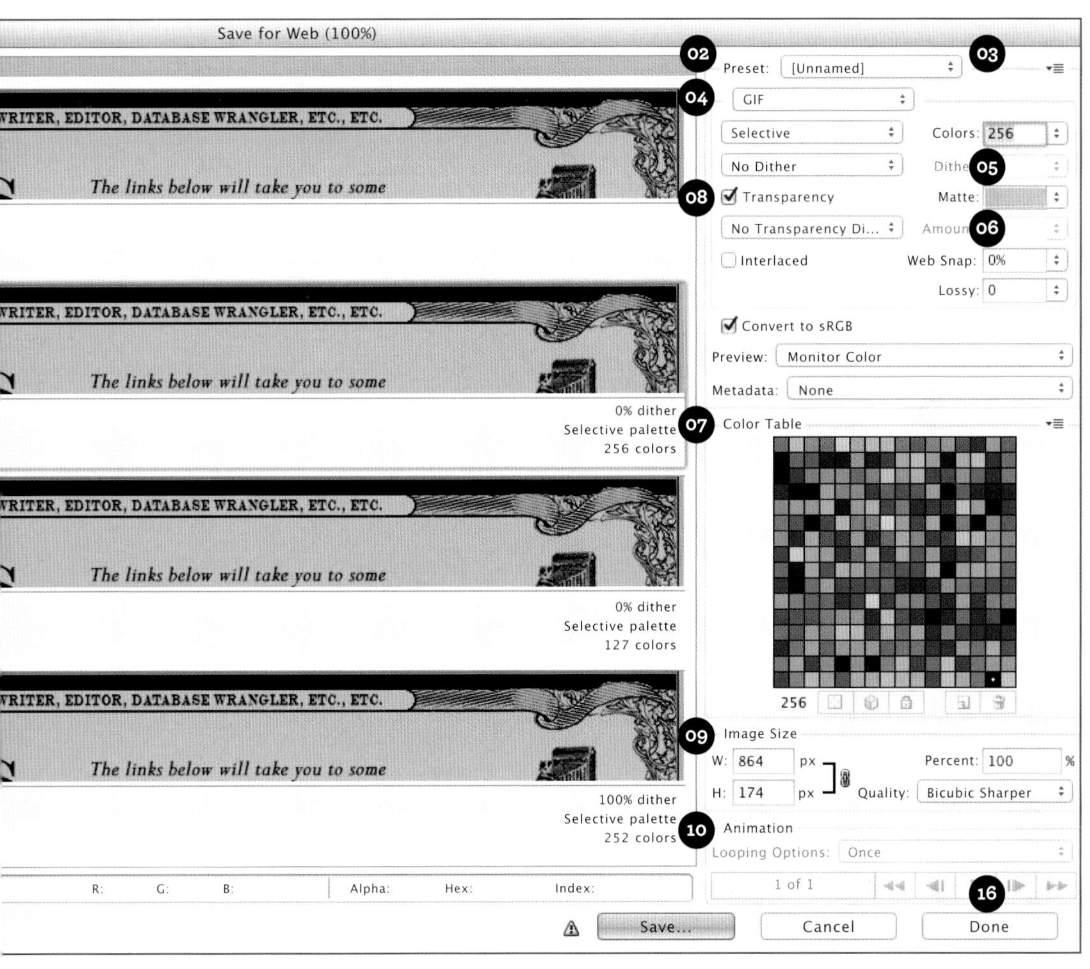
Save for Web (100%)
Preset: [Unnamed]
GIF
Selective
Colors: 256
No Dither
Transparency
Matte:
No Transparency Di...
Interlaced
Web Snap: 0%
Lossy: 0
Convert to sRGB
Preview: Monitor Color
Metadata: None
Color Table
Image Size
W: 864 px
H: 174 px
Percent: 100 %
Quality: Bicubic Sharper
Animation
Looping Options: Once
1 of 1
Save...
Cancel
Done
WRITER, EDITOR, DATABASE WRANGLER, ETC., ETC.
The links below will take you to some
0% dither
Selective palette
256 colors
0% dither
Selective palette
127 colors
100% dither
Selective palette
252 colors
R: G: B: Alpha: Hex: Index:
02
03
04
05
06
07
08
09
10
16

10→60 mins

Medium Savers

CSS Coding in Dreamweaver

Whether you want to dive into the code or let Dreamweaver do the work, the program offers many time-savers for CSS design. Use these features to modify existing style sheets or build new ones from scratch.

The CSS Styles Panel

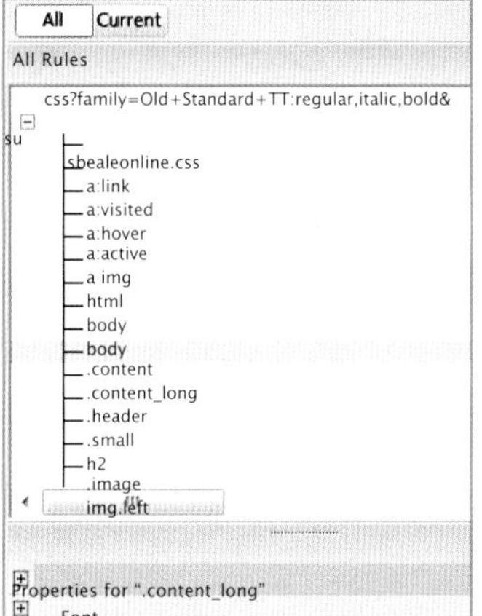

This panel is your command center for managing CSS styles. If it's not already open, go to Window > CSS Styles or hit Shift-F11. The All mode (above) shows all available CSS rules, allowing you to navigate through them and change their properties. This mode also provides a quick way to move rules between style sheets. Current Selection mode (right) lets you see how CSS rules and properties affect specific parts of your design. In both views, you can quickly navigate to any rule to change its properties.

01. Summary Pane: Shows CSS properties that apply to the selected HTML tags. Mouse over the property to see the CSS rule and style sheet it belongs to. You can change its settings by double-clicking here, or enter a new value in the Properties pane.

02. Property Information and Cascade: The middle pane has two views, Property Information and Cascade. Cascade view (the second button) is more useful. It shows the cascade of rules that affect the current selection. As you click on properties in the Summary pane, the rule they belong to will be highlighted. Double-click on the rule to change its properties settings, or use the Properties panel.

03. Properties Panel: Shows all properties for the selected rule organized by category. Click on the + and - buttons to expand or collapse categories. Click in the column next to the property to change its value. Most changes are instantly reflected in the Design view in the main editing window.

04. New CSS Rule: Click on this icon to create a new rule.

Creating a New Rule

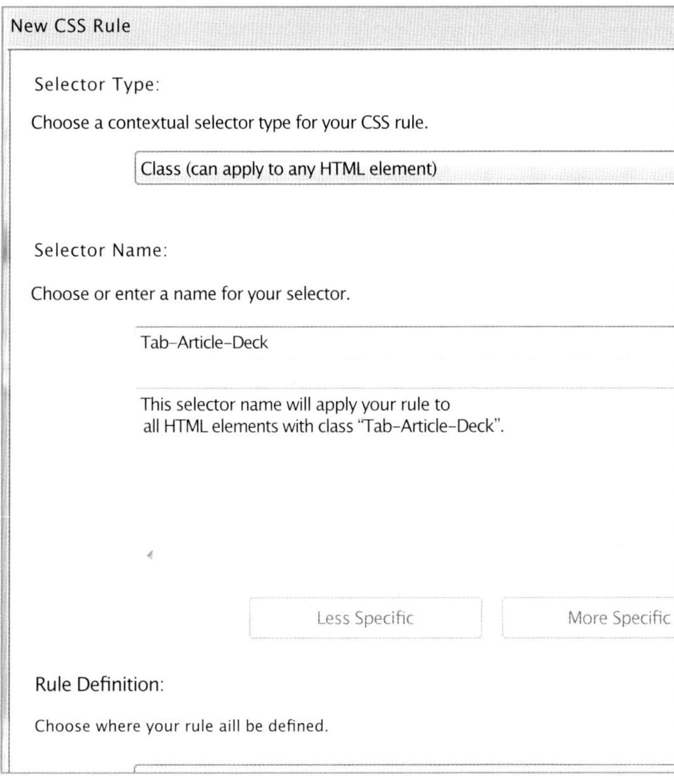

The New CSS Rule dialog is a good starting point for creating a rule. Open it by choosing New in the CSS Styles panel menu or by clicking on the New CSS Rule icon at the bottom of the panel.

Choose a selector type, selector name, and the style sheet where you want the rule to reside. You also have the option to create a new style sheet or place the rule in the current HTML document. Click OK when you're done to begin assigning properties.

The CSS Rule Definition dialog lets you set properties for the rule. Click through the categories on the left to find the properties you want to define. The box appears when you create a new rule or double-click on an existing rule or property in the CSS Styles panel.

10→60 mins

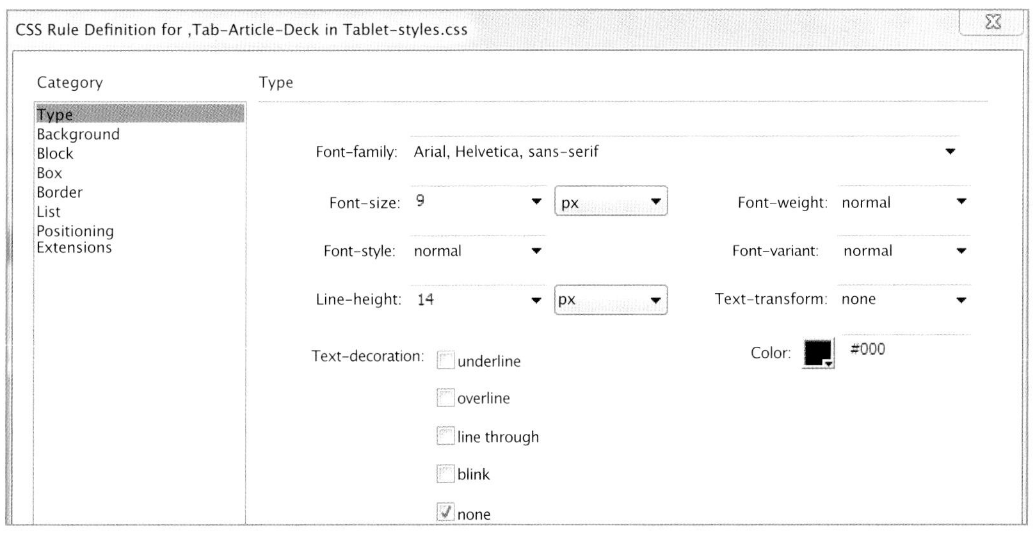

Medium Savers

Code Hinting

Instead of using panels or dialog boxes, an experienced web designer may prefer to dive into the code. Rather than entering code manually, and running the risk of typos, use Dreamweaver's code-hinting features to define CSS properties.

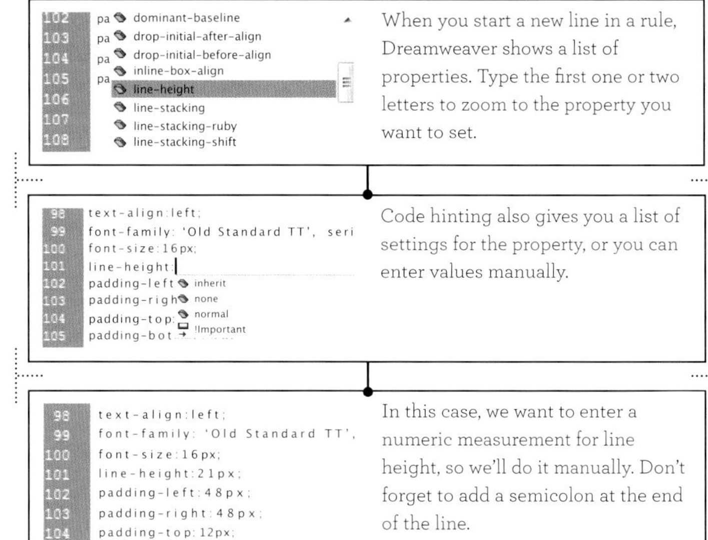

When you start a new line in a rule, Dreamweaver shows a list of properties. Type the first one or two letters to zoom to the property you want to set.

Code hinting also gives you a list of settings for the property, or you can enter values manually.

In this case, we want to enter a numeric measurement for line height, so we'll do it manually. Don't forget to add a semicolon at the end of the line.

Convert Inline CSS

Old HTML coding habits can be hard to break. Here, we placed a style inside an HTML tag instead of using a CSS rule. Dreamweaver's Convert Inline CSS feature makes this easy to fix by automatically creating a CSS rule based on the inline style.

01. If the Coding toolbar is turned off, open it by going to View >Toolbars > Coding (you can also right-click or Ctrl-click on any of the toolbars).

02. Click within the line that contains the offending code.

03. Click on the Move or Convert CSS icon in the Coding Toolbar. It's the one that looks like stairsteps. We want the Convert Inline CSS to Rule... option.

04. Choose your conversion options. You can create a new selector or add the properties to an existing one. The Create Rule In... option lets you insert the rule in an external CSS file or the head of the current HTML document.

05. Click OK. Dreamweaver removes the styling from the HTML tag and places it in the specified style sheet.

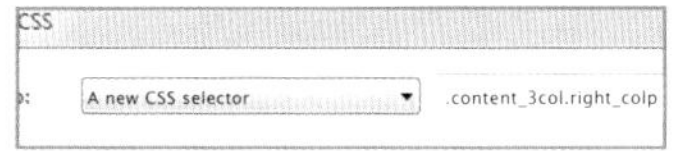

Medium Savers

The Property Inspector

This panel provides a single location from which you can apply settings to web page elements. It's context-sensitive, so the controls change based on what kind of element you've selected.

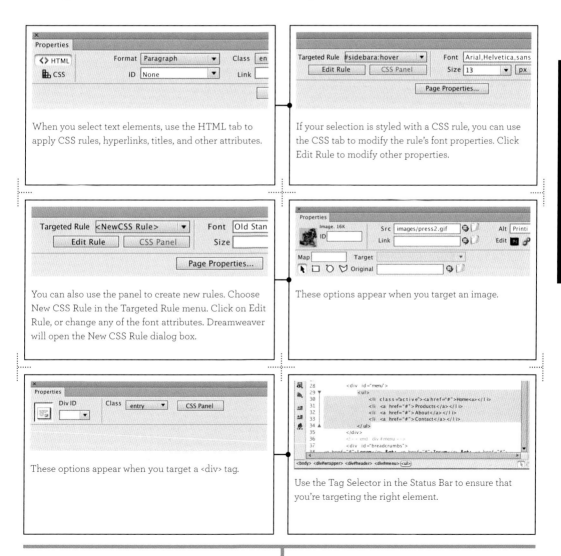

When you select text elements, use the HTML tab to apply CSS rules, hyperlinks, titles, and other attributes.

If your selection is styled with a CSS rule, you can use the CSS tab to modify the rule's font properties. Click Edit Rule to modify other properties.

You can also use the panel to create new rules. Choose New CSS Rule in the Targeted Rule menu. Click on Edit Rule, or change any of the font attributes. Dreamweaver will open the New CSS Rule dialog box.

These options appear when you target an image.

These options appear when you target a <div> tag.

Use the Tag Selector in the Status Bar to ensure that you're targeting the right element.

Medium Savers

Troubleshooting Web Designs

Dreamweaver provides a host of tools that help you identify and fix potential problems in your web pages. Here are a few of the most useful.

Inspect Mode

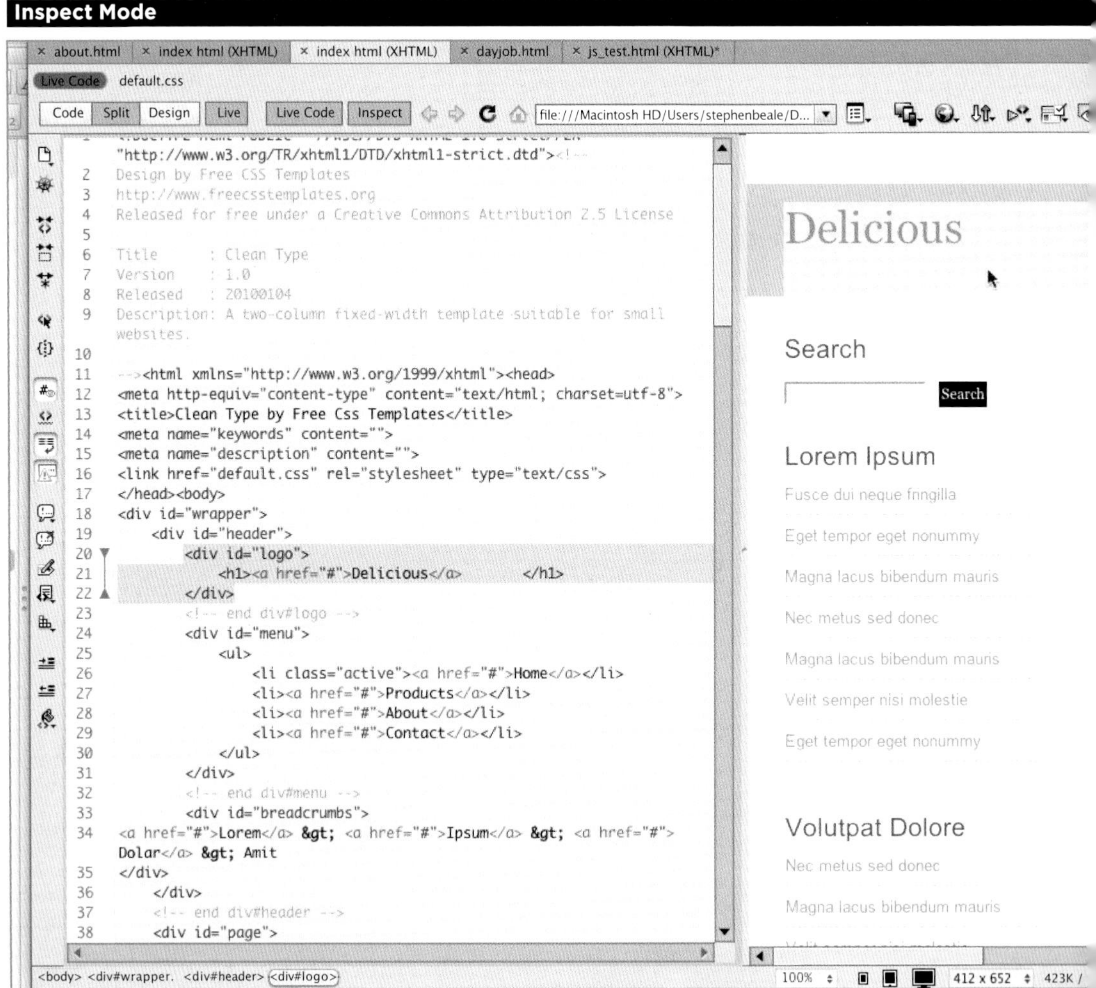

Free Utilities

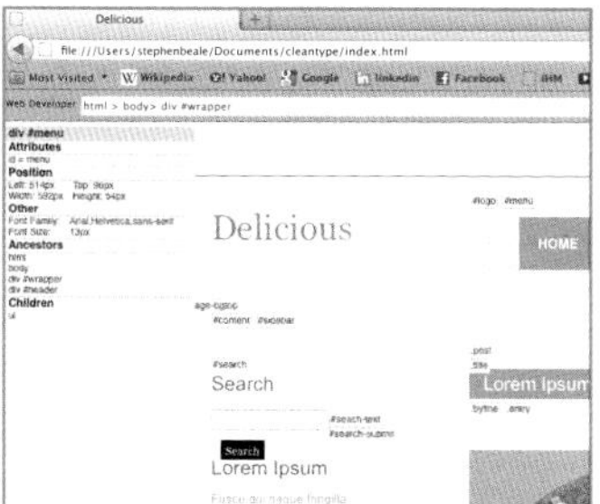

Firebug, a free add-on for Mozilla Firefox, is an essential troubleshooting tool for web developers. Its Inspect Element option is similar to Dreamweaver's Inspect mode, but it offers other useful features as well.

Another useful Firefox add-on is Chris Pederick's Web Developer (shown on left). When you open a web page in Firefox, it can generate labels on top of HTML elements indicating tag names, CSS rules, box dimensions, and other information. If you click on an element on the web page, it displays helpful formatting information. You can also use it to validate links, CSS, HTML, and RSS feeds.

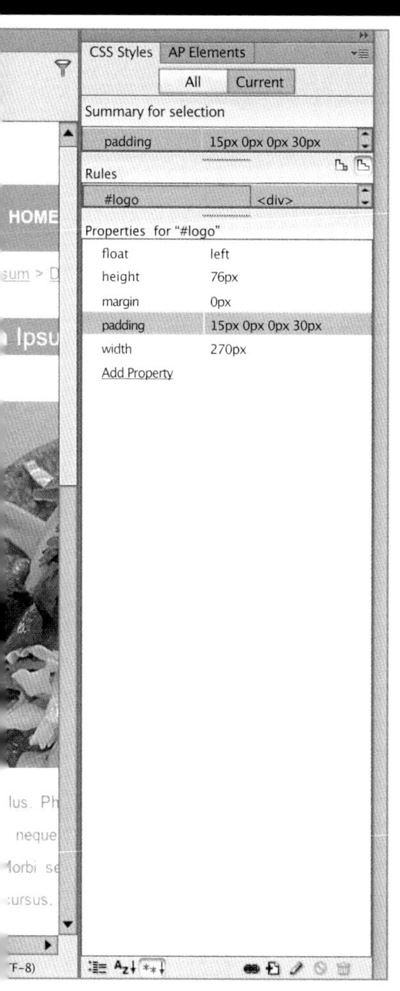

Using Inspect mode, you can hover over different parts of a web page and see which HTML elements and CSS styles apply. It also makes it easy to see how the padding and margin properties in CSS styles affect the page layout. It works in conjunction with Dreamweaver's Live View feature, which renders web pages as they would appear in a browser. Live View is based on WebKit, an open-source rendering engine that's also the foundation for Google Chrome and Apple Safari.

01. Click the Live button in the toolbar to enter Live View mode, then click the Inspect button.
02. Dreamweaver may notify you that the feature works best with certain workspace settings. Click "Switch now" to enable those settings. The document will appear in Split view with the CSS Styles panel open.
03. In the Design view, hover over different parts of the web page—don't click, or Dreamweaver will exit Inspect mode. As you do this, each box element is highlighted, with colors indicating the dimensions of the content (blue), margins (yellow), and padding (purple). In the Code view, the program highlights the associated HTML code. And in the CSS Styles panel, it shows the CSS rules and properties that apply to the highlighted element.
04. To highlight the parent of an element, press the left arrow key. Press the right arrow key to go back to the previous element.
05. To modify CSS properties for a highlighted element, click on it and make the changes in the CSS Styles panel (see page 126). This disables Inspect mode—if you want to continue inspecting the page, click the Inspect button again.

Medium Savers

Validation

This feature, available in Dreamweaver CS5.5 and CS6, checks your HTML code for invalid syntax. It does so by automatically uploading the page to an online HTML validator hosted by the World Wide Web Consortium (W3C), the organization that governs HTML. Browsers will often display pages properly even if they have bad syntax, but validation is still an important step for ensuring quality web design.

01. Open the document.
02. Choose File › Validate › Validate Current Document (W3C). Dreamweaver tells you that it's about to upload your document. Click OK.

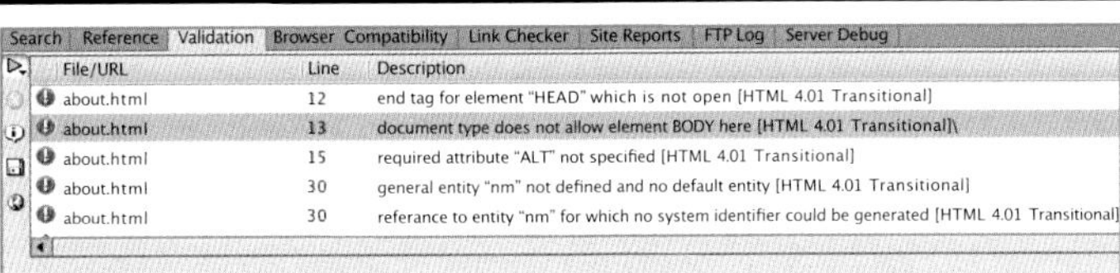

03. The results appear in the Validation panel (CS6) or W3C Validation panel (CS5.5). Each problem is listed with its line number and a description. A red icon indicates the most serious problems.
04. To learn more about an error—and to get clues for potential solutions—select it and click on the More Info button in the Validation panel.

> **Tip**
> To validate CSS style sheets, go to http://jigsaw.w3.org/css-validator/. You can validate external style sheets or HTML files with internal CSS. To validate HTML documents without using Dreamweaver, go to http://validator.w3.org.

Previewing Multiple Screens

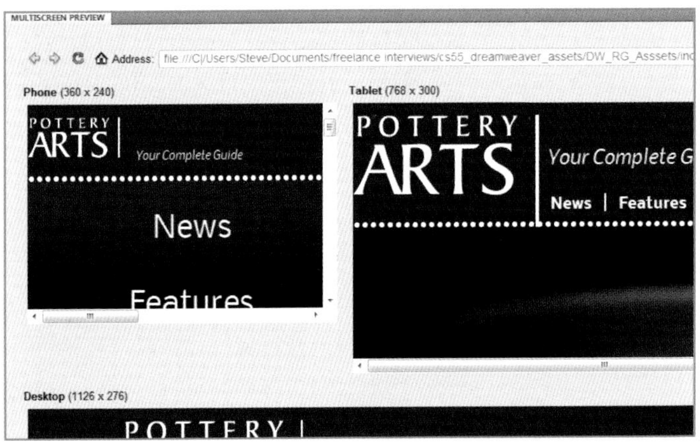

The new Fluid Grid Layouts feature in Dreamweaver CS6 (File › New Fluid Grid Layout) provides a good starting point for creating CSS layouts that automatically adjust themselves to the end-user's browser size, whether it's running on a smartphone, tablet, or desktop computer. Once you've created web pages optimized for multiple screens, Dreamweaver provides several ways to preview your layouts:

- The Multiscreen Preview panel (Window › Multiscreen Preview) displays the current document at three screen sizes.
- You can preview a wider range of screen sizes directly in the document window via the Multiscreen menu in the toolbar.
- The "Device Size" buttons in the status bar provide a quick way to preview pages as they will appear on a phone, tablet, and desktop. These previews appear in the document window.

Checking Links

Dreamweaver's Check Links feature helps you spot broken links within your site. It also identifies "orphaned" files that are no longer linked to by other pages.

Before checking links, you have to set up a site. Choose Site > New Site, enter the site name, and specify the folder containing the site's files. Next, open the Files panel (Window > Files) and Link Checker panel (Window > Results > Link Checker).

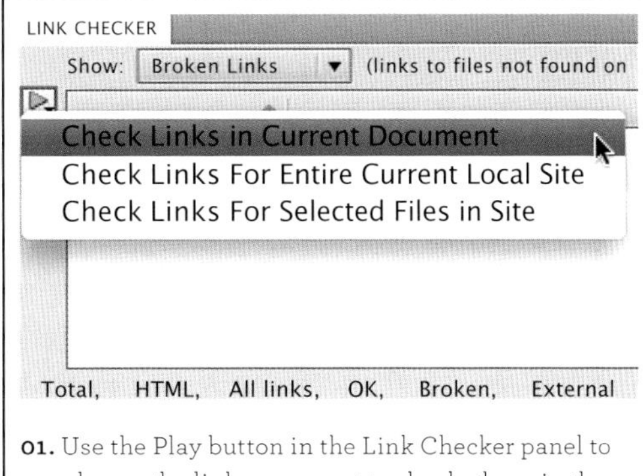

01. Use the Play button in the Link Checker panel to choose the links you want to check: those in the current document, all links sitewide or links in selected files. Choose files for the latter option in the Files panel.

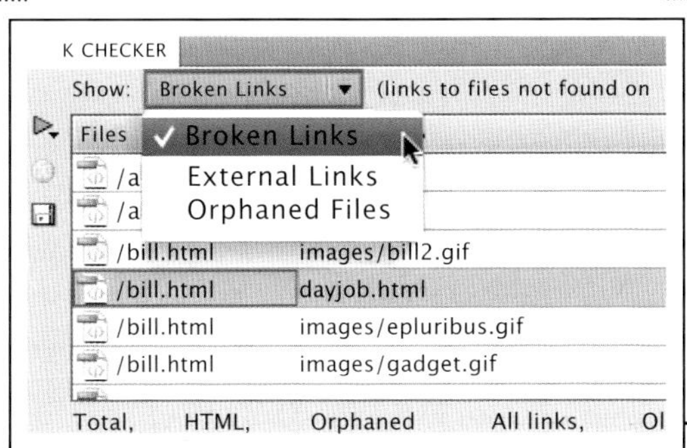

02. Results are listed in the Link Checker panel. Use the View menu to choose whether you want to see broken links, external links or orphaned files. The external links list shows all external links—it doesn't check for broken ones.

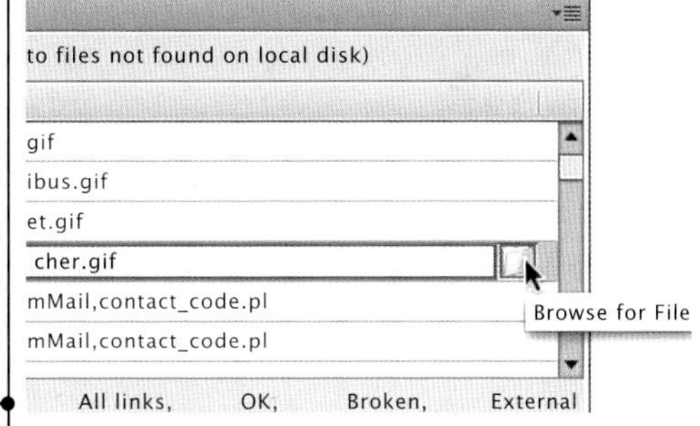

03. To fix a broken link, click on the link's name in the Broken Links column, then click on the folder icon on the right.

> **Tip**
> To check external links in live websites, go to http://validator.w3.org/checklink

Medium Savers

Test Websites with BrowserLab

Adobe's BrowserLab provides a quick way to preview web designs as they will appear in popular browsers on the Mac and Windows. It's an online service that you can access from within Dreamweaver.

Setting Up BrowserLab

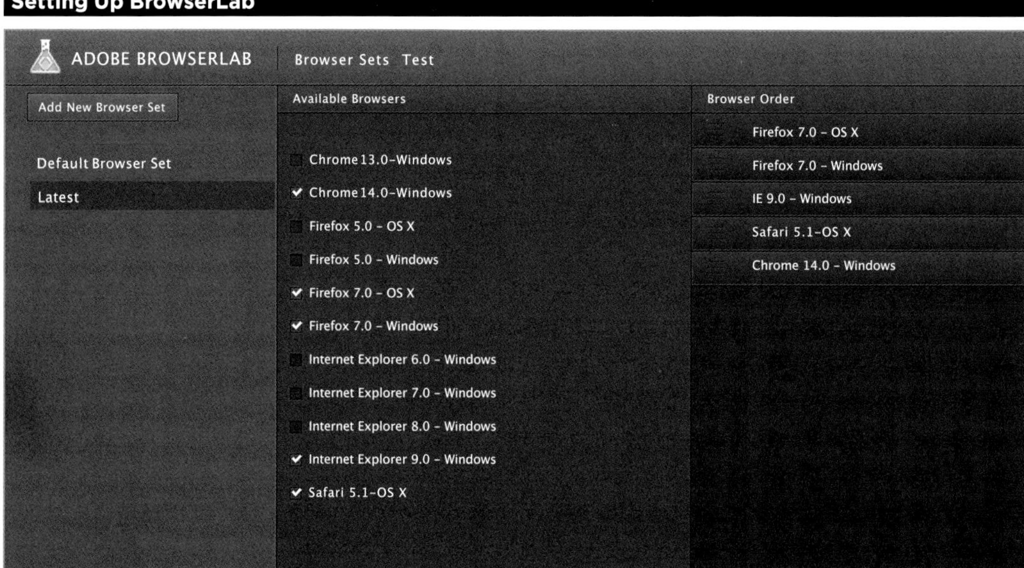

01. Open the Files panel (Windows > Files) and double-click on the HTML file you want to preview.

02. Open the BrowserLab panel (Window > Extensions > Adobe BrowserLab) and click the Preview button. Dreamweaver will attempt to log into the BrowserLab website via your default browser.

03. To use BrowserLab, you must have an Adobe Live account. You'll be prompted to enter your log-in info, or to set up a new account.

04. Once you're logged in, the first step is to create a Browser Set listing the browsers you want to test. Click on Browser Sets.

05. Select the browsers you want to include in your default browser set. You also have the option to set up additional browser sets.

Using BrowserLab

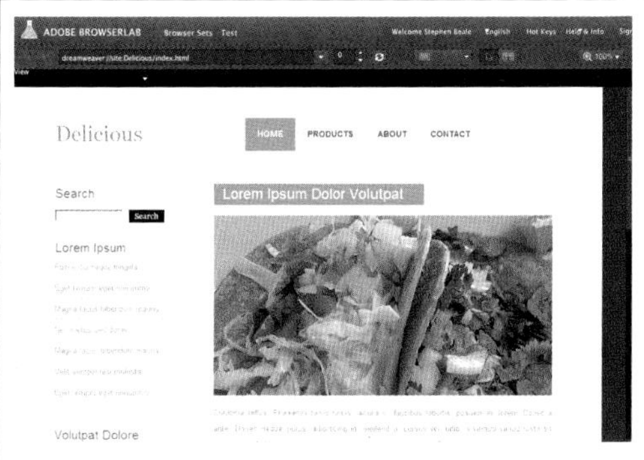

Click on Test. BrowserLab will generate a screen shot simulating how the first browser in your default set displays the web page. Click on the browser name to open a menu that lets you select other browsers.

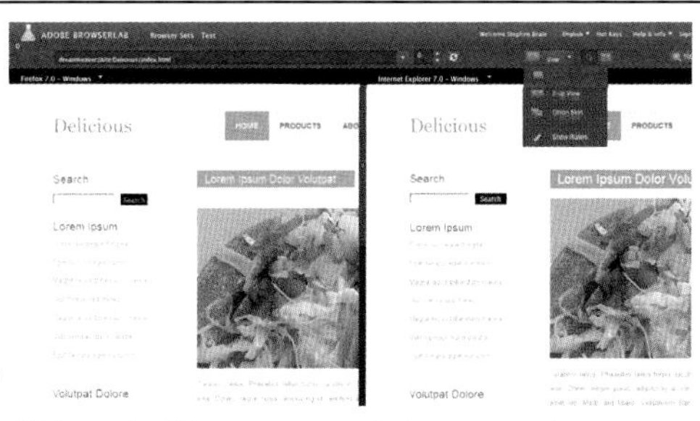

Click on the View menu to switch to a 2-up view or Onion Skin.

If you choose Onion Skin, BrowserLab will overlay one screen shot over another so you can see how the spacing differs.

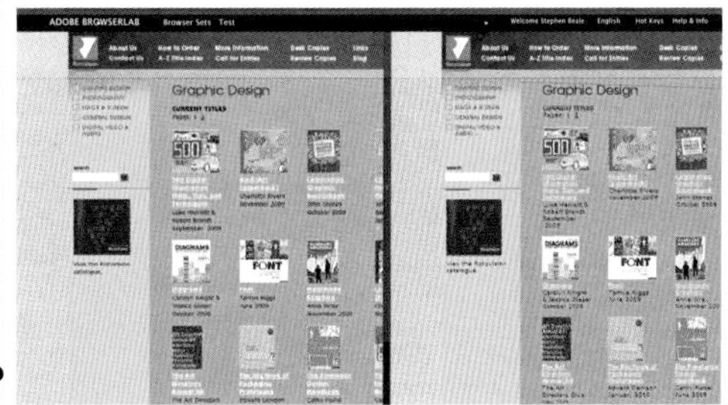

You're not limited to previewing local web pages—you can also enter URLs for live websites in BrowserLab's address bar.

Tip

BrowserLab can simulate how JavaScript effects such as drop-down menus will appear in different browsers. In Dreamweaver, enable Live View mode and test the JavaScript effect. While the effect is still active, press F6 to freeze JavaScript. Click on the Preview button in the BrowserLab panel. A snapshot of the web page with the JavaScript effect will appear in the BrowserLab window.

Medium Savers

Create e-Books in InDesign

e-Books are increasingly popular, but they present numerous design challenges. Fortunately, InDesign CS5.5 and CS6 provide tools that make it much easier to generate e-Books from the same documents you use for print layouts.

Flexible Image Sizes

One challenge of designing for e-Book readers is that they come in a wide range of screen sizes. Using InDesign's Object Export Options dialog box, you can ensure that images in your layout will be automatically resized to fit the end-user's device:

01. Select the image you want to adjust.

02. Open the dialog box (Object > Object Export Options) and click the EPUB and HTML tab.

03. Under Custom Rasterization, choose Relative to Page Width for size. You can also set the file format, resolution, and JPEG compression options.

04. Without closing the dialog box, select the next image to set export options. Apply the settings. Continue with other images you want to adjust.

05. Click Done when you're finished.

Tips

- If you want every image in your document to be automatically resized, you can specify that option in the EPUB Export dialog box.
- If you want the image to occupy its own page, click Insert Page Break and choose Before and After Image from the drop-down menu.
- Keep in mind that these settings will apply only when the document is exported to the EPUB or HTML format. To get a quick preview, export the document to HTML (File > Export) and test it in a browser. Make the browser window smaller, and the images should automatically resize so they fit.

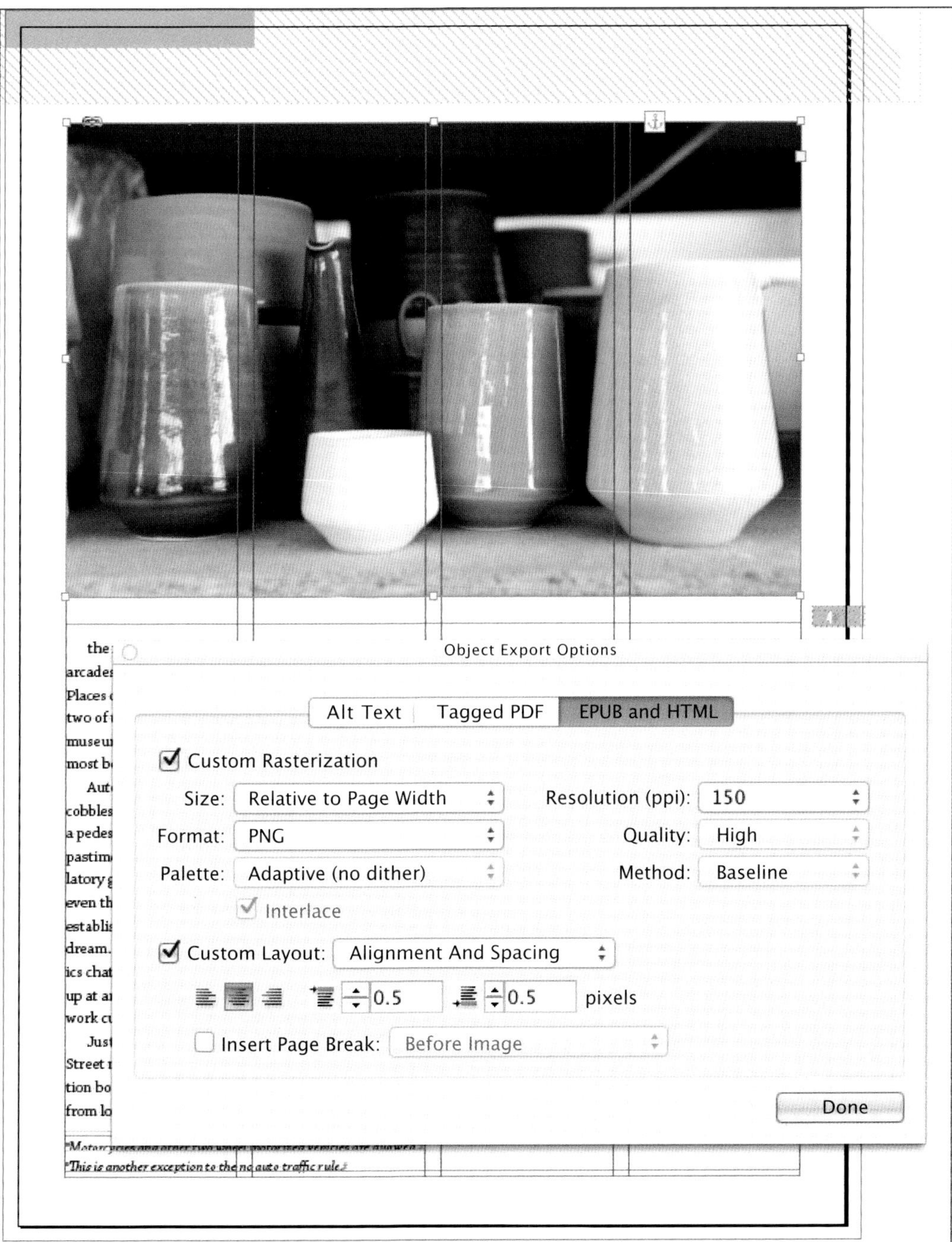
Object Export Options
Alt Text
Tagged PDF
EPUB and HTML
Custom Rasterization
Size: Relative to Page Width
Resolution (ppi): 150
Format: PNG
Quality: High
Palette: Adaptive (no dither)
Method: Baseline
Interlace
Custom Layout: Alignment And Spacing
0.5
0.5
pixels
Insert Page Break: Before Image
Done

Medium Savers

Style Mapping

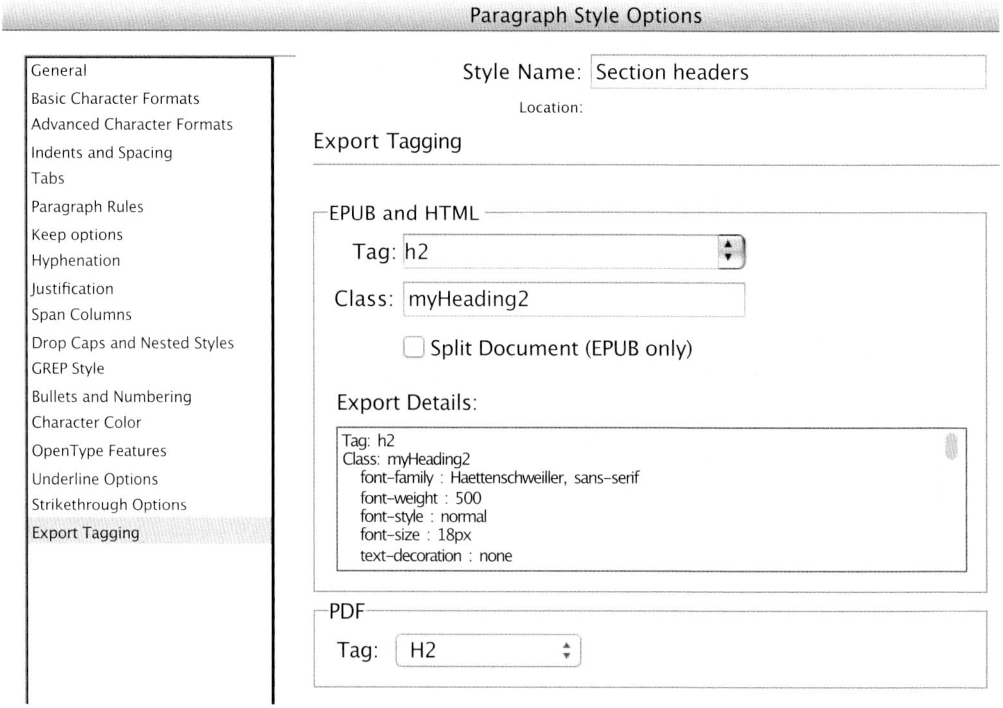

Paragraph Style Options

General
Basic Character Formats
Advanced Character Formats
Indents and Spacing
Tabs
Paragraph Rules
Keep options
Hyphenation
Justification
Span Columns
Drop Caps and Nested Styles
GREP Style
Bullets and Numbering
Character Color
OpenType Features
Underline Options
Strikethrough Options
Export Tagging

Style Name: Section headers

Location:

Export Tagging

EPUB and HTML

Tag: h2

Class: myHeading2

Split Document (EPUB only)

Export Details:

Tag: h2
Class: myHeading2
font-family : Haettenschweiller, sans-serif
font-weight : 500
font-style : normal
font-size : 18px
text-decoration : none

PDF

Tag: H2

The EPUB format uses HTML tags and CSS rules to define the e-Book's appearance. InDesign will handle this automatically, but you can also customize how your document's character and paragraph styles are mapped to HTML tags:

01. Open the Paragraph Styles panel (Window > Styles > Paragraph Styles). Be sure that no text is selected in the document.

02. Double-click on a style you want to map. This opens the Paragraph Styles Options dialog box.

03. Click on Export Tagging at the bottom of the list.

04. Use the drop-down menu to select a tag. When the document is exported, InDesign will apply that tag to all paragraphs with the selected style.

05. You can also specify a CSS class. Choose a descriptive name, such as "MyHeader1." InDesign will add a CSS rule with properties corresponding to the style definition.

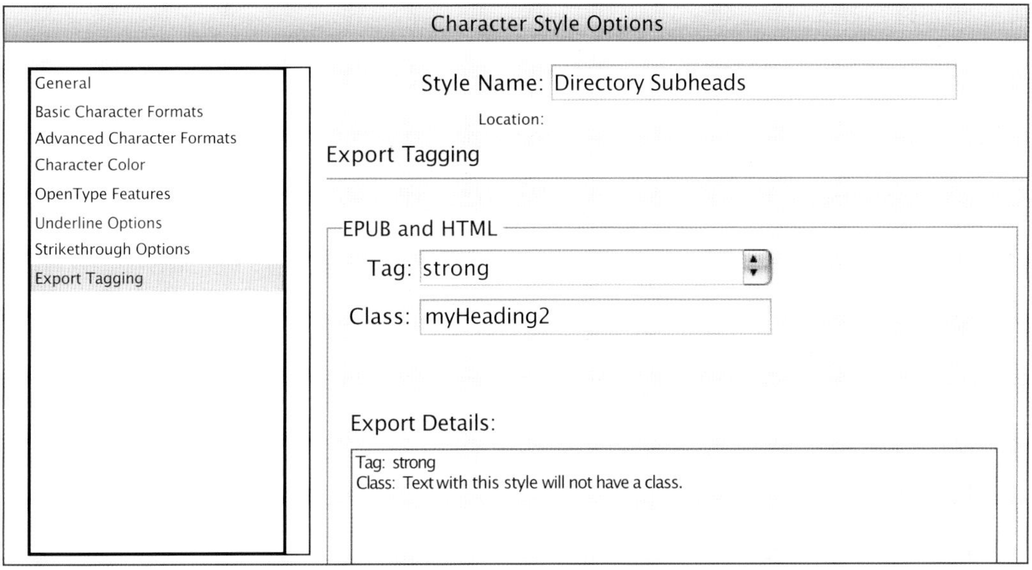

Character Style Options

General
Basic Character Formats
Advanced Character Formats
Character Color
OpenType Features
Underline Options
Strikethrough Options
Export Tagging

Style Name: Directory Subheads
Location:

Export Tagging

EPUB and HTML
Tag: strong
Class: myHeading2

Export Details:
Tag: strong
Class: Text with this style will not have a class.

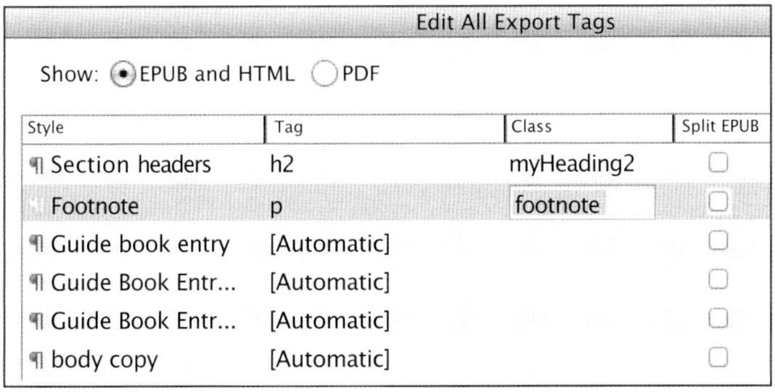

Edit All Export Tags

Show: EPUB and HTML PDF

Style	Tag	Class	Split EPUB
¶ Section headers	h2	myHeading2	☐
Footnote	p	footnote	☐
¶ Guide book entry	[Automatic]		☐
¶ Guide Book Entr...	[Automatic]		☐
¶ Guide Book Entr...	[Automatic]		☐
¶ body copy	[Automatic]		☐

You can also map character styles to <span>, <em> or <strong> tabs.

To quickly map all styles in your document to HTML tags, choose Edit All Export Tags from the panel menu for Paragraph Styles or Character Styles.

Medium Savers

Anchoring Images to Text

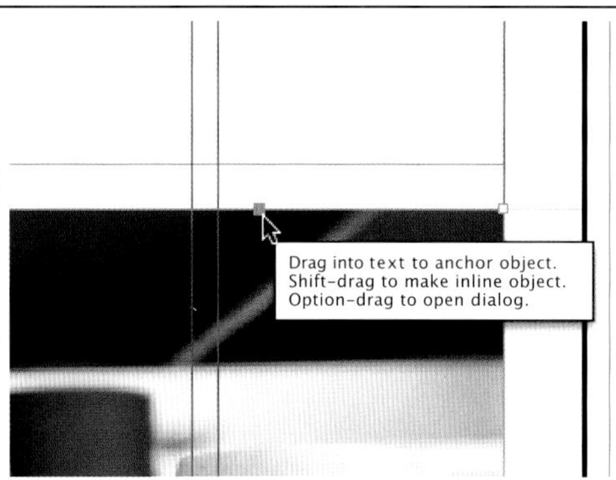

Unlike printed books, e-Books don't have static pages—the text flows differently from one device to another depending on the screen format and the user's chosen font size. So it's important to anchor images and other elements so they flow along with the text. InDesign CS5.5 and CS6 make this much easier:

01. Select an image you want to anchor. In the upper-right, you'll see a small solid blue box.

02. Drag the box to the portion of text you want to use as the anchor point.

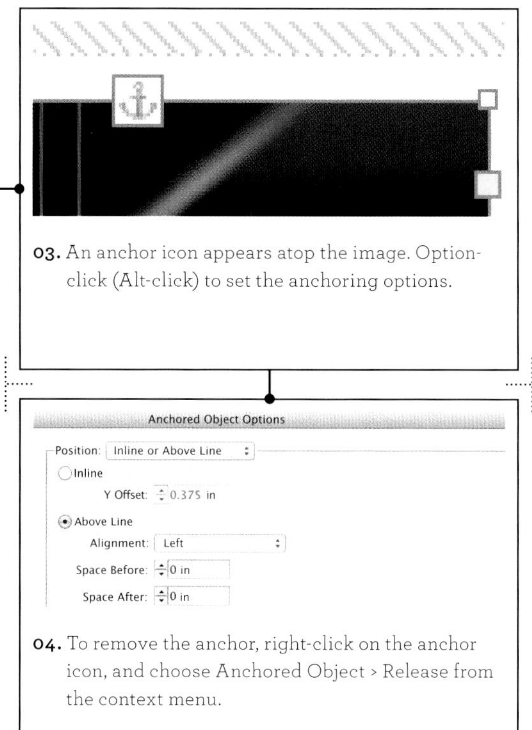

03. An anchor icon appears atop the image. Option-click (Alt-click) to set the anchoring options.

04. To remove the anchor, right-click on the anchor icon, and choose Anchored Object > Release from the context menu.

Articles Panel

Use the Articles panel to specify the stories, images, and other elements that will appear in your e-Book. You can also change the order in which they run:

- To add the entire document as a single article, ⌘-click (Ctrl-click) on the + (plus) sign. Each story and image in the document will appear as a separate item within the article. Rearrange these elements by dragging them up or down. Remove them from the panel by clicking on the trashcan.
- You can also add items to articles by dragging them from the layout. To create a new article, drag the item so it's below the other articles.
- Anchored images are added along with the text to which they're anchored—you don't have to add them separately. If you add a text frame, any other text frames linked to it are also added.

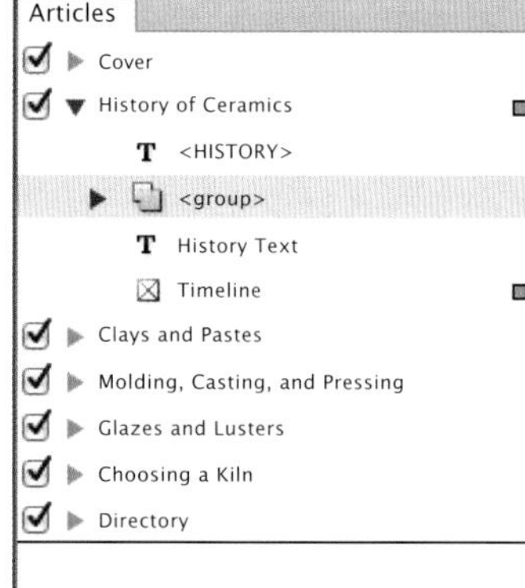

Export to EPUB

Finally, use the File > Export command to generate the e-Book. Choose EPUB as the format and specify the export options:

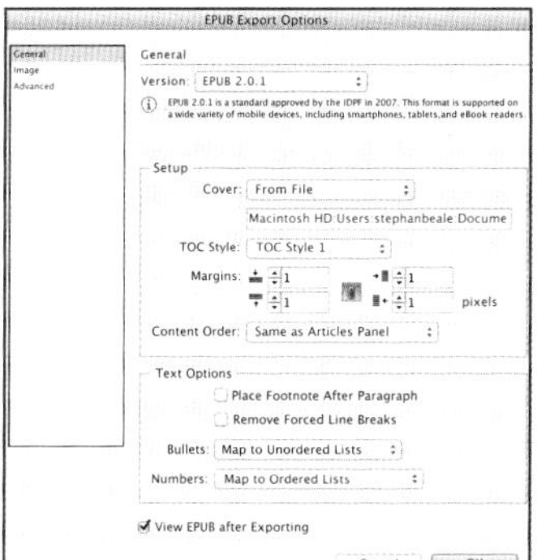

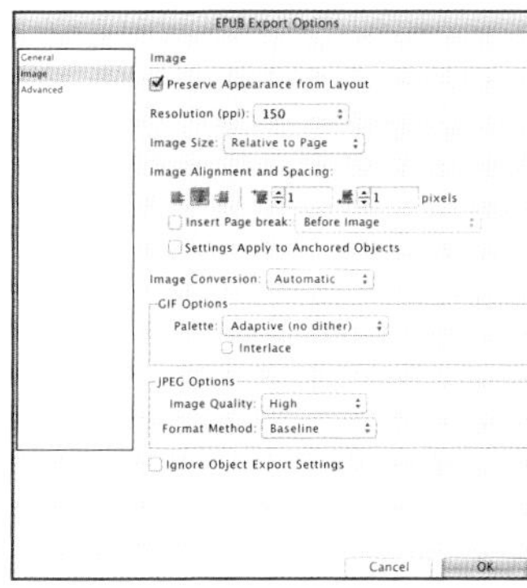

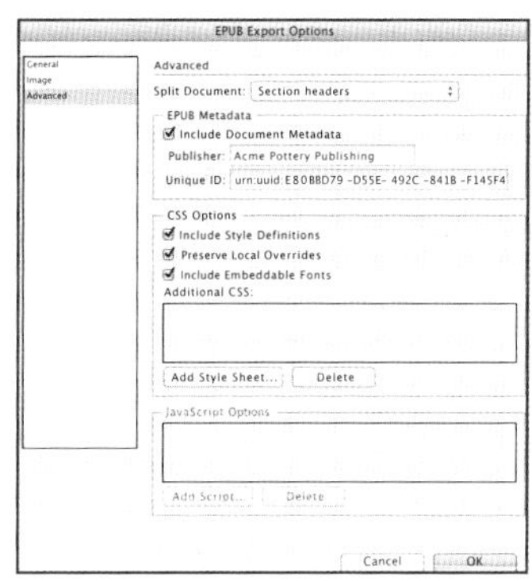

Cover Image: This determines the cover as seen in the user's e-Book library. Select Choose Image from the drop-down to specify a JPEG file.

TOC Style: This lets you specify any TOC style you've created with InDesign's Layout > Table of Contents Styles feature. You don't actually have to generate a TOC—just choose a style, and InDesign will add a TOC that enables users to navigate through each section of the book.

Image Pane: This provides export options that apply to every image in your document. Use the Object Export Options dialog box to set options for individual images.

The Advanced pane in CS6 replaces the Content pane in CS5.5:

Split Document: InDesign will add a page break before any text that's tagged with the selected style. You can also specify a style for page breaks when mapping paragraph styles to tags.

CSS Options: Check Include Style Definitions to apply any CSS styles you specified when mapping Paragraph or Character styles. You can also attach additional style sheets.

Tip

You can convert EPUB files generated by InDesign into the popular MOBI format using free e-book packages such as Kovid Goyal's Calibre (http://calibre-ebook.com/). MOBI is the format used by Amazon's Kindle.

Medium Savers

Creating Tablet Publications with InDesign

The iPad, Kindle Fire, and other tablets have opened new avenues for creating digital publications, but also pose unique challenges. InDesign's new digital publishing tools promise dramatic productivity benefits for anyone who wants to work in this new medium.

Alternate Layouts

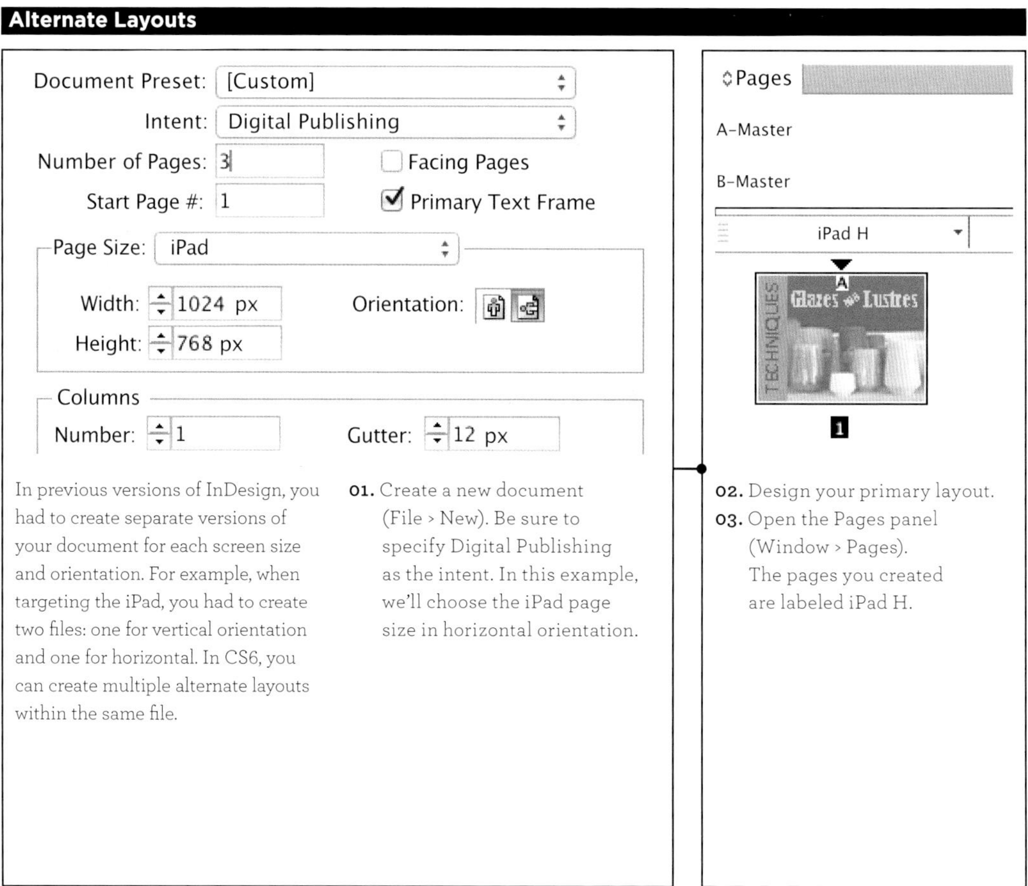

In previous versions of InDesign, you had to create separate versions of your document for each screen size and orientation. For example, when targeting the iPad, you had to create two files: one for vertical orientation and one for horizontal. In CS6, you can create multiple alternate layouts within the same file.

01. Create a new document (File › New). Be sure to specify Digital Publishing as the intent. In this example, we'll choose the iPad page size in horizontal orientation.

02. Design your primary layout.

03. Open the Pages panel (Window › Pages). The pages you created are labeled iPad H.

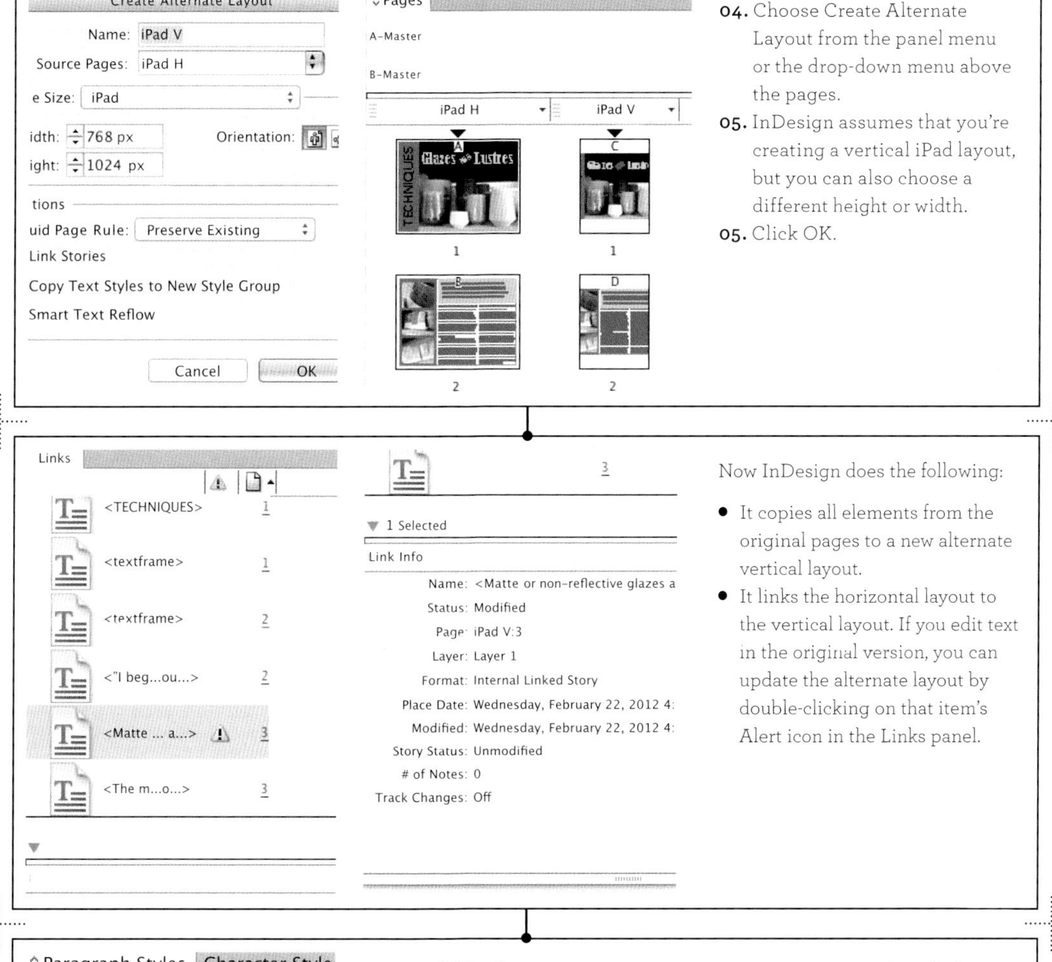

04. Choose Create Alternate Layout from the panel menu or the drop-down menu above the pages.

05. InDesign assumes that you're creating a vertical iPad layout, but you can also choose a different height or width.

05. Click OK.

Now InDesign does the following:

- It copies all elements from the original pages to a new alternate vertical layout.
- It links the horizontal layout to the vertical layout. If you edit text in the original version, you can update the alternate layout by double-clicking on that item's Alert icon in the Links panel.

Paragraph Styles | Character Style
Pull Quote (iPad H)
[Basic Paragraph]
iPad H
Department Head
Paragraph intro
First Paragraph no indent
Paragraph Indent
Pull Quote
Subhead
Call out header
Subhead
Call out header
Normal
iPad V
Basic Paragraph
Department Head
Paragraph intro
First Paragraph no indent
Paragraph Indent

- It copies Paragraph and Character Styles into a new folder for the vertical layout, allowing you to edit the styles to better fit the new orientation.

Medium Savers

Liquid Layouts

InDesign's Liquid Layout features make it even easier to create alternate layouts. You can choose one of four "rules" that will determine how elements on each page are transformed to accommodate each new size and orientation. You apply these rules using the Page Tool in combination with the Options bar or the new Liquid Layout panel (Window >Interactive > Liquid Layout).

First, repeat steps 1-3 in the previous example. Now you can apply the rules. They may be difficult to grasp at first, but the Page tool provides an easy way to see how they work. When you click on a page, drag the handles on the page edges to approximate the size and orientation of the alternate layout. InDesign provides a quick preview of the alternate layout. You can also get a quick preview by adjusting the size and orientation settings in the Options bar.

The Rules

- Resize scales the content to fit the new dimensions of the alternate layout.
- Recenter positions the elements in the center without resizing them.
- Object-based lets you pin objects to specified edges of the page. You can also determine whether an object should be resized horizontally or vertically.
- Guide-based lets you place vertical and horizontal Liquid Layout guides across elements you want to resize.

Once you've set up the rules, use the Create Alternate Layout command to create the new layouts. In the Liquid Rule drop-down, choose "Preserve Existing" to ensure that InDesign applies the rules you just created

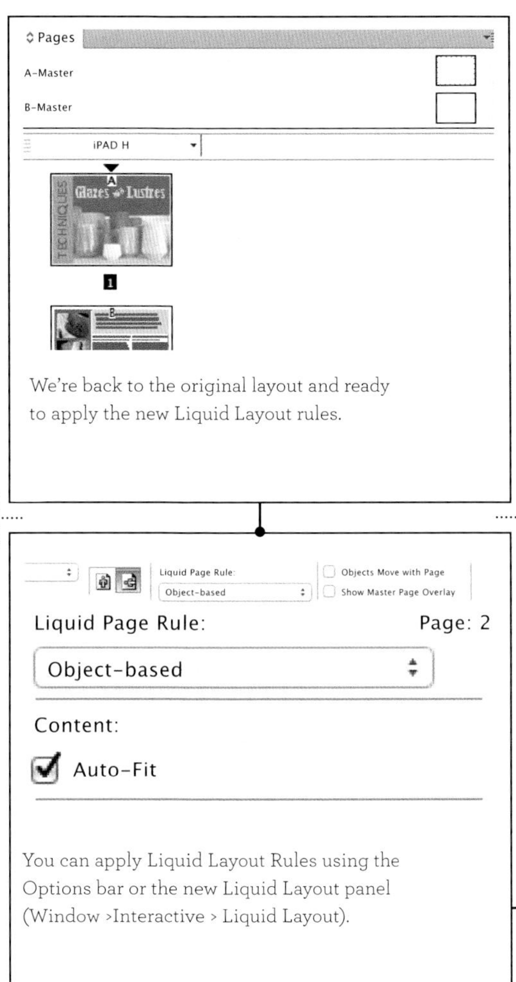

We're back to the original layout and ready to apply the new Liquid Layout rules.

You can apply Liquid Layout Rules using the Options bar or the new Liquid Layout panel (Window >Interactive > Liquid Layout).

Tip
Use the new Flexible Width feature (Object > Text Frame Options) to automatically add or remove columns in text frames as they're resized.

When you click on a page with the Page tool, handles appear on the edges. Drag the handles to approximate the dimensions of the alternate layout, and InDesign will provide a quick preview of the selected rule. Release the mouse button to revert to the current layout. You can scale the page permanently by pressing Option (Alt) as you drag.

Use the Object-based rule to pin frames to specified page edges and determine whether the frames should be resized vertically or horizontally. In the example here, the solid circles indicate that the pull-quote will be pinned to the top and right edges. The lock icons in the center are disabled, so InDesign will resize the object to accommodate the new layout dimensions. You can also choose these settings in the Liquid Layout panel.

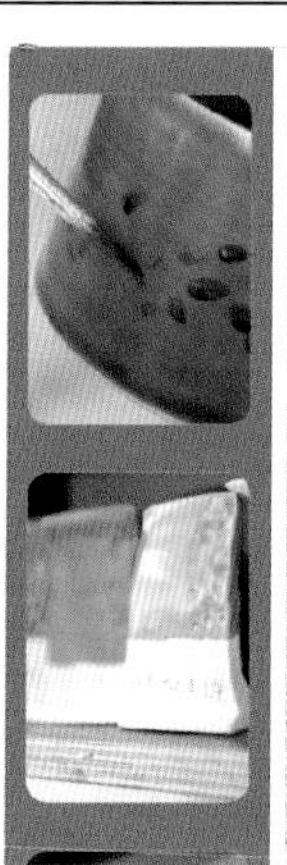

In the alternate layout, the pullquote is automatically resized to accommodate the vertical orientation. The layout still needs some work, but we're closer to the final product.

The Guide-based rule lets you drag Liquid Layout guides over the objects you want to resize. The guides appear as dotted lines. Be sure to choose the Page tool before dragging the guides. You'll also want to use the Page tool to preview this rule, because its actions are not all that intuitive.

Medium Savers

Collecting and Placing Content

InDesign's new Content Collector and Content Placer tools provide a quick way to reuse content within a document or between documents. For example, you can use these tools to grab text and graphics from a print publication and drop them into a digital edition targeted at tablet devices.

The tools work in combination with the new Content Conveyor, which provides a temporary storage area for items you want to reuse. You have the option of linking the content, so that changes made in the original "parent" version are updated in the "child" versions. You can also map styles from parents to children.

Collecting Content

First, open a document from which you want to reuse content and choose the Content Collector tool. This will automatically open the Content Conveyor.

InDesign provides several ways to grab content:

- Click on items to load them individually.
- Marquee-select items to load them as a set.
- Click the Load Conveyor button on the bottom-right of the conveyor.

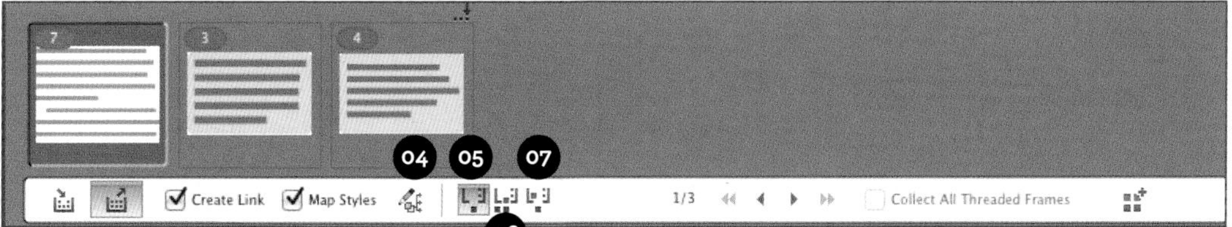

Placing Content

Now you're ready to place the content into another document.

01. Open the document and click the Content Placer tool in the Content Conveyor.
02. Check Create Link if you want to link the placed items to their parents. If items are linked, you can edit the original parent item and then use the Links panel to update the child version.
03. Check Map Styles to enable style mapping between the source document and the current document.
04. Click here to open the Custom Style Mapping dialog box. This lets you determine how the styles will be mapped.

The next three buttons let you determine how content in the conveyor is placed:

05. Click here to place the first item, remove it from the ribbon, and then load the next item.
06. Click here to load all items into the place cursor—just like the Multiple Place option.
07. Click here to place the items one at a time without removing them from the ribbon.

Folio Builder

In print publishing, each document contains a single article, and you use the Folio Builder to assemble the articles into a "folio," which is equivalent to a single issue of a publication.

To use the Folio Builder, you'll need access to Adobe's Digital Publishing Suite. But even if you don't have, you can create articles in InDesign and then pass them on to a client or colleague who will assemble them into the finished product.

Medium Savers

Reusable Content in InDesign

Store frequently used layout elements in libraries—or save them as snippets—so they're always at your fingertips.

Libraries

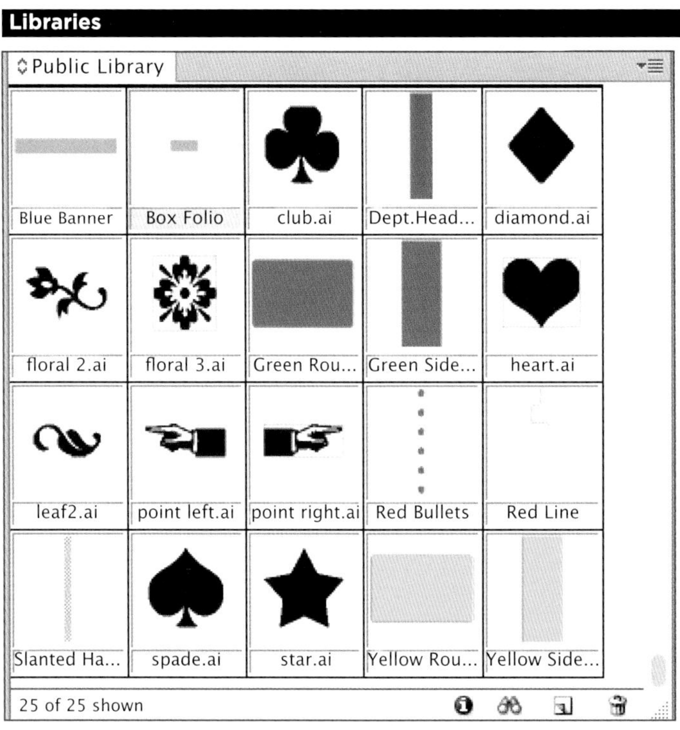

An InDesign library is a collection of layout elements that you can share among multiple documents. Any item that you place on a page—including artwork, guides, text frames, and shapes—can be stored in a library. You can also store the entire contents of a page.

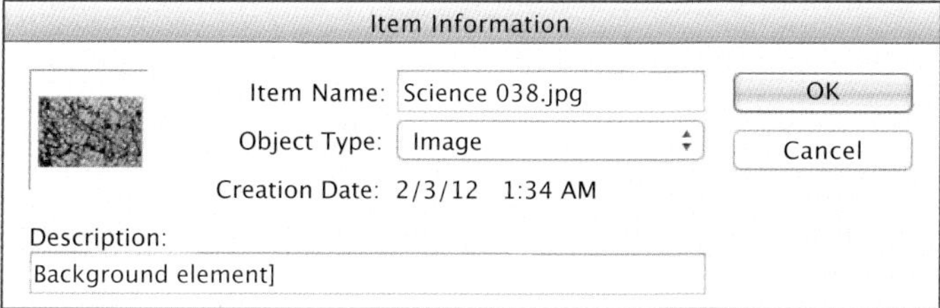

- To create a library, choose File > New > Library. Give it a name, specify a folder location, and click save. You can create as many libraries as you'd like, but using a single library makes it easier to search for items via the Show Subset command.
- You can open libraries via Bridge or the File > Open command.
- To add an item to a library, drag it from the page or choose Add Item from the panel menu.
- To add an entire page as a single object, choose Add Items on Page from the panel menu. You can also add each item as separate objects.
- To place a library item, drag it from the panel or choose Place Item(s) from the panel menu. If you use the latter option, InDesign will place it at the original location on the page.
- If you add a linked graphic to the library, InDesign will maintain the link to the original artwork. If you delete the original or move it to a different location, you'll get a Missing Link error when you drag the item into your layout.
- Use the Item Information command to rename the item, assign it to a category, or give it a description.

- Use the Show Subset dialog box to filter the library by specified attributes. Open it via the panel menu or by clicking on the binoculars at the bottom of the panel. Click on More Choices to add new search criteria.

Snippets

InDesign Snippets are layout elements that you can save to a folder. One advantage over libraries is that you can preview snippets at various sizes in MiniBridge. Another is that all members of a design team can access a snippets folder over a network. You can exchange a library with other users, but only one can have it open.

To create a snippet, select the items you want to save and do one of the following:

- Drag the selection to an open folder, the desktop or MiniBridge. If you do this, InDesign will assign a serialized file name.
- Use the File > Export command and specify InDesign Snippet as the format. This gives you the opportunity to assign a more descriptive filename.

You can place snippets by dragging them from Bridge or MiniBridge, or via the File > Place command.

Medium Savers

Profiles, Templates, and Custom Views in Illustrator

Illustrator's Document Profiles and Templates provide quick ways to customize the program for common design projects. Custom Views make it easier to navigate to different parts of the document.

Document Profiles

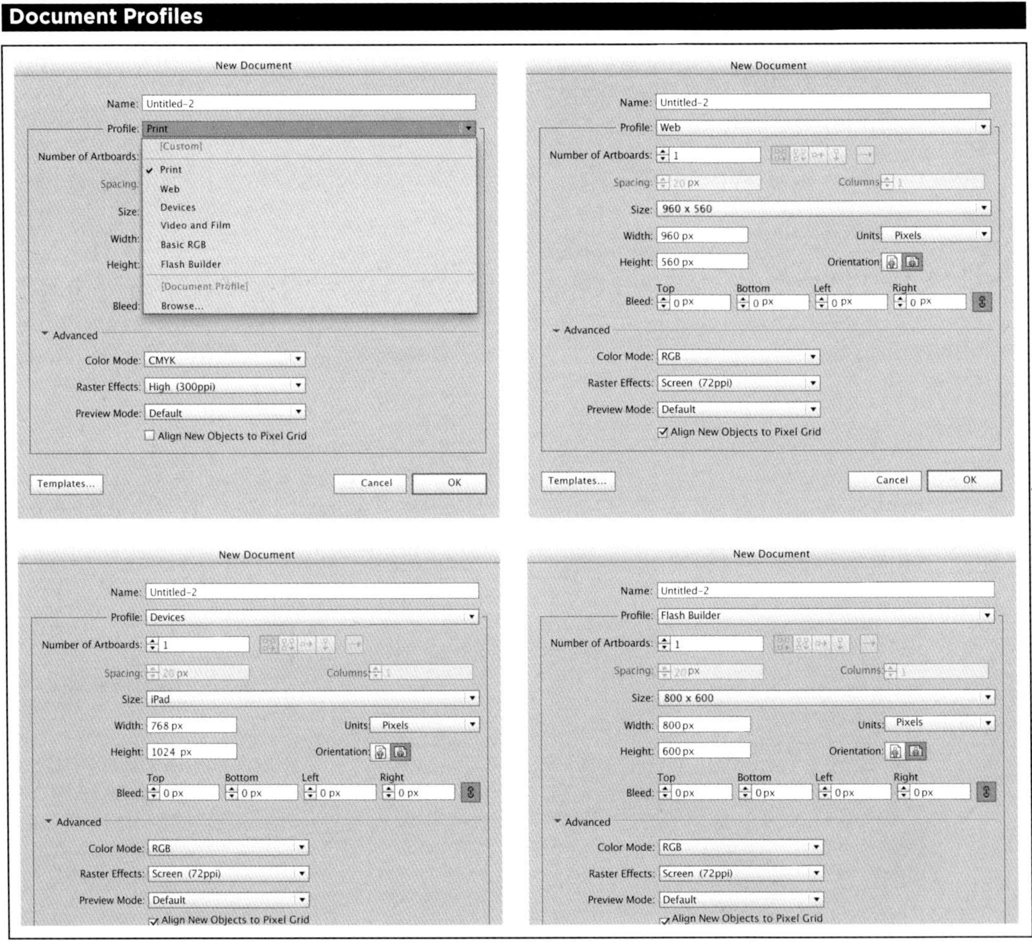

A document profile contains basic settings that apply when you create a new document. Illustrator ships with seven predefined profiles: Basic RGB, Basic CMYK, Print, Web, Flash Catalyst, Mobile and Devices, and Video and Film. However, you can create your own and have it appear as a preset in the New Document dialog box.

01. Choose File > New or hit ⌘-N (Ctrl-N) to open the New Document dialog box.
02. Choose the profile that most closely matches the one you want to create.
03. You can modify other settings in the dialog box, including size, orientation, bleeds, number of artboards, color mode, raster effects, and preview mode. The latter three are available when you click on the Advanced disclosure triangle. Click OK when you're done.
04. Modify other settings you'd like to include in the profile. These can include settings in the Document Setup dialog box as well as rulers, brushes, swatches, and symbols.
05. Save the file in Adobe Illustrator format to one of these locations:

Mac: username/Library/Application Support/Adobe/Adobe Illustrator CS6/en_US/New Document Profiles.

Windows: C:\Users\Username\Roaming\Adobe\Adobe Illustrator CS6 Settings\en_US\New Document Profiles.

Custom Views

Illustrator's Custom Views feature lets you save multiple views of a document, including pan and zoom settings as well as layer visibility. For example, you could have one view in which the entire document fits in the window, and other views that zoom in on various artboards or sections, each with different layers that are shown or hidden.

To create a custom view, choose View > New View and give it a name. It will be listed at the bottom of the View menu. Illustrator saves custom views as part of the document.

Templates

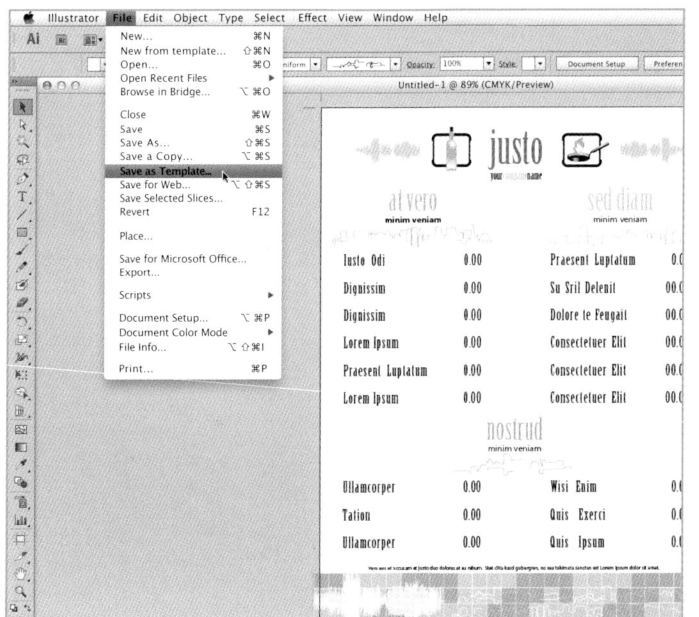

For greater customization, you can save any Illustrator document as a template that includes custom views, grids and guides, print options, crop marks, styles, recurring artwork, and other elements. For example, you can set up templates for business cards, stationery, or specific ad formats and recall them with all settings intact.

To save a document as a template, choose File > Save as Template. These files have an .AIT extension and open as untitled documents. To open a template, choose File > New From Template or click on Templates in the New Document dialog box.

Illustrator ships with a large number of prebuilt templates that can be used if you want to learn more about its features.

Medium Savers

Using Symbols in Illustrator

In Illustrator, a symbol is an object that you can store in a library and reuse in multiple instances. Symbols are not only great time-savers, but also keep file sizes small regardless of how many instances you use.

The Symbols Panel

This is where you manage symbols in Illustrator. It's similar in many ways to the Brushes, Swatches, and Graphic Styles panels. You can load symbols from one of the many built-in libraries or define your own.

- To place a symbol in your document, drag it from the Symbols panel.
- Each use of a symbol is known as an "instance." Each instance is linked to the symbol. You can apply transformations and graphic styles to instances, but you cannot edit the instance's paths, strokes, or fills.
- To edit the original artwork, double-click on the symbol or an instance. When you're finished, press Esc. Any changes will be reflected in all instances of that symbol.

01. **Symbol Libraries Menu**
02. **Place Symbol Instance**
03. **Break Link to Symbol**
04. **Symbol Options**
05. **New Symbol**
06. **Delete Symbol**

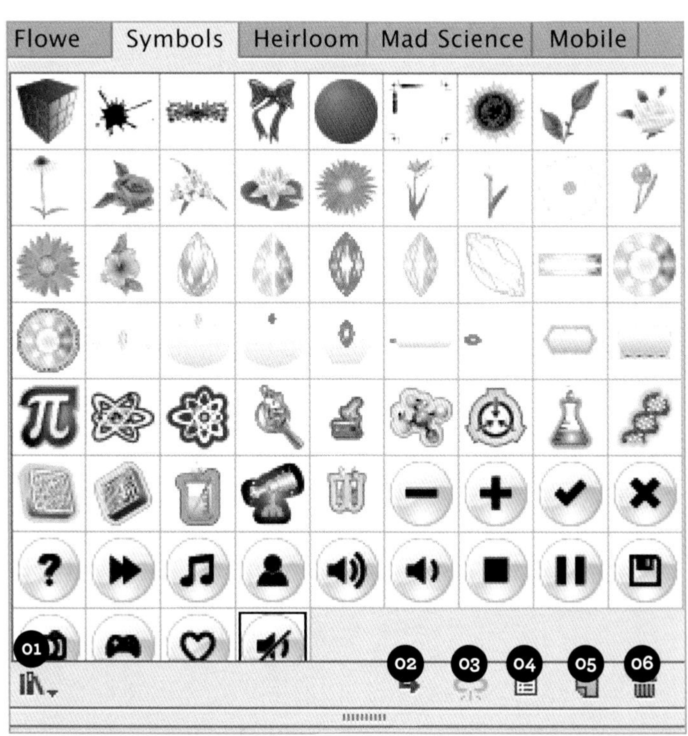

Creating Symbols

01. Select the object you want to convert to a symbol. You can use any kind of artwork except linked images or groups of graphs.

02. Drag the object to the Symbols panel. You can also click on the New Symbol button.

03. Give the Symbol a name. You can define the symbol as a Movie Clip or Graphic, but these settings are important only if you plan to use the artwork in Flash Professional. Click OK.

Symbolism Tools

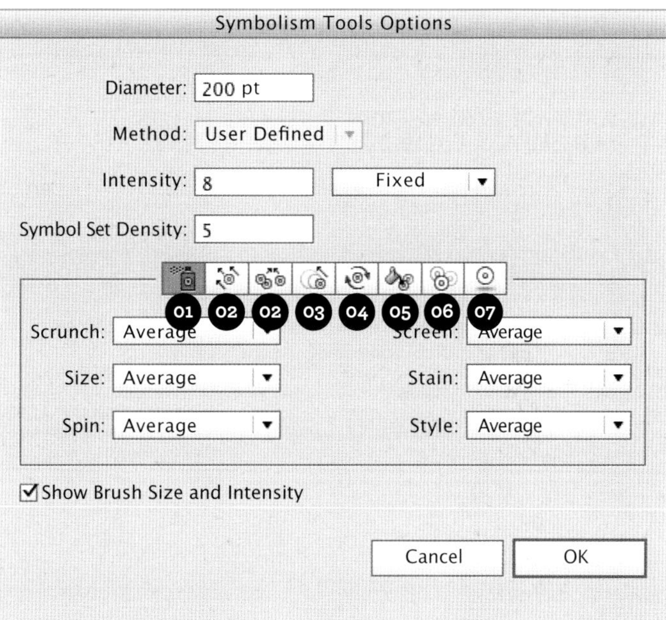

In addition to placing symbols in your document, you can use Illustrator's Symbolism tools to apply the symbols in various ways. For example:

01. Symbol Sprayer: Sprays multiple instances of a symbol.

02. Symbol Shifter and Symbol Scruncher: Move the instances in various ways.

03. Symbol Sizer: Scales the instances up or down.

04. Symbol Spinner: Rotates the instances.

05. Symbol Stainer: Colorizes the instances.

06. Symbol Screener: Makes the instances more or less transparent.

07. Symbol Styler: Applies the currently selected graphic style.

Medium Savers

Reusable Content in Dreamweaver

Customize Dreamweaver's Insert, Snippets, or Library panels for instant access to frequently used design elements.

The Insert Panel

This panel (Window > Insert) provides a quick way to add frequently used Dreamweaver objects to web pages: <div> tags, navigation elements, email links, and much more. Better yet, you can customize the panel by assigning Favorites:

01. Right-click any place on the Insert panel and choose Customize Favorites from the context menu. This opens the Customize Favorite Objects dialog box.

02. Navigate through the list of available objects and click on the arrows to add them to the Favorite objects column.

03. When you're done, click OK. Your selections appear in the panel's Favorites category.

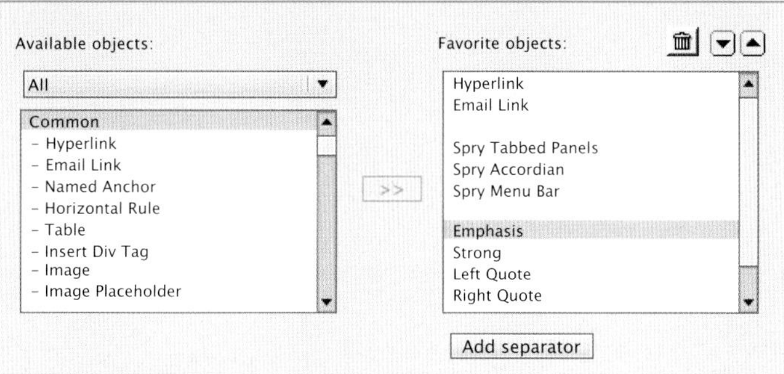

Tip

You can also create Favorites for most items in the Assets panel (Window > Assets). Right-click on the item and choose Add to Favorites from the context menu. Templates and library items can't be saved as Favorites.

Snippets

Dreamweaver Snippets are pieces of code—usually HTML, CSS, or JavaScript—that you can store and reuse. The Snippets panel (Window > Snippets) includes prebuilt snippets, but you can also add your own.

To Create a Snippet

01. Select the code you want to reuse. You can do so in the Code view or Design view.
02. Click the New Snippet button in the Snippets panel.
03. The code appears in the New Snippet dialog. Give it a name and description, and choose whether to insert it as a block or wrap it around a selection. If it's the latter, enter the appropriate code in the Insert Before and Insert After panes. Preview Type indicates how the Snippets panel will preview the content.
04. When you're done, click OK. The snippet appears in the Snippets panel.

To insert a snippet, click on the desired insertion point on the web page. If it's a wraparound snippet, select the item you want to wrap. Then double-click on the snippet or select it and click on the Insert button.

> **Tip**
>
> - Organize snippets using the existing folders, or click the New Folder button to create your own.
> - Avoid using snippets that include links to images or internal web pages, because they won't work on other sites.

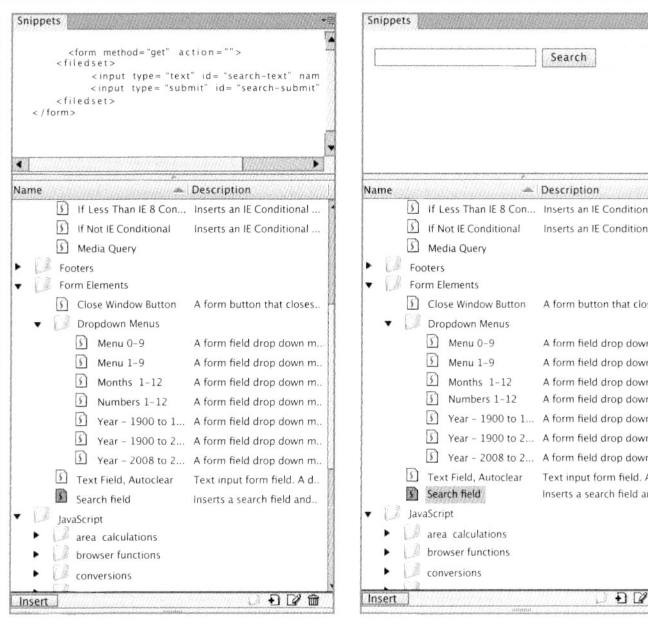

The Snippets Panel

The preview pane shows the snippet's code or a rendered preview depending on the Preview Type selected.

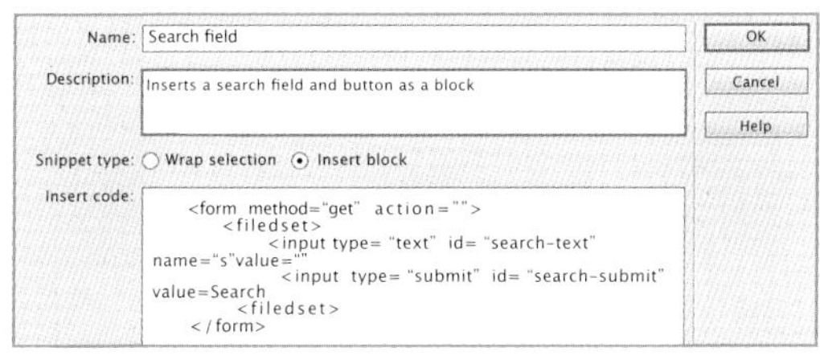

Name: Comment, Multi-Line
Description: Wraps an HTML comment tag around the selection, with a line break before and after the selection.
Snippet type: Wrap selection Insert block
Insert before: <!--
Insert after: -->
OK
Cancel
Help

When creating a snippet, you can have it inserted as a block (left) or wrap it around a selection (below left).

10→60 mins

Medium Savers

Libraries

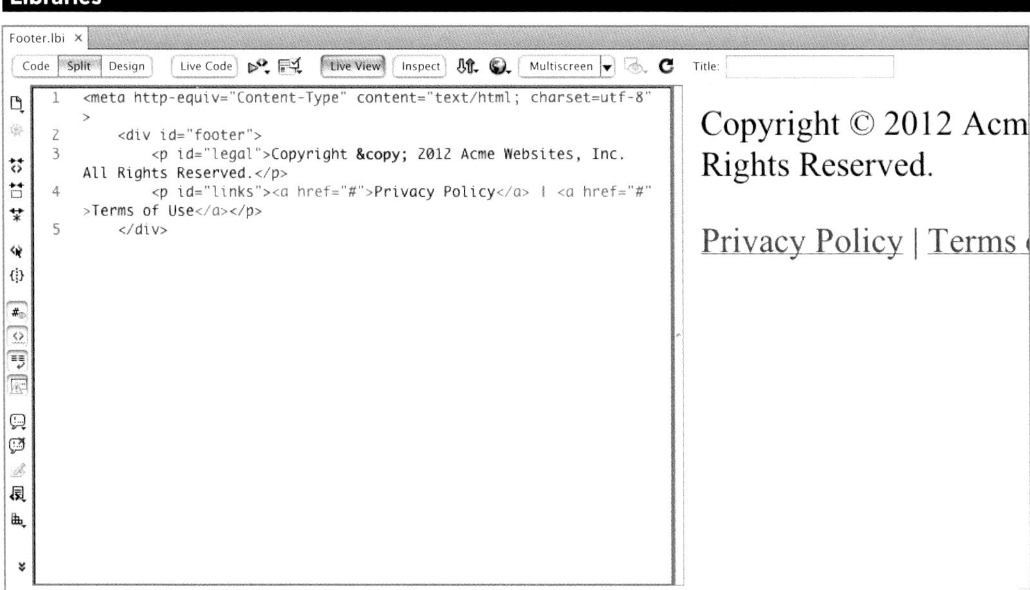

A library is a collection of reusable assets such as images, text blocks, audio clips, tables, and navigation elements. Each library item is stored as HTML code in a text file with an .lbi extension. Dreamweaver places these files in a Library folder within your site folder.

Each library item placed on a page is linked to the .lbi file containing the original HTML code. If you edit the original, the changes are reflected throughout the site.

It's important to keep the following in mind:

- Library items are limited to storing HTML elements contained within the <body> tag of a web page. You cannot include elements placed within the <head> tag.
- Each library item must include all HTML code needed to display that asset, including the opening and closing tags.
- If a library item contains images or other multimedia content, the .lbi file will include the HTML tag linking to those assets. The image or media file remains in its original location. If you move it or rename it, you must edit the library item to reflect the change.
- You cannot use the same library folder on multiple sites. You can copy a library folder from one site to another, but internal links within library items may be broken.
- To manage the library for your site, go to Window > Assets and click on the book icon (it's the last one in the left margin).

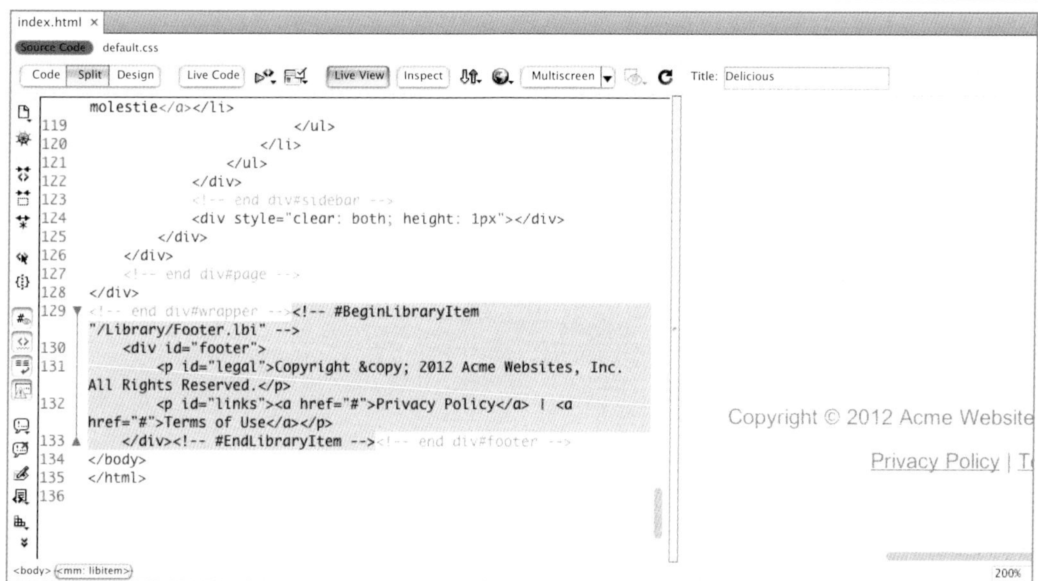

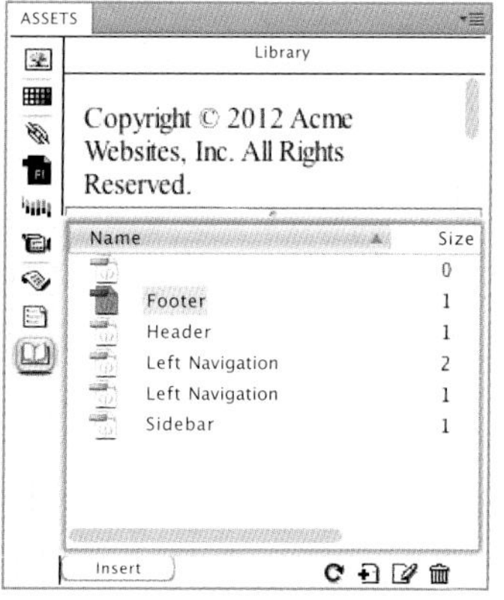

To Create a Library Item

01. Open a page on your site and select an HTML element in Code view or Design view. Use the Tag Selector in the Status Bar to ensure you're selecting the entire element.
02. Click on New Library Item in the Assets > Library panel. Dreamweaver will warn you that your selection may not look the same elsewhere on your site. Click OK.
03. It now appears in the panel as an untitled Library item. Give it a name and hit Return. In Code view, you'll see that Dreamweaver has wrapped the original selection with HTML comments noting that it's now a library item. The comment includes a link to the .lbi file containing that item.
04. To insert a library item, drag it into the Code or Design view, or place the cursor at the desired insertion point and click on the Insert button.
05. To edit a library item, double-click on it. This opens the .lbi file in a separate window. Make your edits, and press ⌘-S (Ctrl+S) to save them. Dreamweaver will alert you that it is about to update that item throughout the site.

Creative Suite 6
Photoshop
Illustrator
InDesign
Dreamweaver
Flash Professional
Edge
Fireworks
Muse
Acrobat Professional
Bridge
Kuler
Online
Mac
Windows

Chapter Four. Long-term Solutions

02→24 hrs

Long-term Solutions

Find and Replace in Dreamweaver

Dreamweaver's powerful Find and Replace function makes it easy to fix tags in a single web page or an entire site. Or use Regular Expressions to create complex pattern-matching queries.

Replacing Tags

Find and Replace (Edit > Find and Replace) can do much more than replace text strings—it can also find and replace tags matching specific criteria. When it does so, it replaces not only the opening tag, but the closing tag as well.

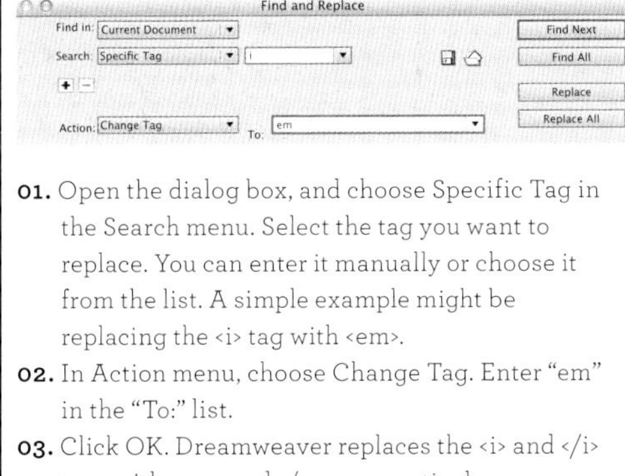

01. Open the dialog box, and choose Specific Tag in the Search menu. Select the tag you want to replace. You can enter it manually or choose it from the list. A simple example might be replacing the <i> tag with <em>.
02. In Action menu, choose Change Tag. Enter "em" in the "To:" list.
03. Click OK. Dreamweaver replaces the <i> and </i> tags with <em> and </em> respectively.

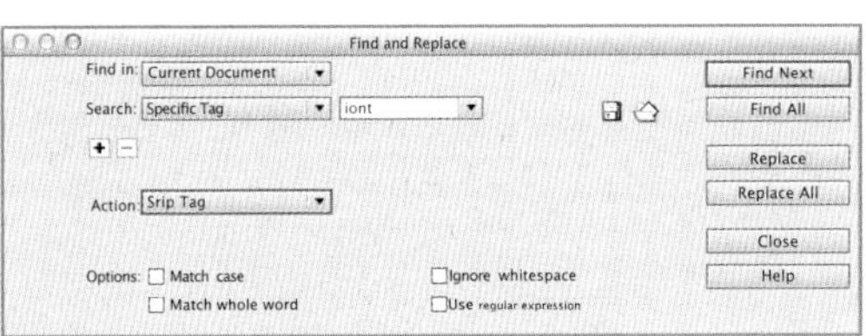

Here's an easy way to strip deprecated <font> tags from your web pages.

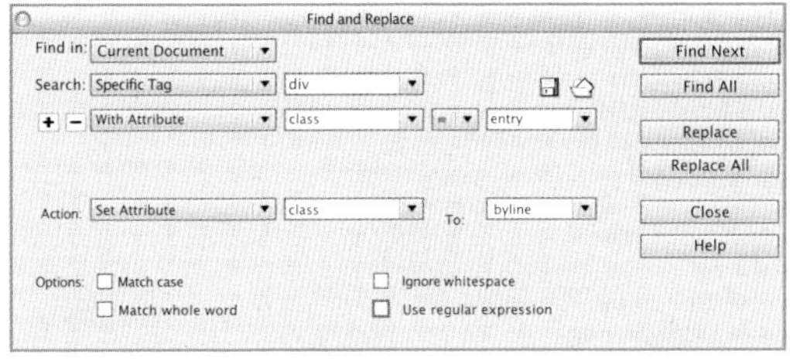

Here's a more complicated example. We'll search for all <div> tags with the CSS class "entry" and change the class to "byline."

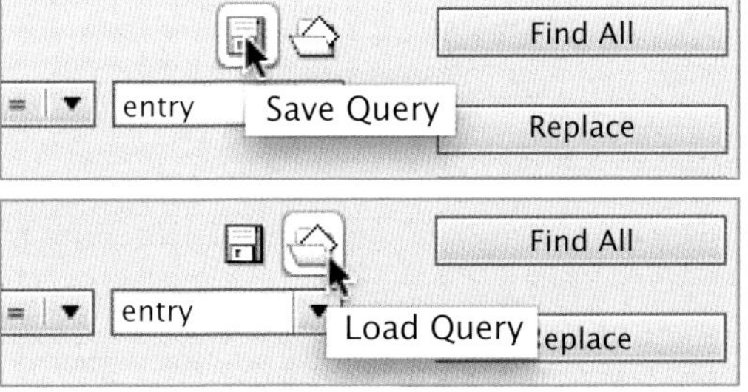

You can save queries to use later. Click the Load button to open saved queries.

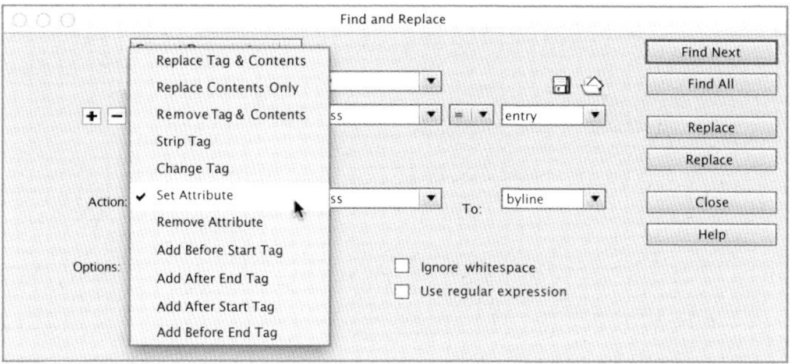

You can choose any of 11 actions to take when Dreamweaver finds a tag matching your search criteria.

Regular Expressions

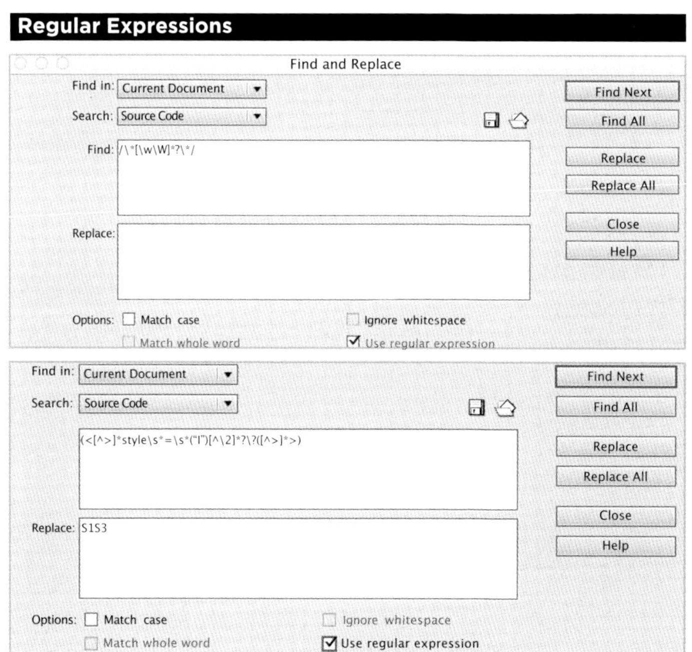

Including Regular Expressions in search queries allows you to perform complex pattern-matching operations. Click the "Use Regular Expressions" option to enable them.

This Regular Expression query strips out all comments in CSS style sheets.

Regular Expressions can be tricky, and can cause unexpected results if not used correctly. It's a good idea to test them first on a backup file. You can find a quick guide to regular expressions in the Dreamweaver help files (press F1) and some tutorials on Adobe.com. You'll also find numerous example queries and guides by searching the web.

Search Multiple Documents

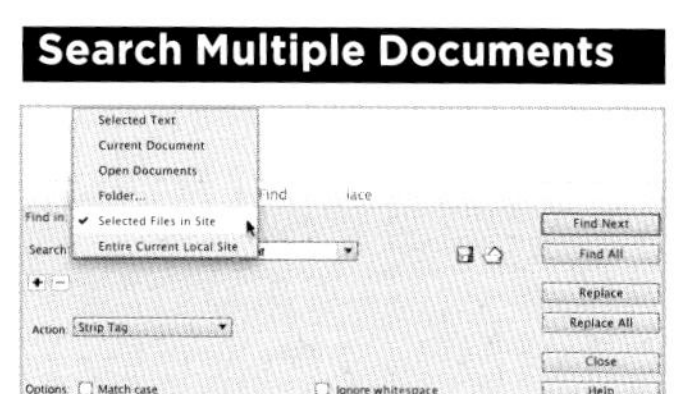

Dreamweaver is not limited to searching the current document. You can also search within a specified folder, selected files or the entire site. Make your choice from the Find In menu.

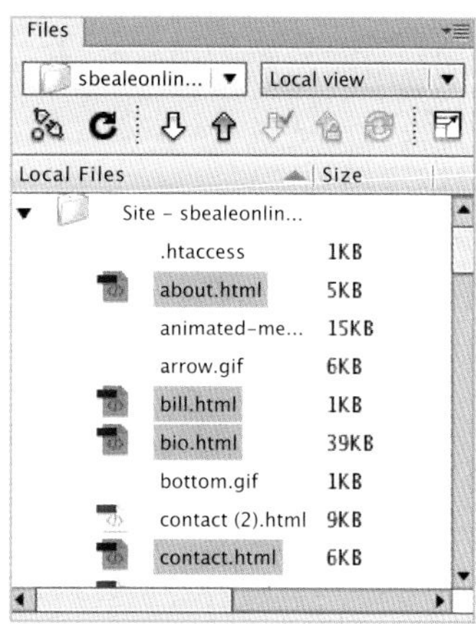

To search a group of files, select them in the Files panel.

Tip

Use caution—when performing Find and Replace operations on multiple files, Dreamweaver cannot undo the action. Be especially careful when executing Regular Expressions queries.

Long-term Solutions

Find/Change in InDesign

InDesign's Find/Change function goes far beyond what you'll find in a word processor. You can find and change glyphs, formatting, and even graphics attributes. And with the GREP option, you can find and replace patterns of text.

The Find/Replace Dialog

Choose Edit > Find/Replace or press ⌘-F (Ctrl+F) to open the dialog box.

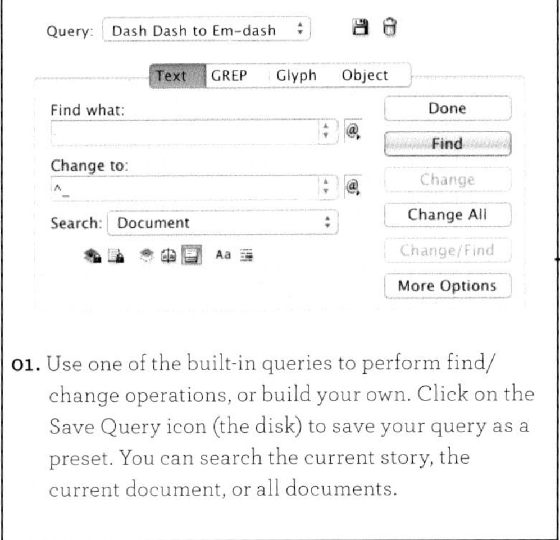

01. Use one of the built-in queries to perform find/change operations, or build your own. Click on the Save Query icon (the disk) to save your query as a preset. You can search the current story, the current document, or all documents.

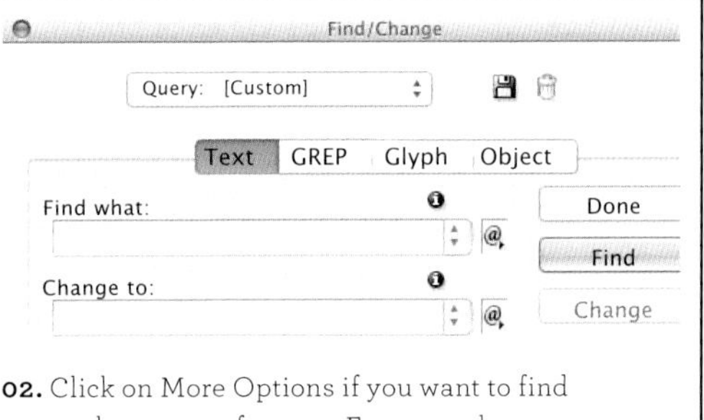

02. Click on More Options if you want to find or change text formats. For example, you can search for all text set in Cambria Bold with no paragraph style, and replace that formatting with the Heading 2 style.

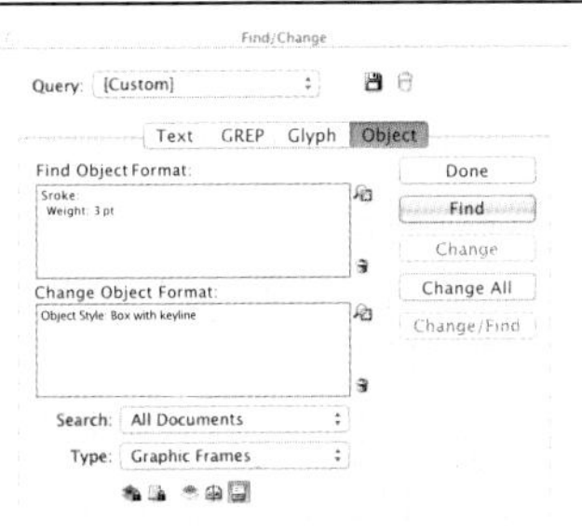

03. Use the Object tab to find/change graphic attributes. For example, you can find all graphics frames with a 3-point stroke and replace them with the Box with Keyline object style.

04. Click on the @ sign to insert special characters, such as tabs or paragraph markers, into the search or replace fields. You can even tell InDesign to replace a string of characters with the contents of the clipboard, including graphics.

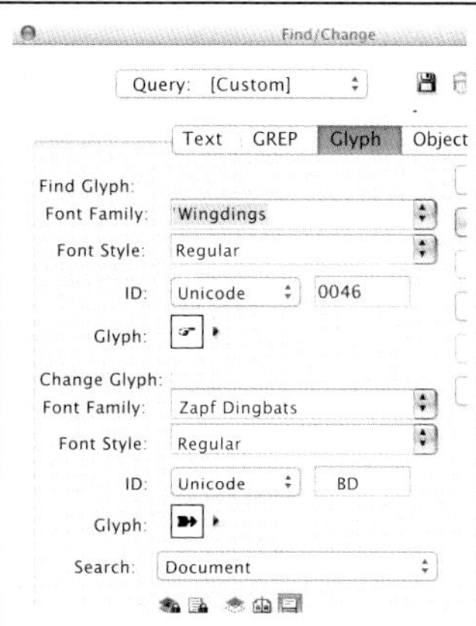

05. Use the Glyph tab to find/change special characters, such as characters from symbol fonts.

GREP

Text GREP Glyph Object
Find what: \(?(\d\d\d)\)?[-.]?(\d\d\d)[-.]?(\d\d
Change to: $1.$2.$3
Search: Story
Done
Find
Change
Change All
Change/Find

GREP, also known as Regular Expressions, is a powerful feature common to many programming languages. It lets you replace one pattern of text with another. For example, with GREP, you can:

- Remove the HTML tags from <b>This is boldface text</b> and apply boldface formatting. Change American-style date formats (mm-dd-yy) to dd-mm-yy.
- Change lastname, firstname to firstname lastname.
- InDesign includes the following built-in GREP search as an example. It changes U.S. phone numbers to the dot format (xxx.xxx.xxxx).

Find what:
\(?(\d\d\d)\)?[-.]?(\d\d\d)[-.]?(\d\d\d\d)

Change to:
$1.$2.$3

As you can see, GREP expressions can appear cryptic, but learning the syntax is not as difficult as you might think. Because GREP is widely used, you can find numerous books and websites that will help you learn more. Some websites include expressions that you can copy and paste. InDesign Secrets (http://indesignsecrets.com/grep) is a good place to start.

Tip

- Use the @ menu in the Find/Change dialog to insert GREP metacharacters.
- Before executing a find/change operation, test the expression on a single instance to see if it works as intended. Until you become comfortable with GREP, it's also a good idea to work on a backup of your document.
- Once you're confident that an expression works as intended, click the Save Query button to save it as a preset.
- You can use the GREP Styles option in Paragraph Styles to apply nested character styles based on GREP expressions.
- InDesign's @ menu can automatically insert GREP metacharacters (shown at right).

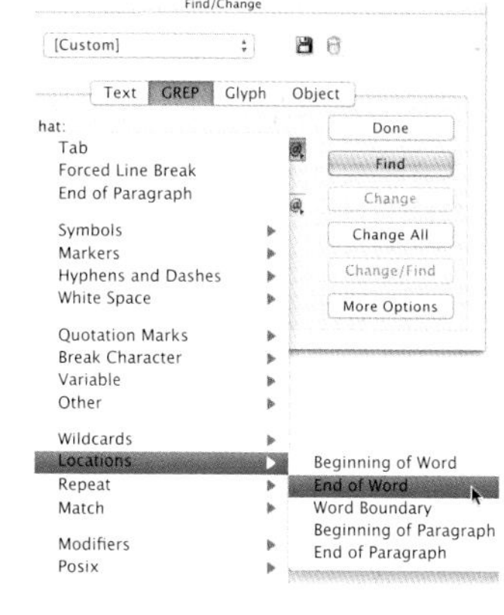

Long-term Solutions

Search Tools

Rather than hunting through folders to find files, use the built-in search functions in Mac OS X or Windows to do the job for you.

Searching for Documents with Windows

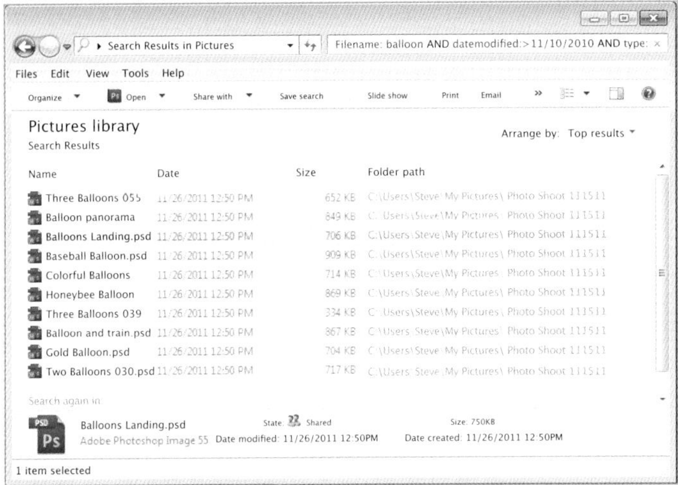

Searches can also use Boolean logic. For example, the following yields all Photoshop documents modified after 11/10/2010 that contain "Balloon" in their filenames:

Filename: balloon AND datemodified:>11/10/2010 AND type: PSD

Boolean operators (AND, OR, NOT) must be all caps. Searches can be saved by clicking on Save Search in the results folder. Learn more about the search function by typing "Advanced tips for searching in Windows" in the Help window.

Windows doesn't have a separate search program like Apple's Spotlight. Instead, you can use the search field in the Start menu or any folder. Use the Start menu if you want to search the entire system (or press ⊞ + F). Use a folder's search field if you're looking for a document in that folder or one of its subfolders.

By default, Windows displays all documents that contain your search terms. However, you can narrow the search by using its built-in query language. For example, if you enter "Name" or "Filename" followed by a colon, you can limit the search to documents whose filenames contain the search term. "Type" followed by a colon limits the search to specific document types, such as Photoshop files. "DateModified" limits the search to files modified on or before a certain date.

Spotlight

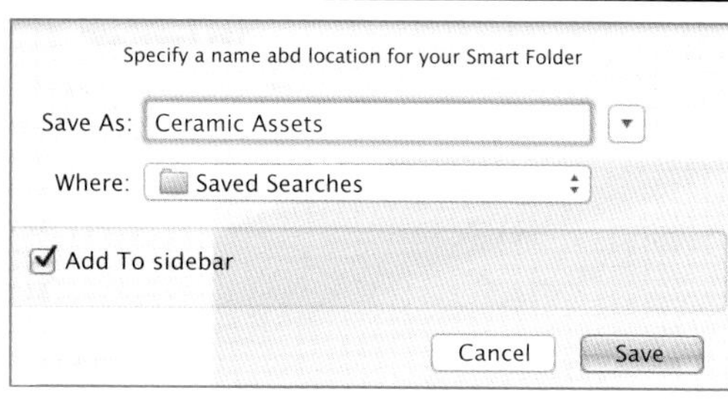

Mac OS X's built-in search feature makes it easy to locate documents based on a wide range of criteria. Use the search box for quick searches, or the Spotlight Window for advanced searches with multiple attributes.

The Spotlight Search Box

To access the search box, press ⌘-Spacebar or click on the magnifying glass on the right of the menu bar. Enter your search term and the matches appear below. Mouse over the search results to see a preview of the contents.

The Spotlight Window

To access the Spotlight Window, press Option-⌘-Spacebar or choose Show All in Finder from the search box results. Click on the plus sign to add new search criteria, such as file type. The "Other" menu option provides access to dozens of search attributes.

Long-term Solutions

Mac OS X's Automator

Automator is a Mac OS X feature that allows users to automate a wide range of functions in the operating system, as well as some applications. You can build Automator workflows or applications via a visual interface—no scripting required.

Document Formats

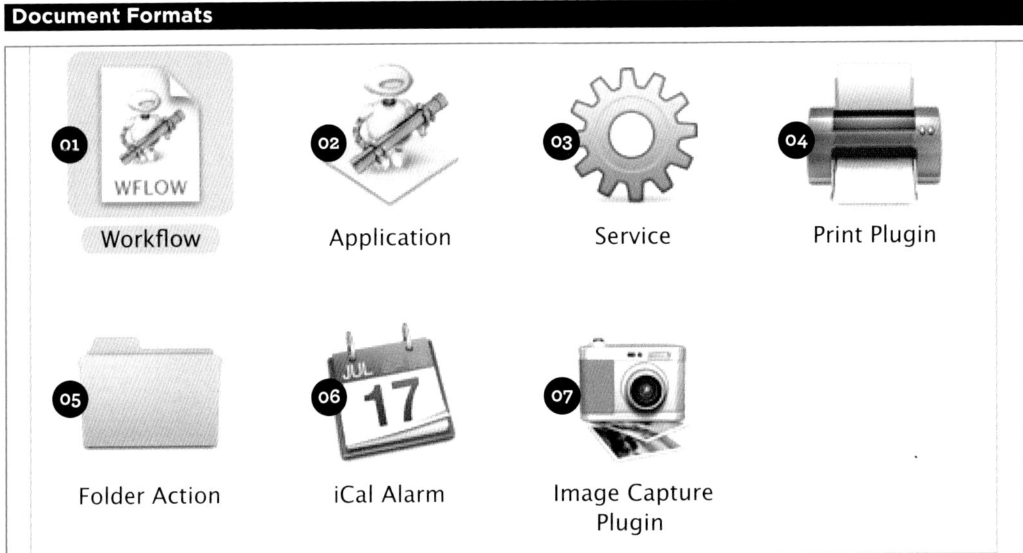

When you launch Automator, it asks you what kind of document you want to create. Your options are:

01. **Workflow:** This is the best starting point for building workflows. Workflows won't run unless Automator is open, so eventually you'll want to convert it to an Application, Service, or Folder Action. To do this, choose File > Duplicate To and select a new format.
02. **Application:** This is a self-running workflow that behaves like any other Mac application.
03. **Service:** This option makes workflows accessible through the Services menu of OS X applications—or via keyboard shortcuts.
04. **Print Plugin:** These workflows are accessible via the PDF menu in the Print dialog box. For example, you can create a plugin that moves newly generated PDF files to a specified folder and renames them.
05. **Folder Action:** These workflows run automatically when you drag files to a specified folder.
06. **iCal Alarm:** These run at specified times and days automatically.
07. **Image Capture Plugin:** These run when you import images via OS X's Image Capture program.

The Automator Interface

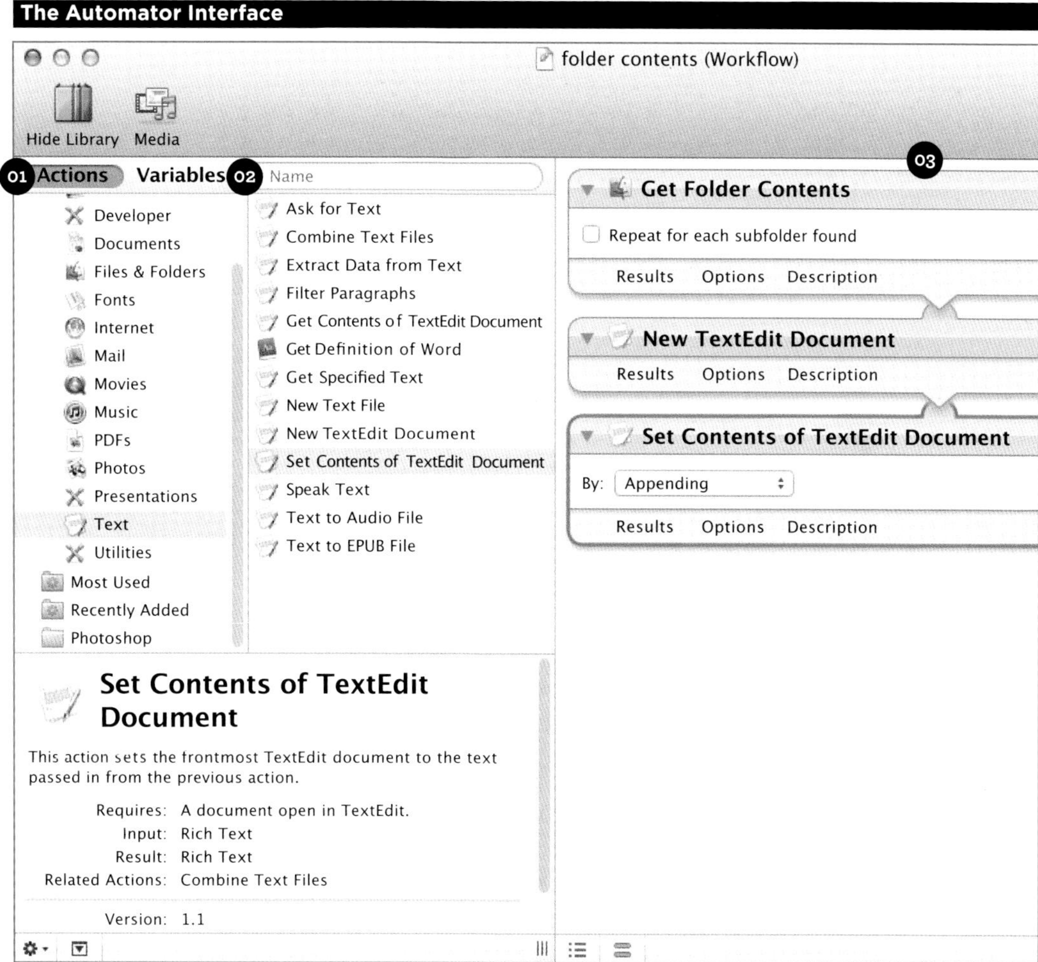

01. Actions Tab: Contains actions that you can drag into a workflow. Click on the categories in the Library pane to filter the list. Click on an action to see a brief description. Each action performs a specified function and sends the results to the next action.

02. Variables Tab: Contains variables that you can drag into workflows. For example, you can insert a variable for the current date, and pass it to an Action that uses the date in some way, such as pasting it into a TextEdit document.

03. Workflow Pane: This is where you build your workflows. You can rearrange actions or variables by dragging on their title bars.

Long-term Solutions

Watch Me Do

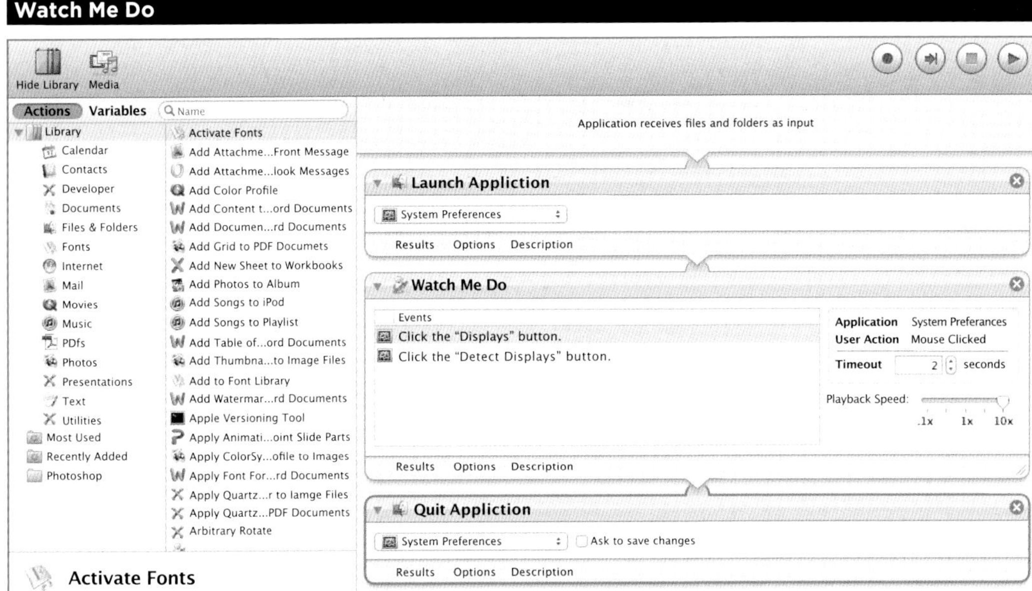

This option lets you record mouse clicks and keystrokes to create actions that otherwise aren't available in the Library.

01. Click the Record button in the toolbar. A recording panel appears.

02. Perform the steps you want to record.

03. Click on the Stop button in the recording panel. This will insert a Watch Me Do action in the current workflow. Each step you performed is listed as an event. You can delete events or rearrange them.

Watch Me Do tends to work better when steps are performed with keystrokes. If you record actions with mouse clicks, they won't run correctly if windows are resized or in different positions.

Creating a Service in Automator

You can use Automator to create Services that launch applications via keyboard shortcuts:

01. Drag Launch Application from the Utilities category to the workflow.

02. In the Service Receives menus, choose No Input in Any Application.

03. Choose the application you want to launch. Click on Other if it doesn't appear in the list.

04. Save the new service.

05. Choose System Preferences > Keyboard to assign a shortcut that launches the application.

Automator and Photoshop

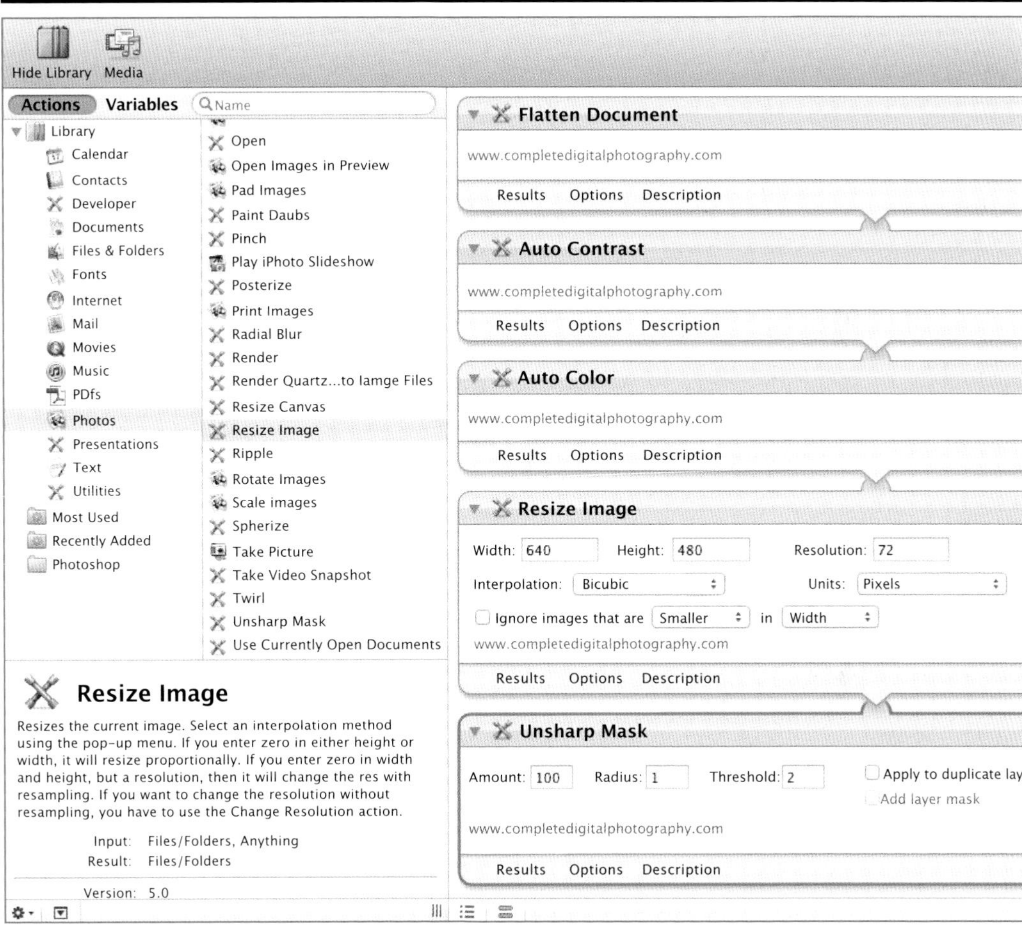

By itself, Automator won't automate Photoshop or other Creative Suite applications. However, Robot Photoshop (http://www.robotphotoshop.com) provides a collection of free and premium Automator Actions that enable you to build workflows that include Photoshop functions. A basic package of 30 actions is available for free. The $20 "Pro" bundle provides 67 additional actions. The website also includes Automator tutorials.

You can find additional websites that offer downloadable actions and workflows by Googling "Automator Actions" or "Automator Workflows."

Long-term Solutions

Photoshop Actions

Photoshop's Actions can save lots of time by automating repetitive tasks. You can run them as you're editing images, or use the Batch function or Image Processor to run them on a folder full of images.

The Actions Panel

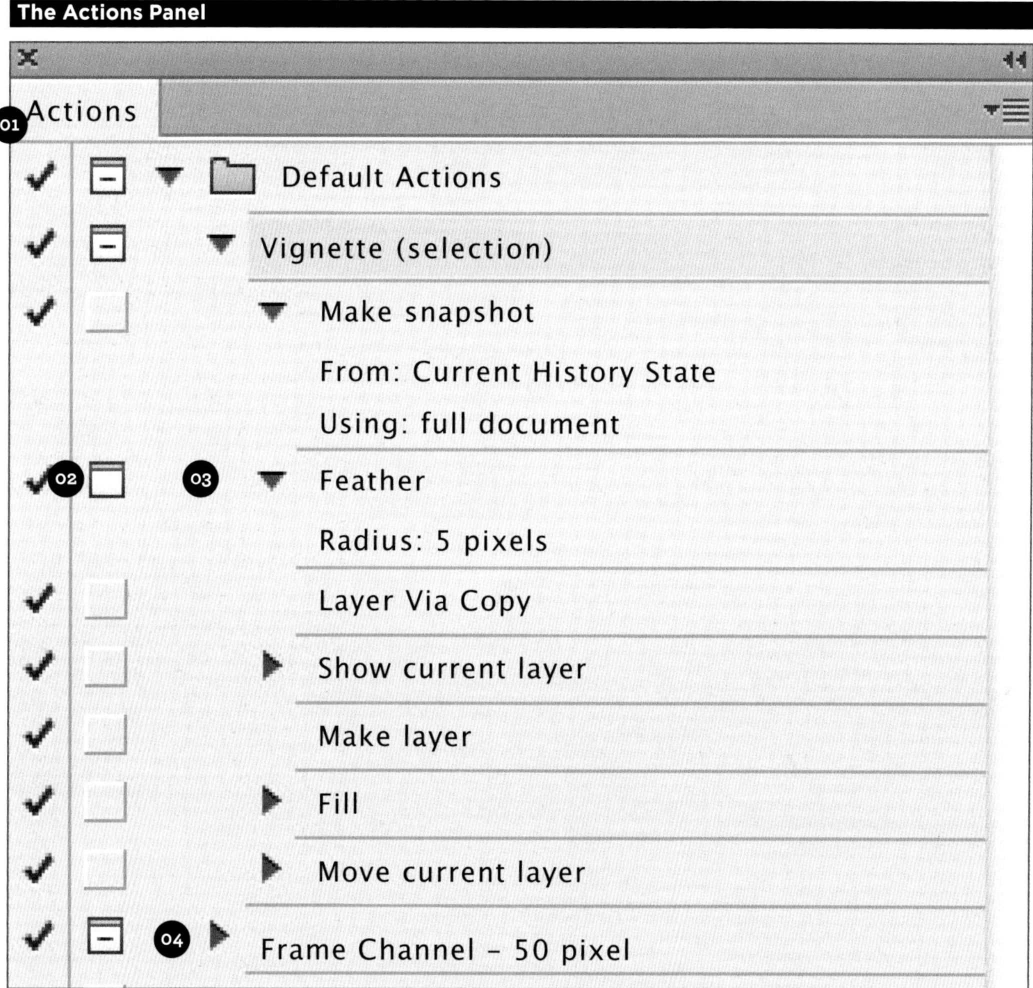

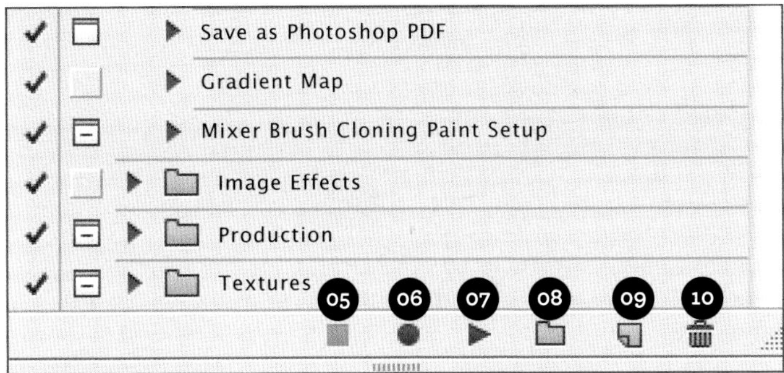

01. **Prevent Play Back:** Uncheck this box to prevent a step from playing back when the action runs.
02. **Modal Control:** Click here to toggle the modal control, which determines whether the action will open a dialog box for this step when it plays back. If the box is empty, Photoshop will use the settings that applied when the action was recorded.
03. **Disclosure Triangles:** Click on these to see the steps contained within an action, and the optional settings for each step. Double-click on the settings to change them. For example, if the step opens the Feather dialog, you can double-click to set a new feather radius.
04. **Disable Modal Controls:** This modal control icon indicates that the action contains at least one step that will open a dialog box. Toggle this off to disable all modal controls in the action.
05. **Stop Recording/Playback**
06. **Begin Recording**
07. **Play Selection**
08. **Create New Set**
09. **Create New Action**
10. **Delete**

Recording Actions

01. Click on the Create New Action button.
02. Give the action a name, and choose which set should contain it. It's a good idea to create a set for your own actions so they're not mixed up with the default set. You can also assign the action to a function key.
03. Click Record to begin recording the action.
04. Perform the steps you want to include in the action.
05. When you're done, click on the Stop Playing/Recording button.

Modifying Actions

You can easily edit actions after you've created them. To delete a step, just select it and click on the trash can. You can rearrange the steps by dragging them up or down within the action. You can even copy steps from one action to another by dragging them while pressing the Option (Alt) key.

To add new steps to an existing action:

01. Select the step preceding the ones you want to add. Or select the action to add steps at the end.
02. Click on the Begin Recording button.
03. Perform the additional steps. When you're done, click on the Stop Playing/Recording button.

Long-term Solutions

Nonrecordable Tools and Commands

Most commands in the View and Window menus are not recordable. However, you can use this alternative to insert any menu item without recording an action:

01. Select the step preceding the menu item you want to add.
02. Choose Insert Menu Item from the panel menu.
03. Choose the menu item you want to add.
04. Click OK. The menu item will be inserted into the action. If the menu item opens a dialog box, you can double-click on the step you just created to modify its settings.

In CS5 and earlier versions, the painting and toning tools are not recordable. In CS6, the new Allow Tool Recording in the panel menu lets you record actions that include these tools.

Another option for including nonrecordable operations is to insert a Stop. This pauses the action, allowing you to apply painting tools or perform other steps before resuming. You can insert a Stop while you're recording the action, or afterward.

01. If you've already recorded the action, select the step preceding the stop you want to add.
02. Choose Insert Stop from the panel menu.
03. You can add a message with instructions about what to do.
04. Check Allow Continue to enable the action to keep playing after the stop.
05. Click OK. The Stop should appear in the Actions panel.

Tips for Working with Actions

Actions		
Vignette (selection)	Frame channel - 50 pixel	Wood frame - 50 pixel
Cast Shadow (type)	Water reflection (type)	Custom RGB to Grayscale
Molten Lead	Make Clip Path (selection)	Sepia Toning (layer)
Quadrant Colors	Save as Photoshop PDF	Gradient Map
Mixer Brush Cloning Pain...	Aged Photo	Blizzard
Light Rain	Lizard Skin	Neon Nights
Oil Pastel	Quadrant Colors	Sepia Toning (grayscale)
Sepia Toning (layer)	Soft Edge Glow	Soft Flat Color
Soft Focus	Neon edges	Soft Posterize
Colorful Center (color)	Horizontal Color fade (co...	Vertical Color fade (color)
Gradient Maps	Fluorescent Chalk	Letter Canvas 150
Letter R	Tabloid Canvas 150	Tabloid R Canvas 150
Legal Canvas 150	Legal R Canvas 150	640 x 480
Save As GIF89a Web Palette	Conditional Mode Change	Batch Processing
Reduced Color Palette	Fit Image	Custom RGB to Grayscale
Custom CMYK to Grayscale	Make Clip Path (selection)	Save As JPEG Medium
Save As Photoshop PDF	Make Button	Parchment Paper
Recycled Paper	Sandpaper	Wood - Pine
Wood - Oak	Wood - Rosewood 1	Wood - Rosewood 2
Asphalt	Bricks	Black Granite
Cold Lava	Gold Sprinkles	Green Slime

- When recording actions, work on a copy of your image.
- Pay attention to document settings such as color mode and foreground/background color. For example, an action that runs on a document in RGB mode may not work in CMYK or Indexed Color mode.
- If you plan to run your action on files with different sizes, set the ruler units to Percent (Preferences > Units & Rulers).
- Use keyboard shortcuts rather than the mouse to select layers. For example, to select the top layer, press Option-. (Alt+.) on Windows. Otherwise, Photoshop will record the name of the layer, and you may get an error message when running the action on other documents.
- Choose Button mode in the panel menu (above) to provide one-click access to the Actions. You'll have to exit Button mode to edit the actions or record new ones.

Finding Actions Online

Numerous websites provide free or inexpensive actions that you can download. To install an action from one of these sources, choose Load Actions from the panel menu and navigate to your download folder. Some are quite elaborate, and can help you learn more about actions and Photoshop in general.

See Also page 204

Long-term Solutions

Batch Processing in Photoshop

Photoshop's Batch feature lets you run actions on entire folders containing images. You can also create Droplets, which sit on your desktop and run actions on files or folders you drag to them.

The Batch Dialog

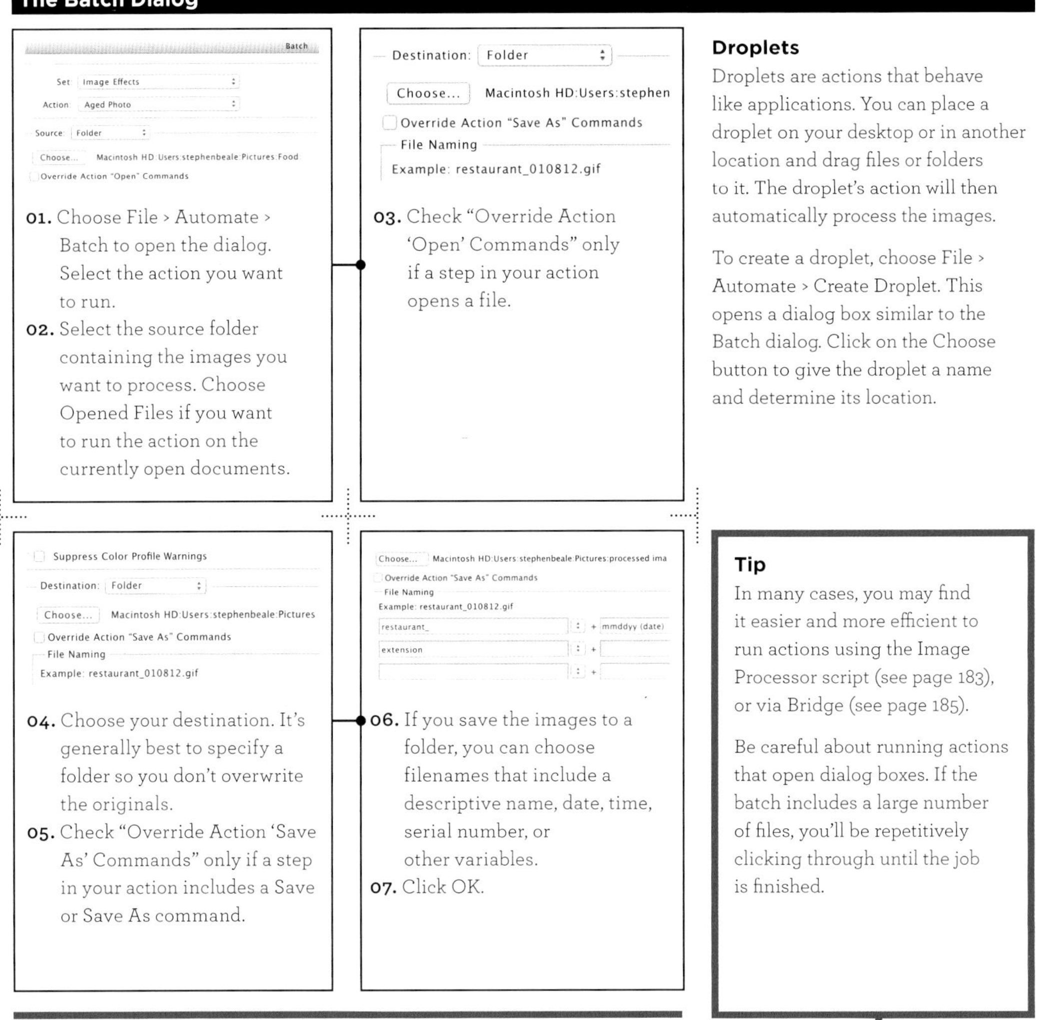

01. Choose File > Automate > Batch to open the dialog. Select the action you want to run.

02. Select the source folder containing the images you want to process. Choose Opened Files if you want to run the action on the currently open documents.

03. Check "Override Action 'Open' Commands" only if a step in your action opens a file.

04. Choose your destination. It's generally best to specify a folder so you don't overwrite the originals.

05. Check "Override Action 'Save As' Commands" only if a step in your action includes a Save or Save As command.

06. If you save the images to a folder, you can choose filenames that include a descriptive name, date, time, serial number, or other variables.

07. Click OK.

Droplets

Droplets are actions that behave like applications. You can place a droplet on your desktop or in another location and drag files or folders to it. The droplet's action will then automatically process the images.

To create a droplet, choose File > Automate > Create Droplet. This opens a dialog box similar to the Batch dialog. Click on the Choose button to give the droplet a name and determine its location.

Tip

In many cases, you may find it easier and more efficient to run actions using the Image Processor script (see page 183), or via Bridge (see page 185).

Be careful about running actions that open dialog boxes. If the batch includes a large number of files, you'll be repetitively clicking through until the job is finished.

Long-term Solutions

Batch Processing in Bridge

With its ability to organize graphics assets, Bridge is ideally suited for batch-processing operations. Rename files, export them to Facebook or Flickr, and apply scripts from Photoshop and other programs.

Batch Rename

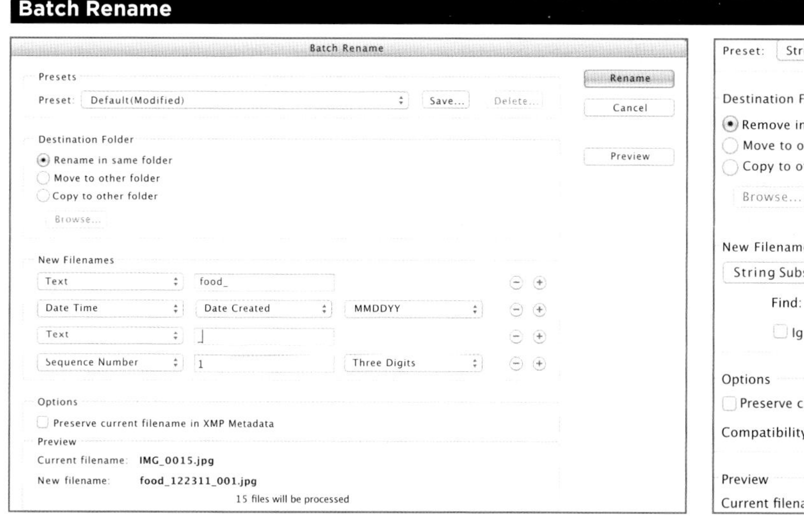

Preset: String Substitution (Modified)
Destination Folder
Remove in same folder
Move to other folder
Copy to other folder
Browse...
New Filenames
String Substitution
Original Filename
Find: __
Repla
Ignore Case
Replace All
Use
Options
Preserve current filename in XMP Metadata
Compatibility: Windows Mac OS Unix
Preview
Current filename: food__15psd

Use this feature to rename groups of files. You can specify descriptive filenames that also include the date, time, and serial numbers.

01. Select the files you want to rename. Press ⌘-A (Ctrl+A) to select all images within the current folder.
02. Choose Tools > Batch Rename or press Shift-⌘-R (Shift+Ctrl+R).
03. Use the drop-down menus to define the new filenames. Use the Text option to include a name that describes the files, or a delimiter such as an underscore. You can also include a date or time stamp and serial numbers. Click on the + (plus) button to add a new segment.
04. The preview section on the bottom shows a sample filename based on your choices. Click on the Preview button to see how all files will be renamed.
05. Click on Save if you'd like to save the formula as a preset.
06. Click on Rename to rename the files as you specified.

You can also use Batch Rename to replace a string of characters within filenames. It works like the Find/Change function in a word processor. First, choose String Substitution as the preset. Then enter the string you want to find and the string to replace it with. In the example above, we want to find two underscores and replace them with a single underscore.

Long-term Solutions

Export

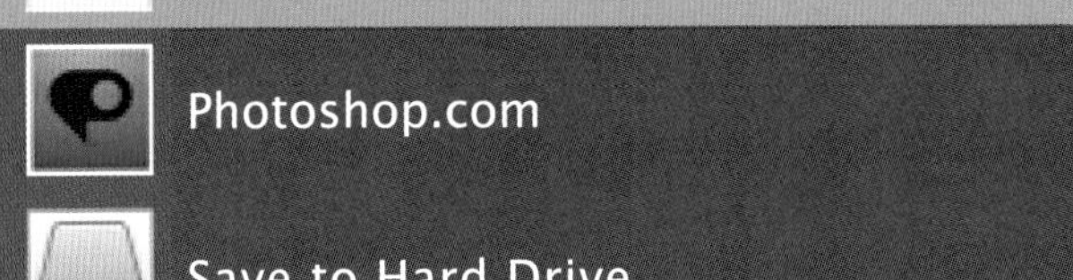

This panel lets you automatically export images to Facebook, Flickr, Photoshop.com, or a specified folder. Images are converted to JPEG format as they're exported. Uploading to file-sharing sites is available only in North America.

01. Double-click on an export module to sign in to your photo-sharing account. You can also customize the export.

02. To set up an export queue, drag images from the Content pane to an export module.

03. To upload the files, click on the diagonal arrow.

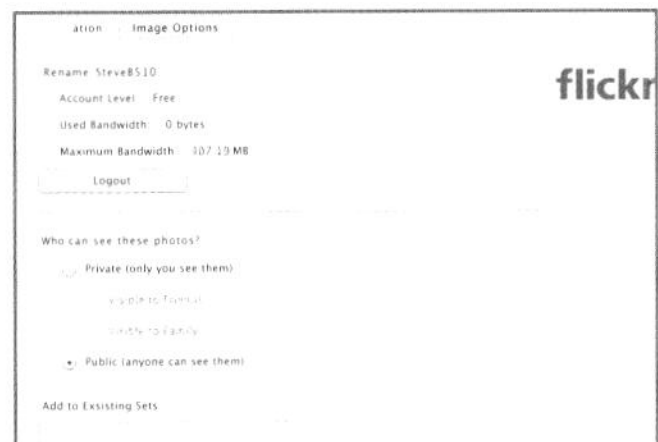

You can sign into a photo-sharing account from within Bridge.

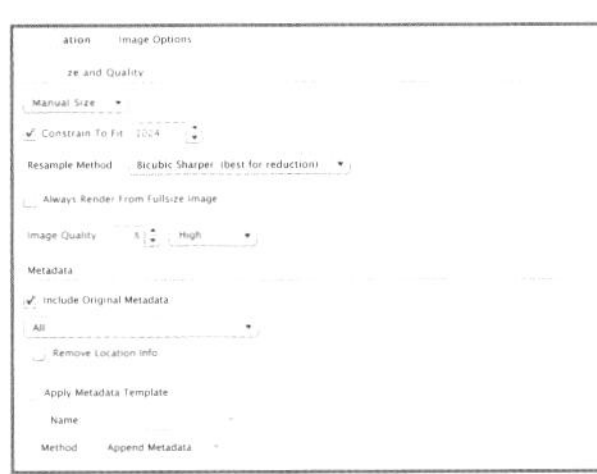

Images are automatically converted to JPEG format before they're uploaded. Use the Image Options tab to choose the image size and JPEG compression level.

Batch-Processing Scripts

Bridge's Tools menu provides access to batch-processing scripts in Photoshop and other CS programs, if they're installed. This is often easier—and faster—than running them from the host program. For example, you can select a group of files and do the following:

- Run Photoshop's Image Processor (Tools > Photoshop > Image Processor) to convert the images to JPEG, PSD, or TIFF format. You can also apply a Photoshop action as the files are converted (see page 170 for details).
- Create a contact sheet (Tools > Photoshop > Contact Sheet II).
- Convert bitmap images into vector graphics (Tools > Illustrator > Trace Image).

Web Galleries and Contact Sheets

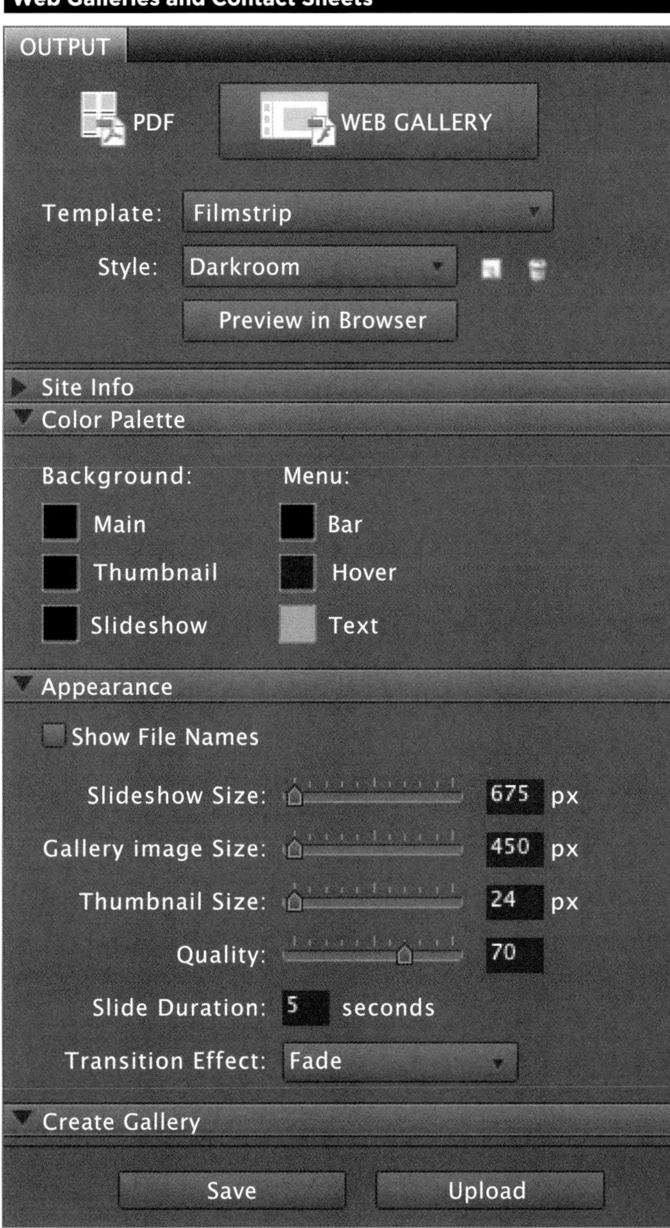

Bridge's Output Module can automatically generate Flash-based web galleries and PDF contact sheets. Either option can be a good way to get quick client approval for images. You can upload web galleries to FTP sites or save them to your hard drive.

Select a folder or a group of images you want to include in the gallery.

Choose Window > Workspace > Output. The images you selected appear in an enlarged preview window.

01. In the Output panel, click on PDF to create a contact sheet, or Web Gallery to create a gallery.

02. Use the Output panel to specify options for your gallery or contact sheet. Choose one of the templates, and then use the panes below to further customize the layout. If you're creating a web gallery, you can specify background colors, thumbnail size, transition effects, and other variables. If you're creating a contact sheet, options include page size, layout dimensions, watermark, and formatting of headers and footers.

03. If you're creating a web gallery, click Preview in Browser to view the gallery before you upload it.

04. Click Save to save your gallery or contact sheet.

Long-term Solutions

Illustrator Actions

Illustrator's Actions can save lots of time by automating repetitive tasks. They're easy to set up and use, especially if you're already familiar with Actions in Photoshop.

The Action Panel

Illustrator's Actions panel (Window > Actions) is virtually identical to the one in Photoshop (see page 170). Use it to record new actions or play back existing ones.

01. Toggle Item On/Off
02. Toggle Dialog On/Off
03. Disclosure Triangles: Click on these to see the steps contained within an action, and the optional settings for each step.
04. Stop Recording/Playback
05. Begin Recording
06. Play Selection
07. Create New Set
08. Create New Action
09. Delete

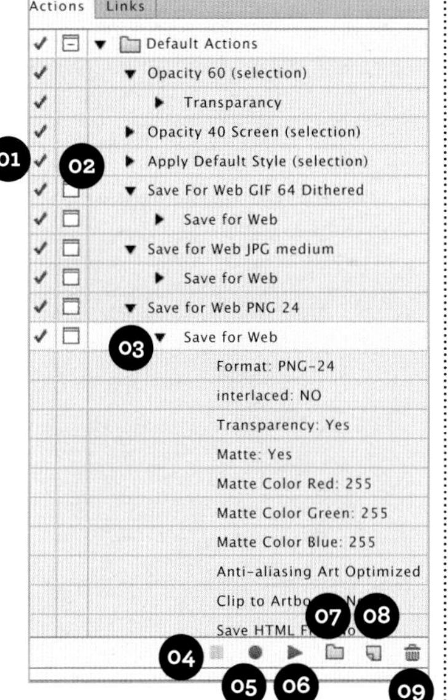

Tip

- Actions with most of the tools are not recordable. These include the Selection, Direct Selection, Pen, Paintbrush, Pencil, Gradient, Mesh, Eyedropper, Live Paint Bucket, Blob Brush, Warp, Symbolism, and Scissors tools.
- Commands in the Effects menus are not recordable. You can add these commands using Insert Menu Item option. However, Illustrator will open the effect's dialog box every time the action plays back, so this is not a good option for actions you plan to apply to a large batch of files.

Batch Processing

As in Photoshop, you can use Illustrator's Batch feature to apply an action to a folder containing artwork.

01. Choose Batch from the panel menu.
02. Select the action you want to run.
03. Select the source and destination folders.
04. Click OK.

Long-term Solutions

Find and Replace in Fireworks

Fireworks' Find and Replace command can replace text, fonts, colors, or URLs in the current document or multiple documents. You can use it with Fireworks PNG files or Illustrator AI files.

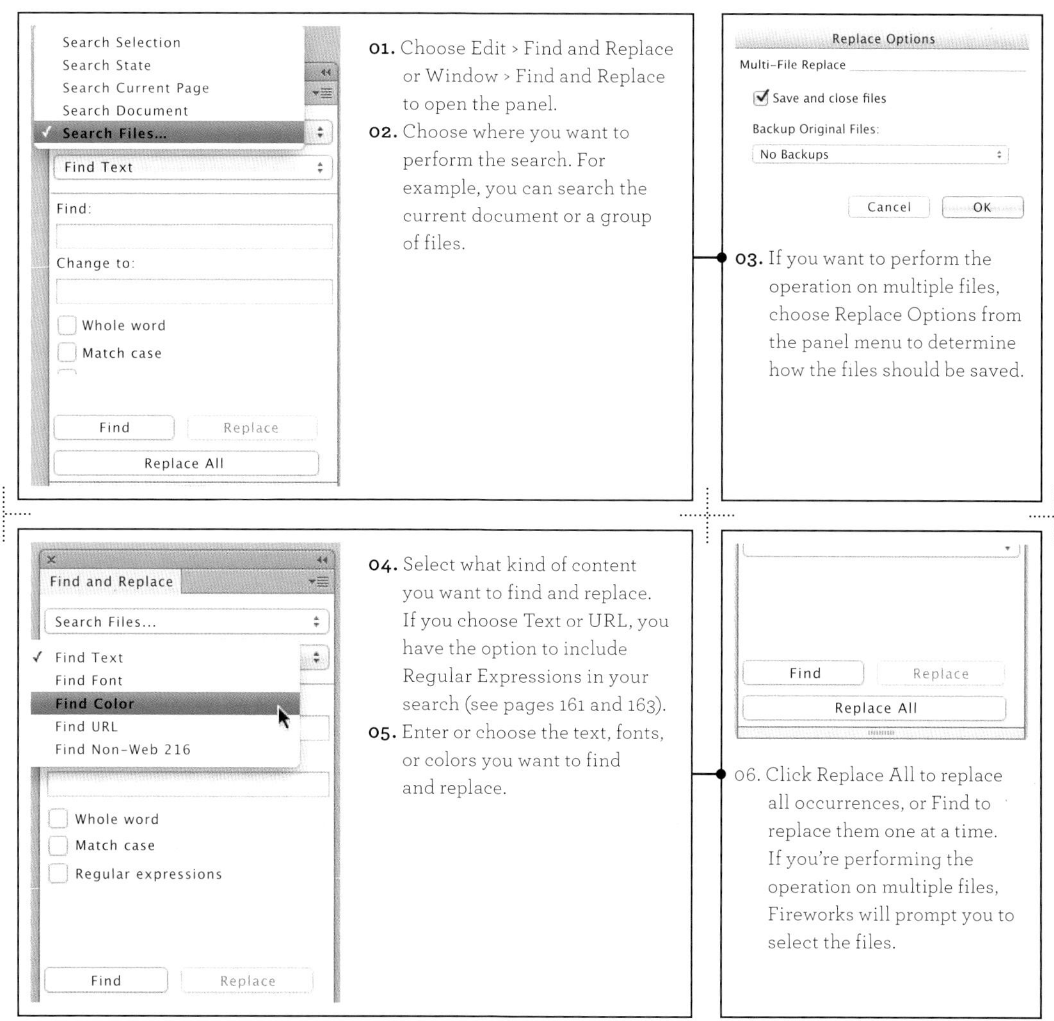

01. Choose Edit > Find and Replace or Window > Find and Replace to open the panel.
02. Choose where you want to perform the search. For example, you can search the current document or a group of files.
03. If you want to perform the operation on multiple files, choose Replace Options from the panel menu to determine how the files should be saved.
04. Select what kind of content you want to find and replace. If you choose Text or URL, you have the option to include Regular Expressions in your search (see pages 161 and 163).
05. Enter or choose the text, fonts, or colors you want to find and replace.
06. Click Replace All to replace all occurrences, or Find to replace them one at a time. If you're performing the operation on multiple files, Fireworks will prompt you to select the files.

Long-term Solutions

Batch Processing in Fireworks

Fireworks' batch-processing function lets you apply selected commands to a group of files. You can run it from Fireworks or Bridge.

BATCH PROCESS

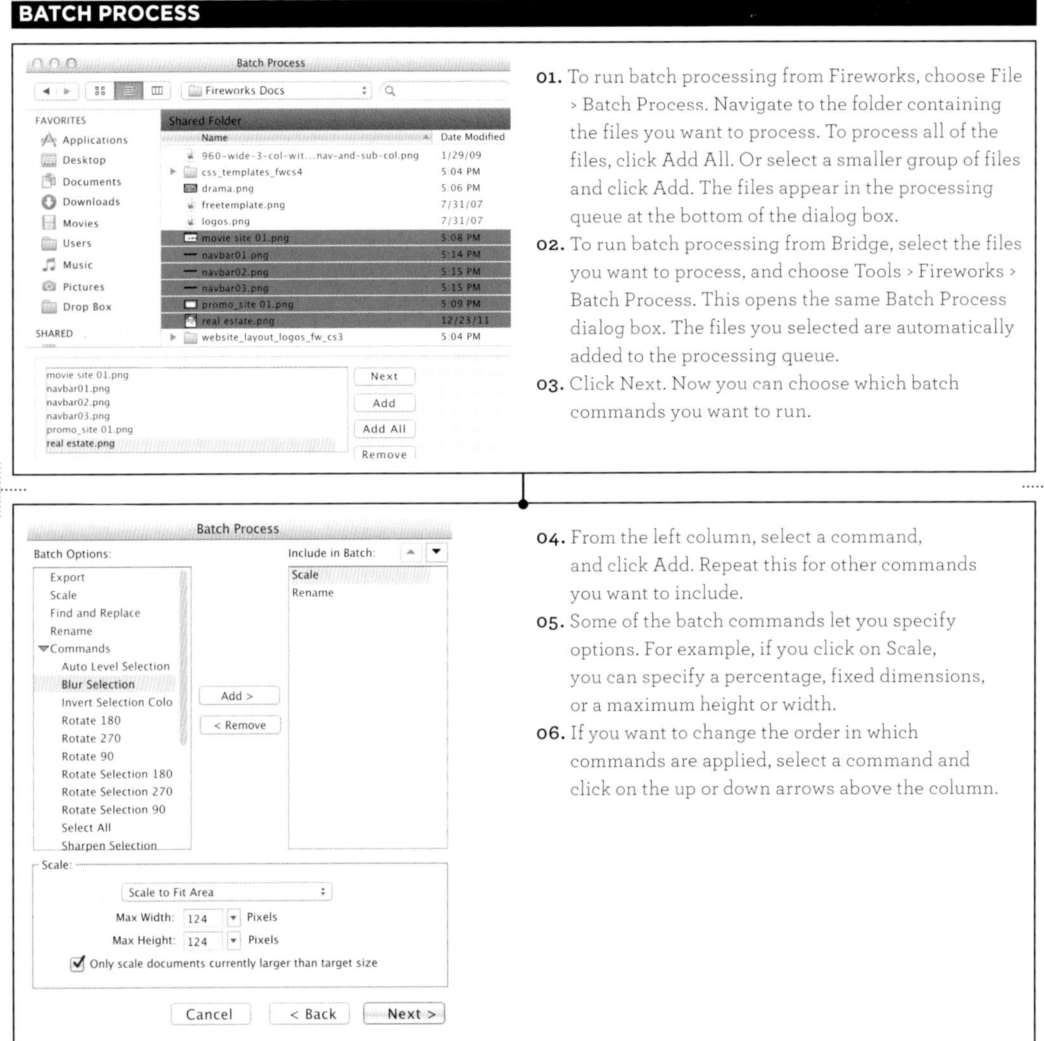

01. To run batch processing from Fireworks, choose File > Batch Process. Navigate to the folder containing the files you want to process. To process all of the files, click Add All. Or select a smaller group of files and click Add. The files appear in the processing queue at the bottom of the dialog box.

02. To run batch processing from Bridge, select the files you want to process, and choose Tools > Fireworks > Batch Process. This opens the same Batch Process dialog box. The files you selected are automatically added to the processing queue.

03. Click Next. Now you can choose which batch commands you want to run.

04. From the left column, select a command, and click Add. Repeat this for other commands you want to include.

05. Some of the batch commands let you specify options. For example, if you click on Scale, you can specify a percentage, fixed dimensions, or a maximum height or width.

06. If you want to change the order in which commands are applied, select a command and click on the up or down arrows above the column.

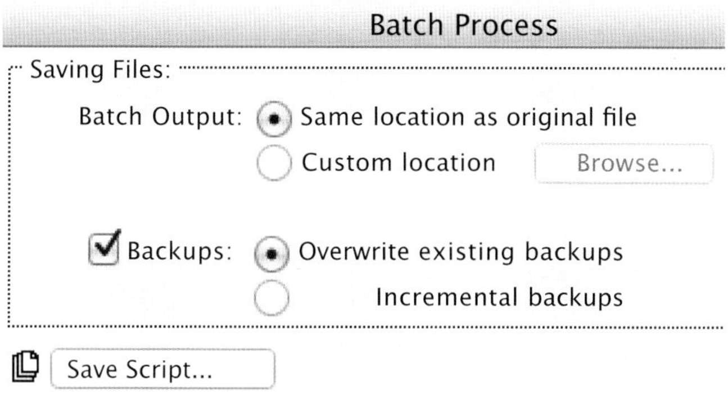

Batch Process

Saving Files:

Batch Output: (•) Same location as original file
( ) Custom location [Browse...]

[✓] Backups: (•) Overwrite existing backups
( ) Incremental backups

[Save Script...]

07. When you're happy with your choices, click Next. Now you can determine how the files will be saved. You can specify a folder, or save the files in their current location. By default, Fireworks will make backup copies of the originals. You can turn this off, but it's a good idea to leave it on. If you specify incremental backups, Fireworks will add numbers to the backup filenames so they don't overwrite previous backups.

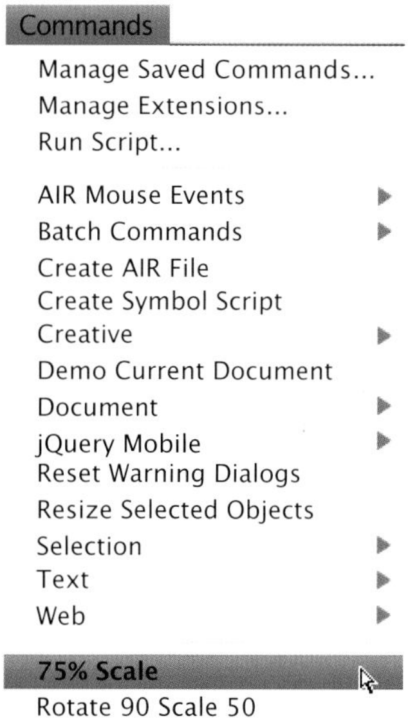

Commands

Manage Saved Commands...
Manage Extensions...
Run Script...

AIR Mouse Events ▶
Batch Commands ▶
Create AIR File
Create Symbol Script
Creative ▶
Demo Current Document
Document ▶
jQuery Mobile ▶
Reset Warning Dialogs
Resize Selected Objects
Selection ▶
Text ▶
Web ▶

75% Scale
Rotate 90 Scale 50

08. If you expect to reuse these batch commands, click the Save Script button. This generates a script that you can access from the Commands > Run Script dialog box.

Tip

Batch-processing operations in Fireworks can include Saved Commands similar to Commands in Dreamweaver (see page 196). You can perform a series of menu operations, such as resizing and rotating an object, and use the History panel to save them as a command. Once you create a Saved Command, it's accessible from the Commands menu and the Batch Processing dialog box.

Long-term Solutions

Scripting

Scripting provides a way to automate, customize, and extend InDesign, Photoshop, and Illustrator. Unlike Actions, scripts behave like real programs, react to user input and perform graphics operations that take advantage of the core capabilities in the host software.

Running Scripts in InDesign

You'll find InDesign scripts in the Window > Utilities > Scripts panel. Open the Application > Samples folder to see the preinstalled scripts. They're intended as learning examples in case you want to create your own scripts, but they also provide useful, time-saving functions.

AdjustLayout: This moves all items in your InDesign layout vertically and/or horizontally by a specified amount. You can set separate values for odd- and even-numbered pages, and limit the adjustment to a specified range of pages.

AlignToPage: Aligns selected objects to the top, bottom, left, or right edge or margin of the page. You can also center objects on the page.

CornerEffects: Applies a variety of corner effects to selected objects. Options are Rounded, Inverse Rounded, Bevel, Inset, and Fancy.

CreateCharacterStyle: Automatically creates a character style based on the formatting of selected text.

CropMarks: Draws crop and registration marks around selected objects.

ImageCatalog: Builds a directory of images from a selected folder, with file names as labels.

Neon: Converts borders of selected objects into gradient fills.

PathEffects: Applies shape distortions to selected objects.

SelectObjects: Selects specified types of objects on the page or spread, such as text frames, groups, or images.

To see descriptions of other scripts, click on the name and choose Edit Script in the panel menu. This opens the ExtendScript Toolkit, Adobe's script-authoring program (see page 185). The script description is near the top, followed by the script itself. Don't try to edit the code, or the script may not run correctly. However, you can save the script under a name and use it as the basis for writing your own.

You'll find more InDesign scripts at the InDesign Exchange on Adobe.com.

Running Scripts in Photoshop

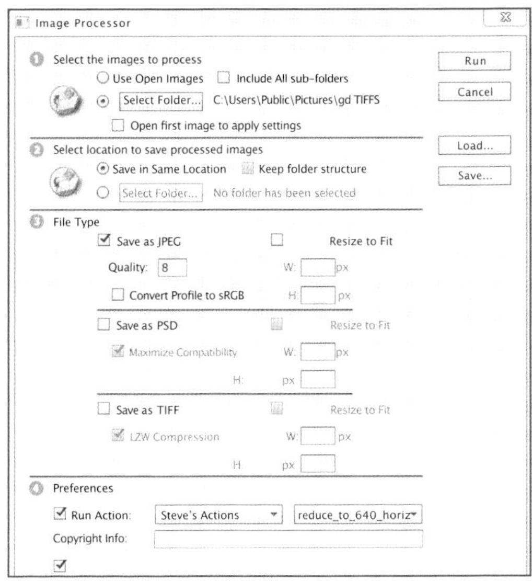

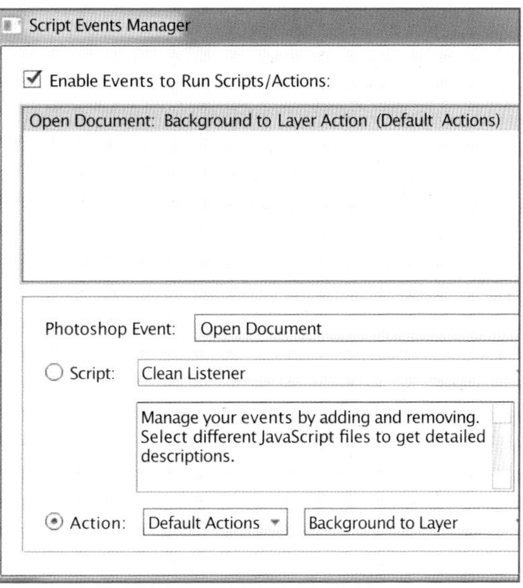

You'll find Photoshop's preinstalled scripts in the File > Automate menu and File > Scripts menu. Some of the most useful ones are listed here.

Image Processor

This script (File > Scripts > Image Processor) is the quickest way to convert a batch of images from one format to another. You can also run it from Bridge (Tools > Photoshop > Image Processor).

01. Select the images to convert.

02. Select a folder to store the converted images, or click on Save in Same Location.

03. Choose the destination formats: JPEG, PSD, or TIFF. You can check as many as you want; files will be converted into each format and stored in separate sub-folders.

04. Under Preferences, you can tell the script to run an action as it performs the conversion. It generally works best with simple actions that don't open dialog boxes.

In addition to format conversions, this script can automatically embed color profiles and add copyright info to each file's metadata.

Script Events Manager

This script (File > Scripts > Scripts Event Manager) lets you use Photoshop events to automatically run a script or action. An event is something that happens in Photoshop, such as launching the program, opening a document, or creating a new document. For example, you might have an action that automatically switches to the Design workspace. Using the Script Events Manager, you can set up Photoshop to run the action whenever it launches. Or an action could automatically convert the background to a layer whenever you open an image.

Here's how it works:

01. In the Scripts Event Manager dialog check Enable Events to Run Scripts/Actions.

02. Use the Photoshop Event pull-down menu to select the event that should trigger the script or action.

03. Click on the Script or Action button and choose the script or action you want to be triggered by the event.

04. Click on the Add button. The script or action you've selected should appear in the list. Then try opening a file or relaunching Photoshop to see what happens.

05. To prevent the action or script from running, use the Remove button to delete it from the list, or uncheck Enable Events to Run Scripts/Actions.

Long-term Solutions

Running Scripts in Photoshop

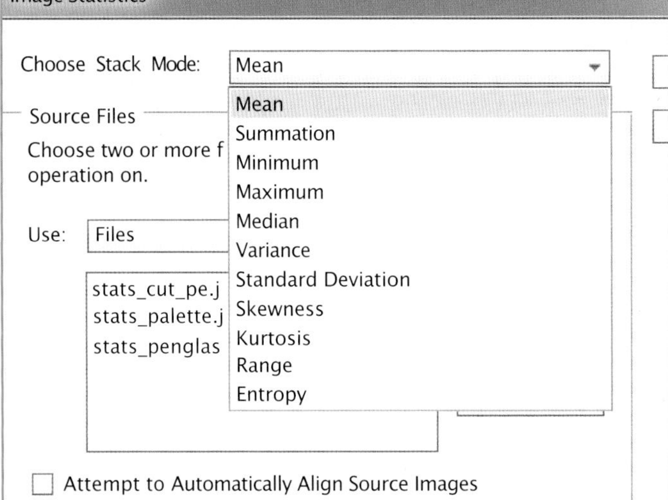

Load Layers

This script (File › Scripts › Load Files Into Stack) automatically opens selected files and stacks them as separate layers in your document. If you're loading multiple versions of the same image, check the Attempt to Automatically Align Source Images option. The script is available only in Photoshop Extended.

Export Layers to Files

This script (File › Scripts › Export Layers to Files) does the reverse of Load Layers; it exports each layer in a Photoshop document into a separate file. Exported file names include the layer name and an automatically generated serial number. You can also add an optional prefix. Files can be exported in BMP, JPEG, PDF, PSD, Targa, TIFF, PNG-8, or PNG-24 format.

Image Statistics

This oddly named script (File › Scripts › Statistics) takes Load Layers a step further. After it imports the layers, it converts them into a Smart Object, and then applies any one of the Stack Modes available in the Layer › Smart Objects › Stack Mode menu. It works best on multiple shots of the same scene. For example, if you choose three photos and the Mean Stack Mode, it adds up the pixel values and divides them by three. It's available only in Photoshop Extended.

Finding Scripts Online

Several websites provide Photoshop scripts that you can download and install. The Photoshop Exchange is a good place to start.

See Also page 202

Running Scripts in Illustrator

As with Photoshop, you run Illustrator scripts from the File › Scripts menu. You'll see a few scripts here that can automatically convert or export documents in various formats. For example, SaveDocsAsPDF converts all open documents to PDFs.

You'll find many more scripts by using File › Scripts › Other Script... to browse to the Sample Scripts folder. This folder is located at C:\Program Files (x86)\Adobe\Adobe Illustrator CSx.x\Scripting (Windows) or Program Files/Adobe/Adobe Illustrator CSx.x/Scripting (Mac).

For the most part, these scripts aren't all that useful on their own. They're intended primarily as starting points for writing your own scripts.

AlignText: Aligns all text to the left.

CountWords: Displays the number of words in the document.

CreateArtboards: Creates a document containing six artboards and adds several star objects.

MakeLinearGradient: Adds a linear gradient to the Swatches panel and applies it to all paths in the document.

Symbols From Styles: Creates a symbol for each object style in the document.

Trees: Randomly draws trees in the document.

Running Scripts in other Programs

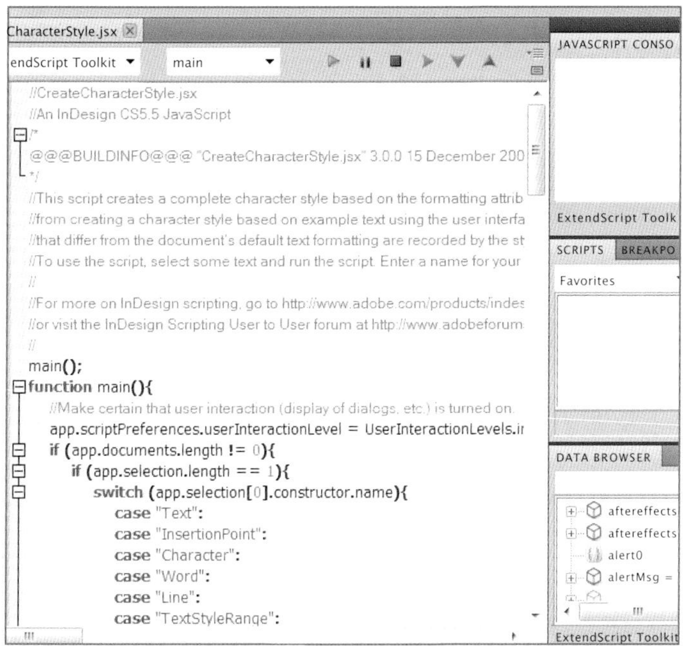

Running Scripts in Bridge

Some Photoshop and Illustrator scripts can be run from the Tools menu in Bridge. This can be an efficient way to apply file conversions or other operations to large groups of selected images:

- Run Photoshop's Image Processor (Tools > Photoshop > Image Processor) to convert images you've selected in Bridge to JPEG, PSD or TIFF formats.
- Use the Live Trace script (Tools > Illustrator > Live Trace) to transform selected bitmap images into vector illustrations. The script includes a dialog box that lets you apply Live Trace presets.

Writing Your Own Scripts

The ExtendScript Toolbox (shown at left) is an environment for writing and editing scripts. Comments at the top of each script usually include a brief description of its function. You can save a script under a different name if you want to try scripting on your own.

You don't have to be a professional software developer to write scripts, but you will need at least a basic understanding of one of three scripting languages (and plenty of patience):

- AppleScript is the easiest for nonprogrammers to learn, but the scripts work only on the Mac. One advantage of AppleScript is that scripts can run from outside of the Creative Suite and interact with other Mac programs.
- VBScript is the Microsoft Windows equivalent to AppleScript. It's similar to the Basic programming language, but runs only on Windows.
- JavaScript is the best choice if you want your scripts to run on Macs and Windows PCs.
- Adobe provides a series of PDF scripting guides for Photoshop, Illustrator and InDesign available from Adobe.com.

Long-term Solutions

Online Sources for Scripts

Ajar Productions
(http://www.ajarproductions.com/pages/products)

This software vendor offers free Illustrator and InDesign scripts, free Flash extensions, and a commercial lip-syncing extension for Flash.

Illustrator Praxis
(http://illustrator.hilfdirselbst.ch/dokuwiki/en/uebersicht)

This Illustrator Wiki site includes free scripts. It's available in English and German.

InDesign Secrets
(http://indesignsecrets.com)

An indispensable resource for InDesign users, the site includes a section containing free scripts and plugins.

Kelso Cartography
(http://kelsocartography.com/scripts)

This website provides links to scripts and plugins for Illustrator and FreeHand.

The Light's Right Studio
(http://www.thelightsrightstudio.com/photoshop-tools.htm)

This photo firm's website includes a section with free Photoshop Actions, scripts and tool presets. The scripts were developed for CS2 and CS3 but also work in later versions.

S.H.'s Page (http://park12.wakwak.com/~shp/lc/et/en_aics_script.html)
This website has free scripts for all recent versions of Illustrator. It's available in Japanese with an English translation.

Scripting Illustrator
(http://js4ai.blogspot.com)

This Illustrator scripting blog also has links to free scripts by the author.

Scriptographer
(http://scriptographer.org)

This website provides an open-source scripting plugin for Illustrator along with a scripting exchange.

Scriptopedia
(http://www.scriptopedia.org)

This website has links to scripts for Photoshop, Illustrator, and InDesign. It also can connect you to developers if you need custom scripts. It's available in French with an English translation.

Trevor Morris Photographics
(http://morris-photographics.com/photoshop/scripts)

This photographer and Photoshop expert offers script development services. His website includes a variety of free scripts.

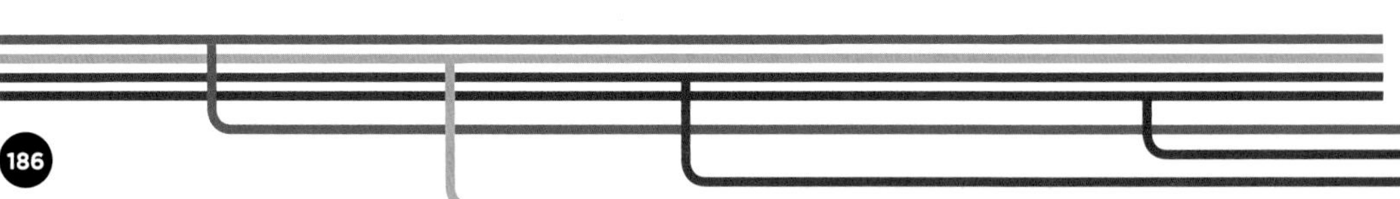

Long-term Solutions

Photoshop Plugins

Photoshop's popularity has spawned an active community of plugin developers. The plugins highlighted here should be especially useful for designers seeking to improve productivity. They're all available as free trial downloads so you can test them yourself.

Perfect Mask

This $100 plugin from onOne Software (www.ononesoftware.com) improves on Photoshop's masking functions, especially if you're working with difficult selections such as those involving hair or fur.

01. You can begin the masking processing by applying features that automatically remove solid backgrounds or make a quick initial selection. Other tools let you refine the mask. For example, you can use Eyedropper tools to create palettes of "Keep" and "Drop" colors for different parts of an image. When you paint over the image with the Magic Brush tool, the "Drop" colors are automatically removed.

02. When you're done, you can apply the mask to the current layer, a new layer, a layer mask, or a copy of the image with a layer mask.

Long-term Solutions

Perfectly Clear

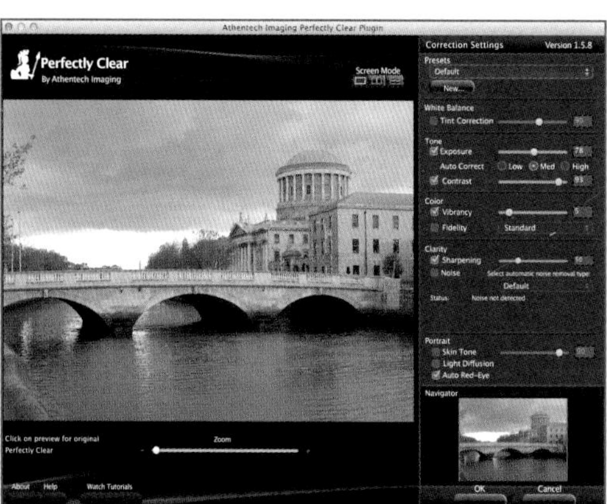

This plugin from Athentech Imaging (www.athentech.com) performs a series of automatic image corrections, including white balance, exposure, contrast, color vibrancy, sharpening, noise reduction, and red-eye removal. With most images, the default settings will noticeably improve quality. However, you can also use built-in presets for portraits, landscapes or dark or noisy images, or tweak the controls to create your own presets.

Correcting an image with Perfectly Clear can be much faster than using Photoshop's built-in adjustment tools. But its real power comes when you run it on batches of images:

01. Create a Photoshop action that runs the plugin (see page 170).

02. Use the Image Processor script (see page 183) to apply the action to a folder containing images.

03. Image Processor will run the action and save copies of the images in separate folders for each format you specified.

04. Use Bridge to inspect the corrected images. Most should look better than before, but you may find a few that you want to correct manually in Photoshop. Because the images are copied into new folders, you will still have access to the original, unmodified versions.

Long-term Solutions

Eye Candy

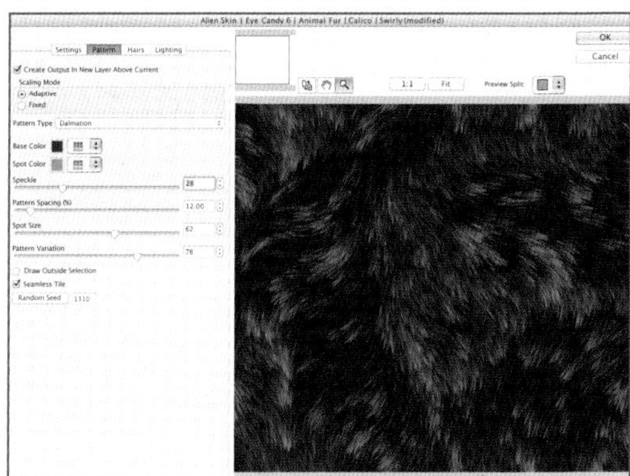

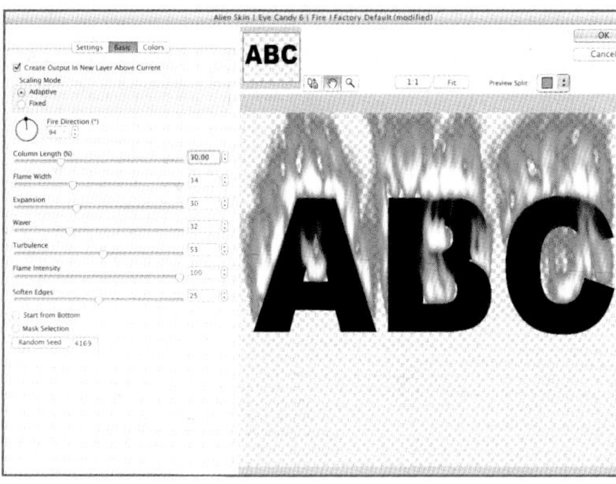

This plugin package from Alien Skin Software (www.alienskin.com) includes 30 filters that make it easy to generate a wide range of photorealistic textures, backgrounds and image effects. They're divided into two sets:

Eye Candy Textures are useful as backgrounds, textures, or fill patterns. The image above left shows the Fur filter in Eye Eye Candy Textures.

The Eye Candy Text & Selection filters work best on text layers and those with layer masks or selections. The image above right shows the Fire filter in Eye Candy Text & Selection.

To use these filters most productively:

01. Begin with a built-in preset that most closely approximates the effect you'd like.

02. Use the plugin's controls to modify the preset. For example, Wood controls include ring thickness, pulp color, bark color, knot size, and grain density.

03. Save your new settings as a preset. They will appear in the User Settings panel whenever you open the filter.

Long-term Solutions

Eye Candy

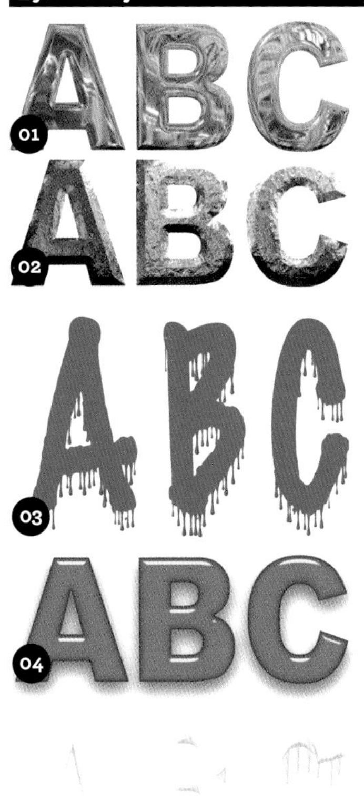

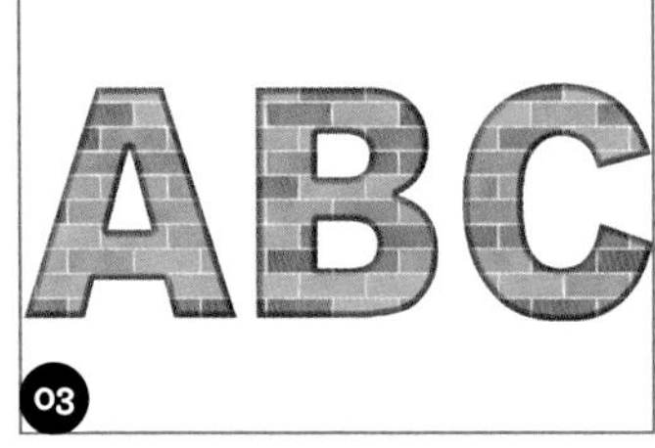

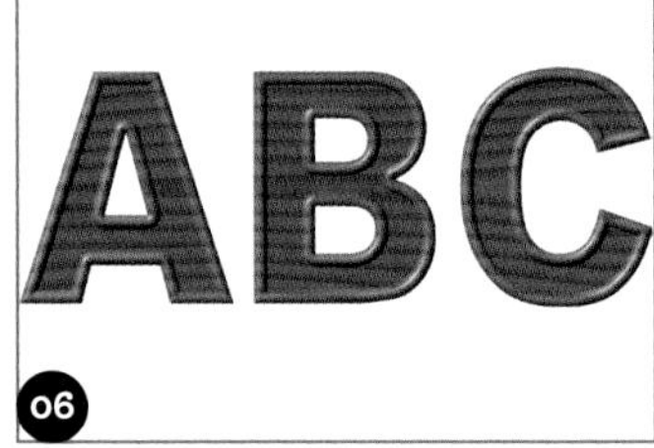

A Sampling of Text & Selection Filters:

01. Chrome with default settings
02. Chrome with Dark Forest preset
03. Drip
04. Glass
05. Snow Drift and Icicles (applied separately to same text)

A Sampling of Textures Filters:

01. Animal Fur (applied separately to the text and background layers)
02. Weave (applied separately to the text and background layers)
03. Brick Wall with Bevel
04. Brushed Metal (Copper preset) with Bevel
05. Stone Wall with Perspective Shadow
06. Wood with Bevel

Long-term Solutions

Snap Art

Also from Alien Skin, Snap Art transforms photos into digital paintings, going far beyond Photoshop's artistic effects filters. It has dozens of presets in categories such as Color Pencil, Comics, Crayon, Oil Paint, Pastel, Pencil Sketch, Stylize, and Watercolor.

As with Eye Candy, the best approach is to begin with a preset and then use the controls to customize it. For example, you can set the paint thickness and amount, so that brush strokes appear to rise from the canvas.

For the best results, images should be printed at 300 dpi or more. You should scale the images to their final size and resolution before applying the filter.

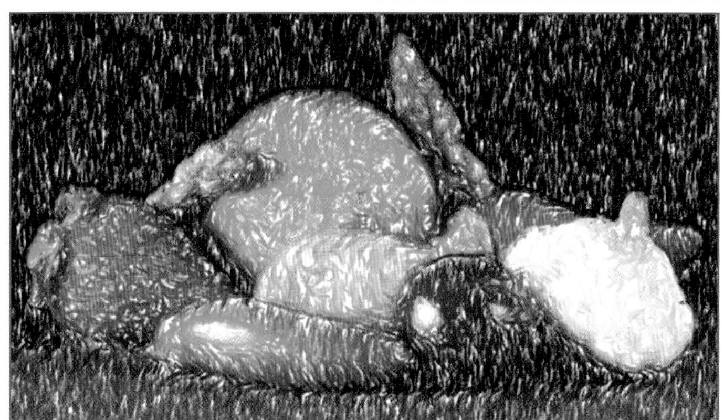

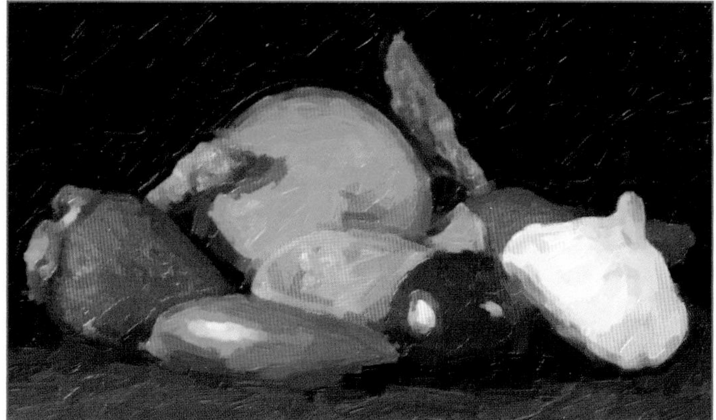

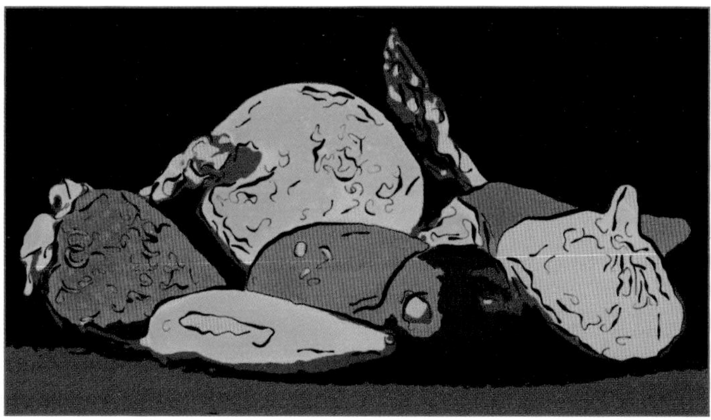

Long-term Solutions

Additional Plugins

Here are some other sources of Photoshop plugins. Most are available as free trial downloads from the websites. You'll find user ratings for some of these at the Adobe Photoshop Marketplace on Adobe.com.

Akvis
(http://akvis.com)
This company provides plugins for sharpening, masking, noise reduction, painting effects, lighting effects, and other image enhancements. They're available individually or in various bundles.

Auto FX Software
(www.autofx.com)
One of the early plugin developers, Auto FX offers a wide range of photo-effects products available separately or in bundles. They include Photo/Graphic Edges for frame effects; the DreamSuite Series of artistic effects; and Mystical Focus, which provides lens effects.

Digital Anarchy
(www.digitalanarchy.com)
Products include 3D Invigorator for creating 3D artwork; Beauty Box Photo for retouching of portraits; Primatte Chromakey for blue-screen and green-screen masking effects; Texture Anarchy for creating textures and borders.

Digital Film Tools, LLC
(www.digitalfilmtools.com)
This company's products were originally developed for video special effects. They include Power Mask, a masking plugin, and Light!, which adds realistic lighting and shadows to photos.

Filter Forge
(www.filterforge.com)
This is a family of products for building and accessing free Photoshop filters. The Basic edition provides access to more than 8,000 user-created filters. The Standard and Professional editions allow users to create their own filters.

Imagenomic
(www.imagenomic.com)
This company is best known for Noiseware, a noise-reduction plugin available in two versions: Standard and Professional. The company also offers Portraiture, a plugin for portrait retouching, and RealGrain, a plugin that simulates film grain.

Nik Software
(www.niksoftware.com)
Products include Viveza for exposure and color correction; Dfine for noise reduction; Sharpener Pro for sharpening; and Color Efex Pro, a collection of 250 filter effects; Silver Efex Pro, for black-and-white conversion, and HDR Efex Pro for HDR image creation.

The Plug In Site
(www.thepluginsite.com)
This site offers a series of free and commercial photo-enhancement plugins, including ColorWasher (color correction), FocalBlade (sharpening), LightMachine (shadow/highlight corrections), B/W Styler (black and white effects), ContrastMaster (contrast enhancement), and Noise Control (noise reduction).

Richard Rosenman
(www.richardrosenman.com/software/downloads)
This design firm offers a series of free and inexpensive Photoshop plugins.

The Tiffen Company
(www.tiffen.com)
A leading manufacturer of lens filters, Tiffen also offers the Dfx family of photo effects, some of which mimic traditional filters. They're available as a Photoshop plugin or a standalone program.

Topaz Labs
(www.topazlabs.com)
This company offers plugins for masking, edge-smoothing, noise reduction, lens effects, exposure control, and other image enhancements. They're available separately or in a bundle.

Long-term Solutions

Illustrator Plugins

These plugins extend the capabilities of Illustrator by adding tools, vector effects, and other features to the program. Many are available as free trial downloads. They run on Mac and Windows unless otherwise noted.

Available Plugins

FILTERiT from Cvalley, Inc. *(www.cvalley.com)*
Adds a variety of vector effects to Illustrator, including lens and 3D transform effects. The company's Xtream Path adds enhanced path-editing functions.

PathToolkit from PointExp *(http://pointexp.com)*
Adds numerous drawing and editing tools to Illustrator, including a Fillet tool for rounded corners, a Straighten tool for aligning segments, and an Orient tool for scaling or rotating objects based on a reference axis. The company also offers Rasterino, which provides enhanced functions for working with raster images.

VectorScribe from Astute Graphics *(www.astutegraphics.com)*
A vector plugin available in two versions: Designer ($65) provides enhanced path-editing and measurement tools. Studio ($119) adds dynamic shape tools. The company also offers **Phantasm CS**, which adds color adjustment functions for vector and raster artwork. It also provides exposure control and relinking for embedded images.

FoldUP 3D from Comnet Co., Ltd. *(www.comnet-network.co.jp)*
Enables previews of 2D packaging designs in 3D.

Productivity Pack from Graffix *(http://rj-graffix.com)*
A set of five Illustrator plugins, including Concatenate (connects multiple paths); Nudge Palette (adjust patterned fill); Proof Block (adds proofing instructions on a separate layer); and Cutting Tools. Proof Block is not available for Windows. Each plugin is also available separately.

Andrew's Vector Plug-Ins Collection from Graphic Xtras *(www.graphicxtras.com)*
Includes more than 40 plugins that add various shape, pattern, gradient, color, and symbol effects. Plugin packs are also available separately. The website also offers inexpensive collections of symbols, swatches, styles, and brushes for Illustrator.

CADtools 7 from Hot Door *(www.hotdoor.com)*
Adds eight groups of tools for drawing, editing, labeling, and dimensioning CAD layouts.

Path Styler Pro from Shinycore Software *(www.shinycore.com)*
A plugin for Illustrator and Photoshop that adds bevels and various surface effects to artwork. Surface effects include metallic materials, textures, and reflections.

Worker72a *(www.worker72a.com)*
Offers a family of Mac-only Illustrator plugins for production artists. They include **Scoop**, which collects fonts and placed images into a folder; **SepPreview**, which previews Illustrator documents as color separations; **QuickCarton**, which creates layouts for corrugated cartons;

Point Control, which adds a path-editing panel; and **Select Effects**, which automatically selects objects with live effects, blend modes, or transparency settings that could cause printing or flattening problems.

Long-term Solutions

InDesign Plug-Ins

These products extend the capabilities of InDesign in many different ways. Some are aimed at specific design or production categories, such as book or catalog publishing. The ones here run on Mac and Windows unless otherwise noted.

Database Publishing

EasyCatalog from 65bit Software Ltd *(www.65bit.com)*
Enables direct links between product databases and InDesign layouts. It's available in full and light versions. Additional modules cost extra.

EmCatalog from Em Software *(http://emsoftware.com)*
Also links InDesign documents to databases or spreadsheets for production of catalogs and other data-driven publications.

Cacidi Extreme from Cacidi Systems *(www.cacidi.com)*
A high-end automated production tool for advertising and catalogs. It's available in light and full versions. The company also offers other less costly plug-ins for print production.

DataLinker from Teacup Software *(www.teacupsoftware.com)*
Another plugin that links databases to InDesign documents. It also enables scripting to modify how imported text is formatted. The company also offers TypeFitter Pro, which fixes text oversets and other fitting problems, and BarcodeMaker, a family of barcode plugins.

Book Publishing

Virginia Systems *(www.virginiasystems.com)*
Provides a family of InDesign plugins for book production:

Sonar Bookends InSeq automatically generates numbers for tables, figures, paragraphs, and other elements in books.

Sonar Bookends InDex is an indexing utility available in a "light" version or a pro version.

Sonar Bookends InFnote automatically numbers, sorts, and assigns styles to footnotes and endnotes.

Sonar Bookends InXref automatically generates cross-references for tables, figures, appendices, and other material.

Productivity Tools

DTP Tools *(www.dtptools.com)* offers a wide range of productivity plugins for InDesign.

Active Tables adds spreadsheet functions to InDesign tables.

Text Count adds an info panel that shows character, word, line, and paragraph counts for contents and overset text. It also provides options for managing overset text.

Layer Comps adds Photoshop-style Layer Comps to InDesign. It's also available in a bundle with Layer Groups, which adds Photoshop-style layer groups.

Blatner Tools is a set of 12 plugins by InDesign author/instructor David Blatner.

Annotations imports notes and comments from PDF versions of InDesign documents.

Cross-References PRO adds various cross-referencing features to InDesign.

Gluon
(www.gluon.com)
Another prolific developer of plugins for InDesign, as well as QuarkXPress. The following are Mac only.

Cropster ID adds registration marks, crop marks, dimension arrows, and other guides to InDesign documents.

Slugger ID places trafficking and document info on each page, including color chips, colorbars and lists of fonts, images, and colors. It also lists info about which team members worked on the page.

Greeker ID automatically greeks selected text in a document. It also adds greeked text to empty text boxes.

ColorBreaker adds labels showing color and font usage in InDesign documents.

Linkster links and unlinks text boxes.

ProScale ID adds enhanced scaling functions to InDesign.

magPeople
(www.magpeople.com/w)
Offers a series of plug-ins previously sold under the Knowbody brand.

SmartAlerts provides live warnings of common mistakes involving images and fonts.

Color Markup generates labels indicating which colors are used on each page.

Cool Kerning adds enhanced kerning functions to InDesign.

Cool Tracking adds enhanced tracking functions to InDesign.

Smart Paste lets you define font and style values when importing text.

StampIt adds labels with date/time stamps, font lists and names of users.

LabelIt adds image labels to printed documents.

Markzware
(http://markzware.com)
Offers two file-conversion plug-ins:

Q2ID converts QuarkXPress files to InDesign.

PUB2ID converts Microsoft Publisher files to InDesign.

Zevrix Solutions
(http://zevrix.com)
Offers two Mac-only plug-ins:

InPreflight packages multiple InDesign jobs and adds enhanced preflight capabilities.

LinkOptimizer optimizes images linked to InDesign documents. It reduces image size based on settings in InDesign documents and converts file formats. It requires Adobe Photoshop. The company offers a similar product for Illustrator.

Long-term Solutions

Dreamweaver Commands

Commands in Dreamweaver are similar to Photoshop Actions, allowing you to save a series of operations and replay them later. The interface isn't as friendly as the one in Photoshop, but this feature can still save time on repetitive tasks.

Creating a Command

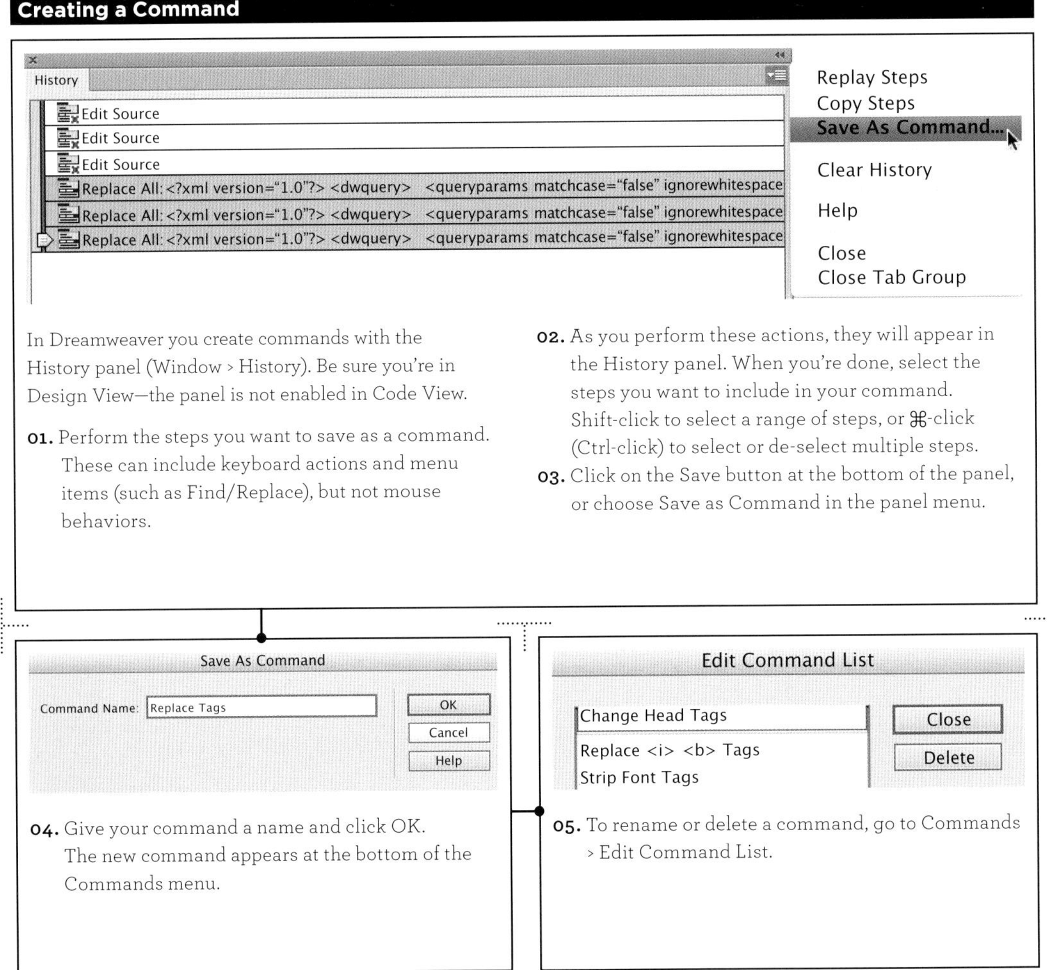

In Dreamweaver you create commands with the History panel (Window > History). Be sure you're in Design View—the panel is not enabled in Code View.

01. Perform the steps you want to save as a command. These can include keyboard actions and menu items (such as Find/Replace), but not mouse behaviors.

02. As you perform these actions, they will appear in the History panel. When you're done, select the steps you want to include in your command. Shift-click to select a range of steps, or ⌘-click (Ctrl-click) to select or de-select multiple steps.

03. Click on the Save button at the bottom of the panel, or choose Save as Command in the panel menu.

04. Give your command a name and click OK. The new command appears at the bottom of the Commands menu.

05. To rename or delete a command, go to Commands > Edit Command List.

Recording Commands

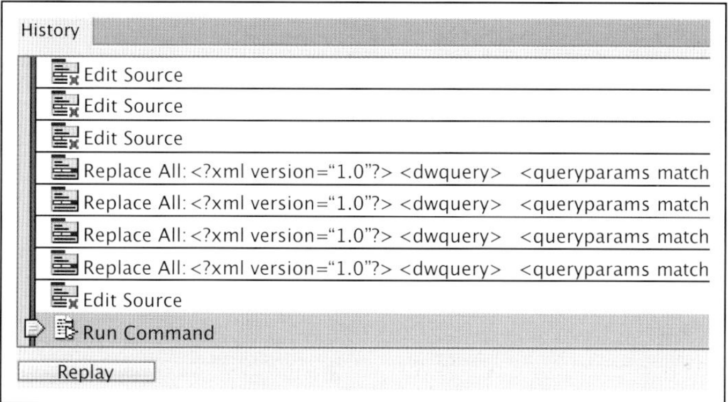

Dreamweaver can record a series of steps for immediate playback. Again, this works only in Design View.

01. Choose Commands > Start Recording.
02. Perform the steps you want to record. Again, you can use keyboard actions and menu commands, but not mouse clicks.
03. When you're done, click Stop Recording. To run the command, choose Commands > Play Recorded Command.

When you record a new command, Dreamweaver overwrites the previous one. However, when you play a recorded command, it appears as a step in the History panel, labeled Run Command. Now you can save the command by clicking on the Save button.

Unlike Photoshop or Illustrator, Dreamweaver does not provide an interface for editing commands. However, each command is saved as an HTML file containing JavaScript code, so experienced JavaScript programmers can modify the commands to suit their needs.

You'll find the files in the following locations:

Mac: /Users/username/Library/Application Support/Adobe/Dreamweaver CS6/en_US/Configuration/Commands/

Windows: C:\Users\Username\AppData\Roaming\Adobe\Dreamweaver CS6\en_US\Configuration\Commands

Tip

Because you cannot include mouse actions in commands, it's a good idea to become familiar with Dreamweaver's keyboard shortcuts. You'll find many on page xx, but to generate a comprehensive list in HTML format, choose Dreamweaver > Keyboard Shortcuts (Mac) or Edit > Keyboard Shortcuts (Windows) and use the Export option.

Long-term Solutions

Dreamweaver Widgets

Widgets make it easy to add sophisticated JavaScript behaviors to your web designs with little or no programming knowledge. Dreamweaver's built-in Spry Widgets let you create elements such as drop-down menus, accordion panels, and tooltips.

Spry Widgets

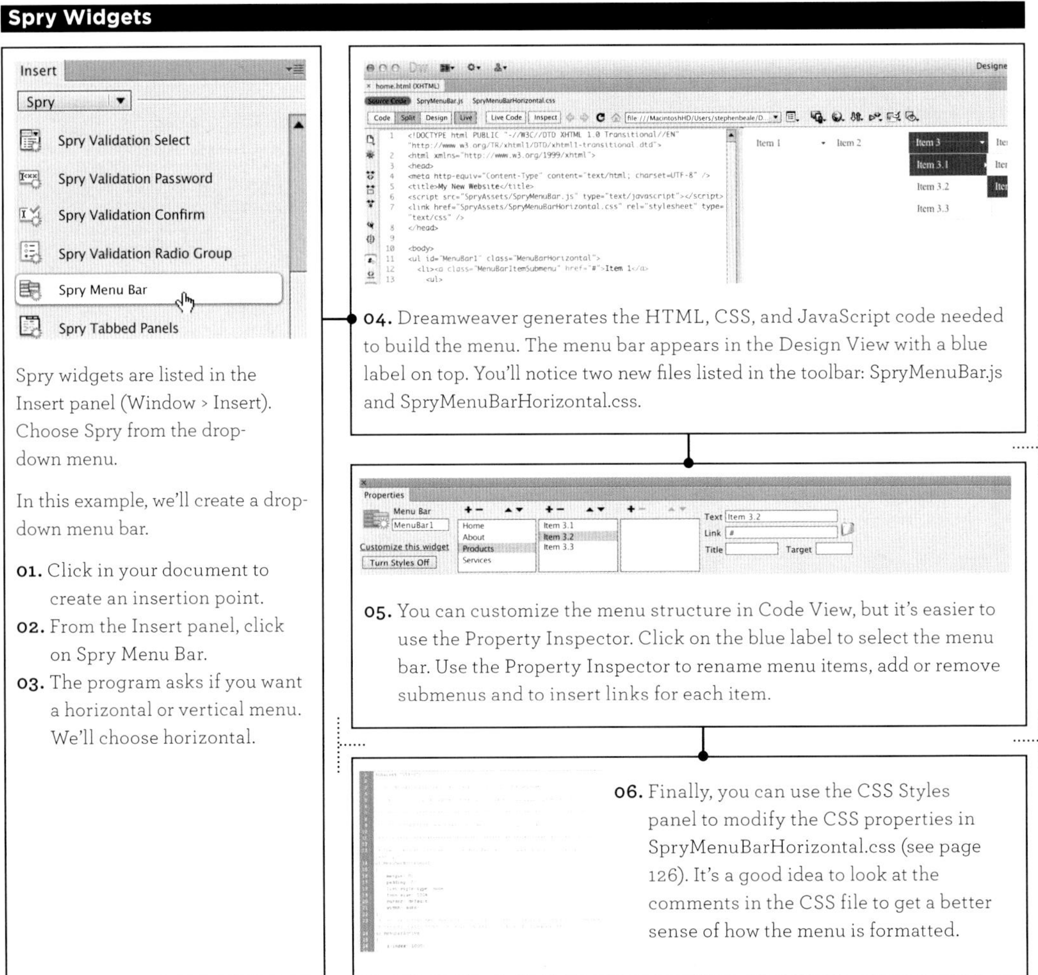

Spry widgets are listed in the Insert panel (Window > Insert). Choose Spry from the drop-down menu.

In this example, we'll create a drop-down menu bar.

01. Click in your document to create an insertion point.
02. From the Insert panel, click on Spry Menu Bar.
03. The program asks if you want a horizontal or vertical menu. We'll choose horizontal.

04. Dreamweaver generates the HTML, CSS, and JavaScript code needed to build the menu. The menu bar appears in the Design View with a blue label on top. You'll notice two new files listed in the toolbar: SpryMenuBar.js and SpryMenuBarHorizontal.css.

05. You can customize the menu structure in Code View, but it's easier to use the Property Inspector. Click on the blue label to select the menu bar. Use the Property Inspector to rename menu items, add or remove submenus and to insert links for each item.

06. Finally, you can use the CSS Styles panel to modify the CSS properties in SpryMenuBarHorizontal.css (see page 126). It's a good idea to look at the comments in the CSS file to get a better sense of how the menu is formatted.

Web Widgets

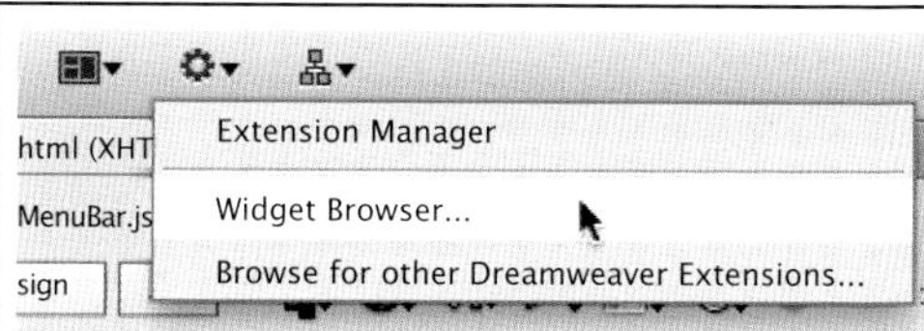

You're not limited to the Spry Widgets—Dreamweaver's Widget Browser helps you find user-contributed "web widgets" posted on the Adobe Exchange.

01. Open the Widget Browser by clicking on the Extend Dreamweaver button (it's the small gear in the Application bar).

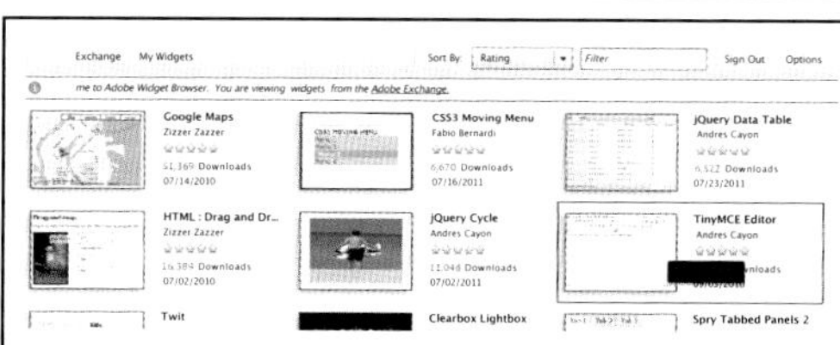

02. The browser has two windows: Adobe Exchange and My Widgets. In the Adobe Exchange window, you'll see each widget listed with a thumbnail, the author's name and other information. Pay attention to the user ratings and number of downloads—that will give you a good sense of the widget's usefulness.

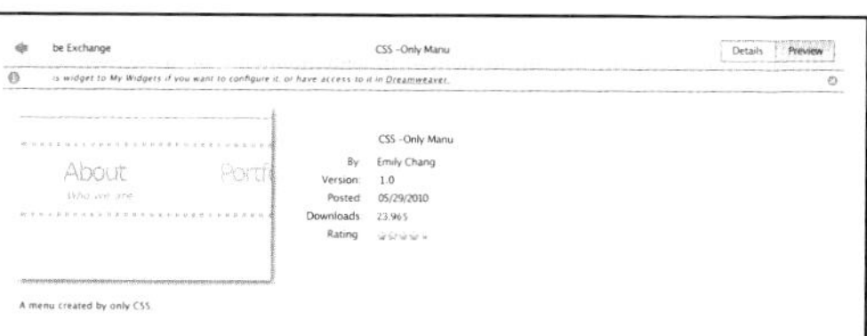

03. Click on a widget to download it. Click on Preview to see how it will appear on your webpage. You can also view the code that generates the widget.

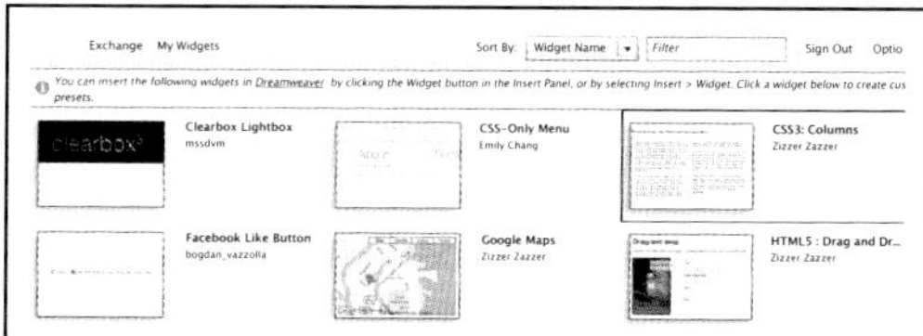

04. If you want to use the widget, click on the Add to My Widgets button. Now it appears in the My Widgets window and the Insert > Widget dialog.

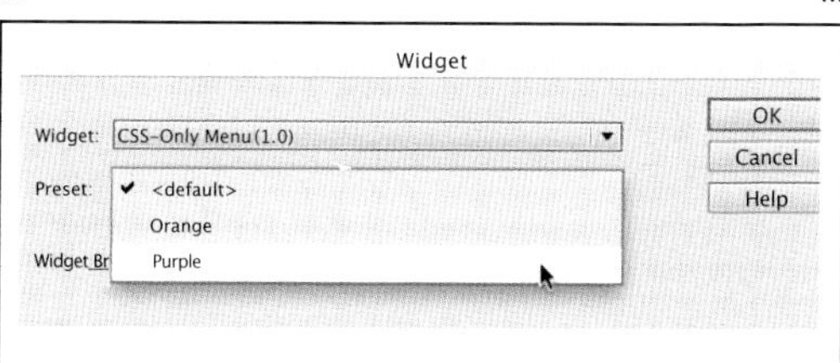

05. Use the Insert > Widget dialog to place the widget on your webpage. When you do so, you can choose from one of the presets.

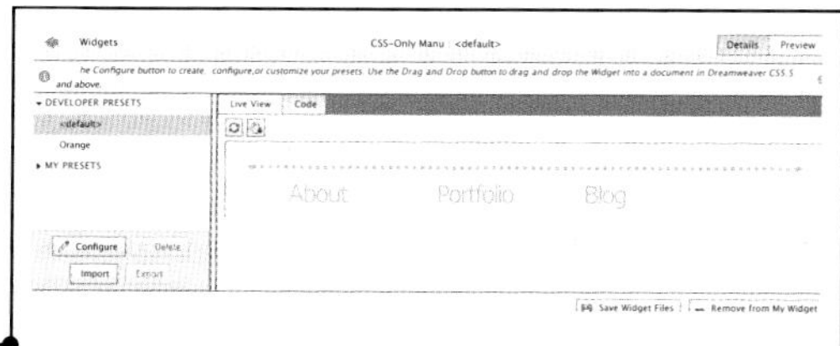

06. To customize the widget, go to My Widgets. Click on its thumbnail, then click on the Configure button. Each widget has its own options, which you can save as a preset.

Long-term Solutions

Dreamweaver Extensions

Dreamweaver Extensions are similar to Photoshop or InDesign plugins, adding useful functionality to the core program. The ones listed here provide tools for rapid website development.

WebAssist

DesignAssist (www.webassist.com) consists of eight Dreamweaver extensions that were previously available separately. The package installs a WebAssist menu in Dreamweaver through which you can access any of the extensions.

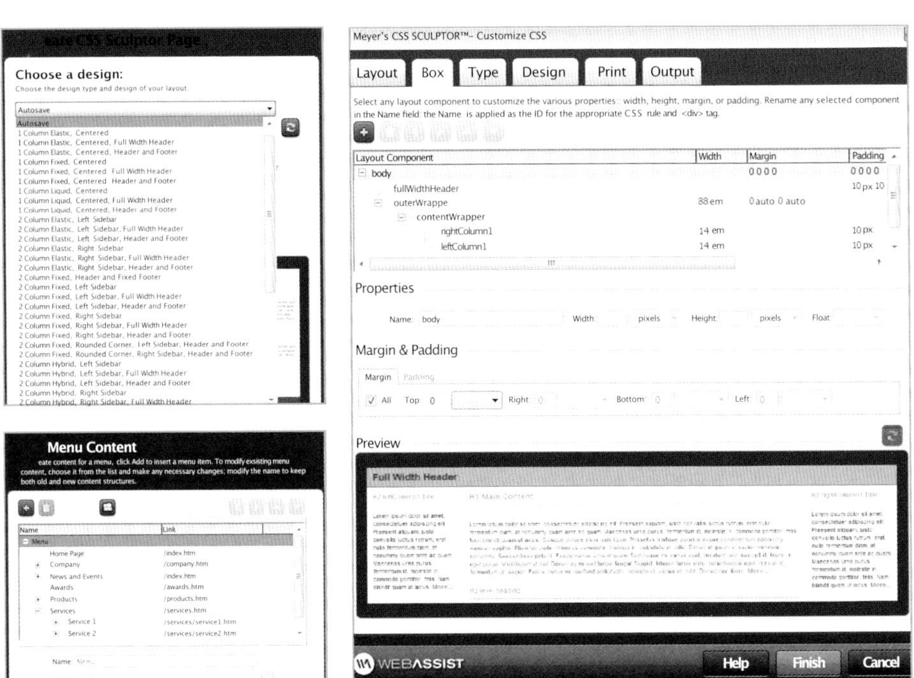

CSS Sculptor: This extension helps you create multi-column CSS layouts. First choose from one of numerous design types. Then customize the layout by navigating through panels that let you set CSS properties, and the program generates the necessary CSS and HTML.

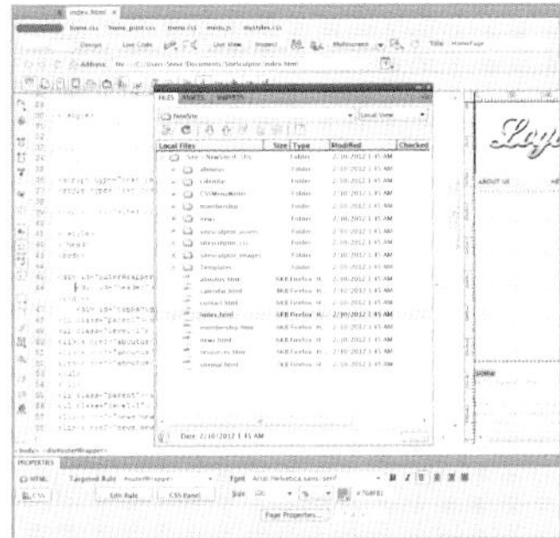

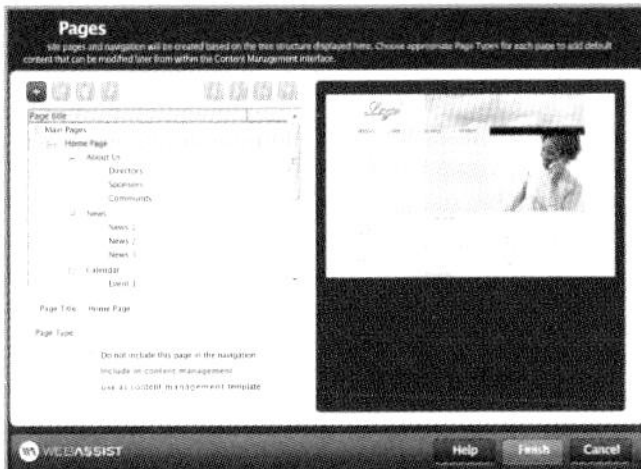

Site Sculptor: The most powerful extension is Site Sculptor, which builds an entire site—including webpages and navigation elements—based on choices you make through a series of wizards. You begin by defining a site type, such as Association, Corporate, Non-Profit, or Special Event, then choose from one of 19 site designs. Each of these is customizable, and once Site Sculptor builds the site, you can further customize it using the tools in Dreamweaver.

Project Seven

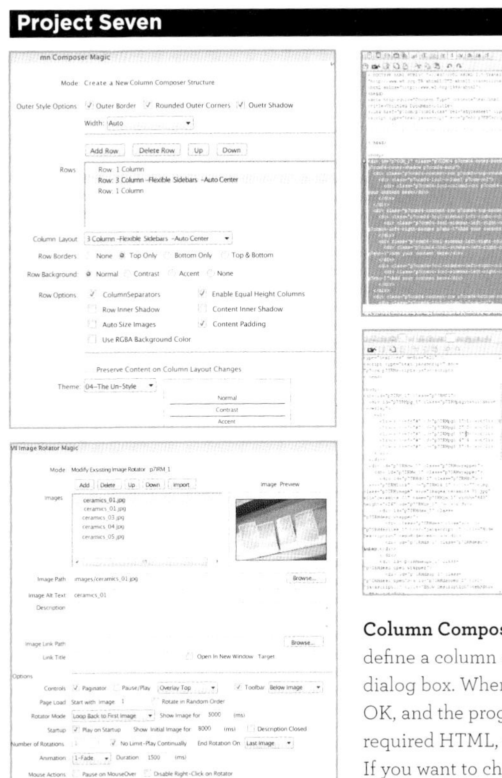

This company (www.projectseven.com) sells extensions for quickly generating CSS layouts, menus, panels, slide shows, galleries, tooltips, and other design elements. You can create many of these elements using free widgets, but the Project Seven extensions can do so more productively and with better results. For example, after you've inserted a widget, you can easily modify your original settings through a user interface instead of wading through CSS or HTML code.

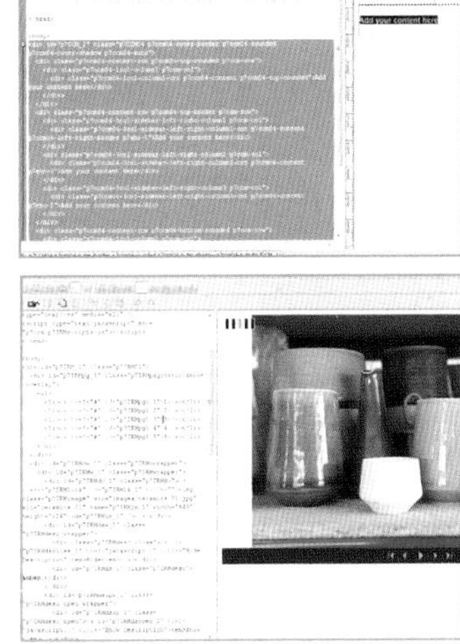

Column Composer Magic: Lets you define a column structure through this dialog box. When you're done, click OK, and the program generates the required HTML, CSS, and JavaScript. If you want to change the structure later, just click on the page and choose Modify > Studio 7 > Modify Column Composer Magic to reopen the dialog box.

Image Rotator Magic: Generates image and banner rotators using CSS and JavaScript. Open a set of images and choose options for navigation and transitions, and you can build a rotator in just a few minutes.

Additional Resources

The more you learn about the Creative Suite and other graphic design applications, the more productive you'll be. Here you'll find information about training resources as well as free or inexpensive products that work with the Creative Suite.

Adobe Resources

Adobe Marketplace & Exchange
www.adobe.com/cfusion/exchange
Clearinghouse for tools and services related to Adobe products. This should be your first port of call when searching for extensions, plugins, scripts, and other resources.

Adobe Labs
labs.adobe.com
Testing ground for new Adobe technologies. Includes public betas of forthcoming products.

Creative Cloud
creative.adobe.com
Adobe's new online service for creative professionals. Subscription plan includes access to the entire Creative Suite.

Russell Brown
russellbrown.com/tips_tech.html
Website featuring tips and techniques from Adobe's Senior Creative Director Russell Brown.

Plugins

Plugins World
www.pluginsworld.com
Website that provides a directory of plugins for Adobe and Apple products.

The Power Exchange
www.thepowerxchange.com
Distributes plugins and extensions for Photoshop and other graphics programs.

Xchange
www.xchangeuk.com
UK-based site that sells a wide range of third-party Photoshop plugins, QuarkXPress Xtensions, and other add-on products for graphics software.

Color Resources

Color Scheme Designer
colorschemedesigner.com
Free online app for generating color themes.

Color Schemer
www.colorschemer.com
Inexpensive color utilities for Macs, PCs, and mobile devices.

GenoPal
www.genopal.com
An inexpensive tool for creating color schemes.

Painter's Picker
old-jewel.com/ppicker
Shareware color wheel for Mac artists.

Font Tools

FontGear Inc.
www.fontgear.net
This vendor's font utilities include FontGenius, a commercial application that identifies fonts based on user-supplied images.

Identifont
www.identifont.com
This site allows users to search for fonts based on various criteria and includes links to websites where the fonts are available for purchase.

Linotype GmbH
www.linotype.com
E-commerce site for fonts. Includes Font Identifier, which identifies fonts based on design characteristics.

MyFonts
www.myfonts.com
Online font service that allows users to purchase desktop and web fonts. Also includes WhatTheFont, a utility that identifies fonts based on images uploaded by users.

What Font is
www.whatfontis.com
Identifies fonts based on images uploaded by users.

Books and Video Training

Adobe Press
www.adobepress.com
Books and video training on Adobe applications, including products such as Fireworks for which few books are available.

Creative Edge
www.creativeedge.com
Online training resources for creative professionals, including books and videos.

Lynda.com
www.lynda.com
wpular video-training site for creative professionals. Subscribers can view all online videos.

Missing Manuals
missingmanuals.com
An excellent book series from David Pogue and O'Reilly Media. Includes titles on Photoshop, Dreamweaver, CSS, Windows 7, and Mac OS X.

Peachpit Press
www.peachpit.com
Publishes the Real World series of books on Photoshop, Illustrator, InDesign, and other topics for creative professionals.

Pixel2Life
www.pixel2life.com
Tutorials for Photoshop, Flash, Illustrator, Fireworks, and other graphics programs.

Online Magazines

A List Apart
www.alistapart.com
Online home of the web design magazine, *A List Apart*.

bitFUUL Magazine
bitfuul.com/bitfuul-design-resources
Online design publication that includes free Photoshop actions, brushes, and other downloads.

CreativePro.com
www.creativepro.com
Online publication that covers all Adobe applications.

Layers Magazine
layersmagazine.com
Articles and tutorials on all Adobe products.

Smashing Media
www.smashingmagazine.com
Produces books and an online magazine for web designers and developers.

Photoshop Resources

Advanced Photoshop
www.advancedphotoshop.co.uk
UK-based magazine for advanced Photoshop users.

Deke.com
www.deke.com
Website for noted author/trainer Deke McClelland. Includes tutorials on Photoshop, Illustrator, and other programs.

Digital Mastery
www.digitalmastery.com
Online home of Photoshop expert Ben Willmore.

National Association of Photoshop Professionals
www.photoshopuser.com
Membership organization, which publishes *Photoshop User* magazine and provides Photoshop training.

Photo Lesa
photolesa.com
Tutorials from Photoshop author Lesa Snider.

Photoshop Café
www.photoshopcafe.com
Includes Photoshop tutorials and other resources.

Photoshop Creative
www.photoshopcreative.co.uk
Online home of *Photoshop Creative* magazine. Includes video tutorials.

Photoshop Killer Tips
kelbytv.com/photoshopkillertips
Photoshop tips from author and trainer Scott Kelby.

Planet Photoshop
www.planetphotoshop.com
Photoshop tutorials, tips, and news.

Scott Kelby's Photoshop Insider
www.scottkelby.com
Daily comments on digital photography from Scott Kelby.

TipSquirrel: Nuts About Photoshop
www.tipsquirrel.com
Website that provides tutorials on Photoshop, Photoshop Extended, Lightroom, Camera Raw, and Photoshop Elements. Includes a comprehensive links directory.

Photoshop Freebies

123FreeBrushes
123freebrushes.com
Free and premium Photoshop brushes.

Action Central
www.atncentral.com
Website that offers free Photoshop Actions and reviews of plugins for Photoshop, Photoshop Elements, Lightroom, and Aperture.

Addicted to Design
addictedtodesign.com
Inexpensive Photoshop Actions plus some freebies.

Brush Portfolio
www.libertiny.com/brushportfolio
Photoshop brushes organized by category.

Brusheezy
www.brusheezy.com
Photoshop brushes, textures, and patterns.

BrushKing
www.brushking.eu
Free Photoshop brushes and tutorials.

ChainStyle
www.chainstyle.com/freebies.html
Photoshop Actions, brushes, layers styles, patterns, gradients, and other resources.

Colorburned
colorburned.com
Brushes, patterns, tutorials, and other graphic design resources.

deviantArt
www.deviantart.com
Online social network for artists. Includes free downloads of Photoshop Actions, Brushes, Shapes, and Patterns, as well as resources for other graphics programs.

Folksnet
folksnetdesktop.com
Website that includes icons, Photoshop actions, textures, backgrounds, and other freebies.

Get Brushes
getbrushes.com
Photoshop brushes organized by category.

Graphic River
graphicriver.net
Inexpensive templates, web elements, and other resources.

MikeW Photoshop Actions
www.mwphotoshopactions.com
Free and commercial Photoshop Actions.

The Light's Right Studio
www.thelightsrightstudio.com/photoshop-tools.htm
Photo firm's website that includes sections with free Photoshop Actions, Scripts, and Tool Presets.

MyPhotoshopBrushes
myphotoshopbrushes.com
Includes brushes, patterns, shapes, styles, gradients, and tutorials.

Photoshop Graphics
photoshopgraphics.com
Royalty-free brushes, textures, backgrounds, templates, and clip art.

Photoshop Pattern
photoshoppattern.com
Seamless patterns and backgrounds for Photoshop.

Photoshop Roadmap
www.photoshoproadmap.com
Photoshop tutorials, brushes, and text effects.

Photoshop Styles
photoshopstyles.net
Royalty-free layer styles, patterns, and textures.

PS Brushes
www.psbrushes.net)
Photoshop brushes organized by category.

Q Brushes
qbrushes.com
Photoshop brushes organized by category.

Wetzel & Company
www.wetzelandcompany.com
Inexpensive backgrounds, patterns, and textures.

Illustrator Resources

Deke.com
www.deke.com
Website for author/trainer Deke McClelland. Includes tutorials on Photoshop, Illustrator, and other programs.

Mordy.com
www.mordy.com
Website for Illustrator author/trainer Mordy Golding.

N.Design Studio
ndesign-studio.com
Toronto-based web designer/illustrator Nick La provides free Illustrator tutorials along with desktop wallpapers and WordPress themes.

Real World Adobe Illustrator
rwillustrator.blogspot.com
Blog associated with the Illustrator book of the same name written by Mordy Golding and published by Peachpit Press.

Scripting Illustrator
js4ai.blogspot.com
Illustrator scripting blog by John Wundes. Includes links to free scripts by the author.

Vectortuts+
vector.tutsplus.com
Tips and tutorials for working with vector graphics.

InDesign Resources

InDesign Secrets
indesignsecrets.com
Clearinghouse for tutorials, scripts, plugins, and other InDesign resources. Includes a guide to using GREP in InDesign's Find-and-Replace function.

InDesign Magazine
www.indesignmag.com
Bimonthly magazine from the publisher of CreativePro.com.

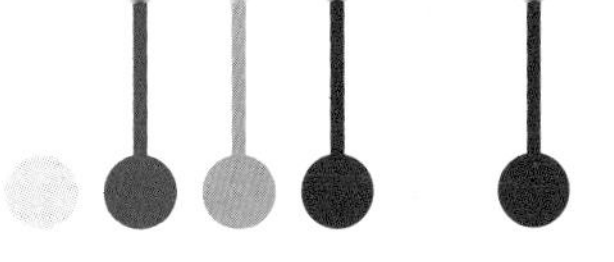

Web Design Resources

Cascading Style Sheets home page
www.w3.org/Style/CSS
Provides information about the development of the CSS standard.

Cold Hard Flash
coldhardflash.com
Website by video producer Aaron Simpson provides news and videos about Flash.

Community MX
www.communitymx.com
Subscription site that provides tutorials, design templates, and other resources for Dreamweaver, Fireworks, Photoshop, Flash, and ColdFusion.

DigitalFamily.com
www.digitalfamily.com
Website for author/instructor Janine Warner, who focuses on web design.

DMXzone
www.dmxzone.com
Website offers tutorials, reviews, extensions, templates and user forums involving Dreamweaver. Has sibling sites covering Flash and Fireworks.

Dynamic Drive
www.dynamicdrive.com
Free DHTML scripts.

Fireworks Guru Forums
www.fireworksguruforum.com
Website that provides user forums, tutorials, extensions, and other resources for Fireworks.

Fireworks Zone
www.fireworkszone.com
Website includes news, tutorials, extensions, symbols, styles, Auto Shapes, and other Fireworks resources.

Flash Daily
flashdaily.net
News and tutorials about Flash.

Flash Magazine
www.flashmagazine.com
News, reviews, and tutorials about Flash, Swift3D, and related technologies.

John Dunning
www.johndunning.com
Developer's site that offers a large number of free Fireworks extensions.

jQuery.org
jquery.org
Online home of the jQuery project. Includes free jQuery plug-ins.

Web Design Ledger
webdesignledger.com
Website provides tips, tutorials, fonts, and other resources for web designers.

World Wide Web Consortium (W3C)
www.w3.org
The organization that oversees development of HTML and other web standards.

Bibliography

Adobe Acrobat X PDF Bible
Ted Padova. Wiley Publishing Co., 2011.

Adobe Creative Suite 5 Bible
Ted Padova and Kelly L. Murdock. Wiley Publishing Co., 2010.

Adobe Fireworks CS5 Classroom in a Book
Adobe Creative Team. Adobe Press, 2010.

The CSS Pocket Guide
Chris Casciano. Peachpit Press, 2011.

Degunking Windows 7
Joli Ballew. McGraw-Hill Osborne Media, 2011.

Dreamweaver CS5.5: The Missing Manual
David Sawyer McFarland. O'Reilly Media, Inc./Pogue Press, 2011.

Mac OS X Lion: The Missing Manual
David Pogue. O'Reilly Media, Inc./ Pogue Press, 2011.

Mac OS X Snow Leopard: The Missing Manual
David Pogue. O'Reilly Media, Inc./Pogue Press, 2009.

Photoshop CS5 Bible
Lisa DaNae Dayley and Brad Dayley. Wiley Publishing Co., 2010.

Photoshop CS5: The Missing Manual
Lesa Snider. O'Reilly Media, Inc./ Pogue Press, 2010.

Real World Adobe Illustrator CS5
Mordy Golding. Peachpit Press, 2010.

Real World Adobe InDesign CS5
Olav Martin Kvern, David Blatner, and Bob Bringhurst. Peachpit Press, 2010.

Windows 7: The Missing Manual
David Pogue. O'Reilly Media, Inc./ Pogue Press, 2010.

Index